C000134785

THE STRUCTURE OF STORY

HOW TO WRITE GREAT STORIES BY FOCUSING ON WHAT REALLY MATTERS

ROSS HARTMANN

KIINGO

Try to leave out the part that readers tend to skip.

— Elmore Leonard

CONTENTS

INTRODUCTION

PART I
THE BLUEPRINTS
Starting With an Idea

PART II
POUR THE FOUNDATION
A Brief Introduction to Story Structure

PART III

PUTTING UP THE FRAMING
Expanding the Story Idea

PART IV
IS THE FOUNDATION STURDY?
Vetting a Story Idea

PART VI

WINDOWS AND DOORS

Dramatic Tools for the Toolbox

PART VII

BRING IN THE FURNITURE!
Dramatization and Scenes

INTRODUCTION

Why Another Storytelling Book?

Storytelling theory isn't new. Aristotle's *Poetics* laid out some of the core principles of drama in 335BC that we still follow today. And yet, the state of story theory is muddled, at best.

One thing's for sure: the writing community certainly doesn't suffer from a lack of writing information. We have at our fingertips more storytelling knowledge than we could ever hope to consume. The trouble is that it's disjointed. There are few resources available that give us a clear, structured storytelling framework that reflects the complicated reality of story. Even though we have, in theory, an endless supply of writing knowledge available to us, it's fragmented and scattered across books and blogs. We, as a community, are sorely lacking a comprehensive toolbox of storytelling tools and techniques.

The challenge is compounded when we realize that we don't even have a common set of terms for our storytelling principles. Is the initial disruption that kicks off a story called the impetus, the inciting incident, the point of first attack, or the catalyst? Is the end of act one called the lock-in moment, plot point one, the predicament, or the dramatic question moment? Is the end of act two called the crisis, the main turning point, or the All Is Lost moment? Is a character's past called their backstory, ghost, or rubber ducky moment? The unfortunate answer is that it depends on whom you're talking to.

Many books that *do* attempt to offer a cohesive storytelling framework typically focus on the *symptoms* of great stories rather than the causes. They focus on the things that happen rather than the *reasons* they happen. They try to explain the surface reality of stories but fail to dive deeper into the underlying first principles.

It seems to often be the case that story analysts will look at existing stories and try to find commonalities. From these commonalities, they'll extrapolate and arrive at a set of story rules that all stories *must* follow in order to be successful. They'll arrive at one pattern that appears to fit *all* stories. And the idea that one pattern will *always* lead to writing success is certainly an attractive idea.

There are a couple of problems with this approach, however. First as mentioned, the analysis is typically based on the symptoms of what makes a story great, not the underlying principles. The analyst might notice that most stories have an active main character who's chasing a goal and then conclude that all stories must have an active main character. They may fail to realize the *function* that an active main character is fulfilling and thus fail to realize that a different dramatic principle could serve the same purpose. We can, in fact, have a story with a passive main character where the story is driven by dramatic irony.

The second problem with this "one-size-fits-all" story approach is that it simply doesn't reflect reality. Not all stories follow the exact same pattern. But why does it feel plausible that all stories *might* follow the same basic set of events? Why does the Hero's Journey feel so compelling? This is typically because the pieces of the Hero's Journey and most other story frameworks are defined broadly and metaphorically. Take the Call to Adventure, for instance. When we interpret "call" metaphorically and "adventure" metaphorically, then *anything* could be a "call" to some sort of "adventure"—even if the character doesn't go anywhere.

The tools that existing storytelling books introduce tend to be defined so broadly that they apply to any and all stories. Any writing tool that can work in all situations is necessarily a blunt tool. If we want to build with a sledgehammer, then maybe that's the way to go. But if we want to craft with the precision and delicacy of a master clocksmith, we must have a toolbox that's not afraid to admit that some tools (and structures) don't work in every situation.

No single storytelling tool (or structure) can be effective in trying to prescribe a one-size-fits-all solution for all stories. Sure we can shoehorn a tool into any situation, but it's to the detriment of the story, the storyteller, and the tool. Part of mastering a storytelling toolbox is mastering the ability to choose the right tool in the right moment.

This book strives to present a comprehensive storytelling toolbox that offers practical, well-defined tools to be used when—and only when—they serve the story. We must choose the tool for the story we want to craft, not the story for the tools we have.

There are few fundamentally new ideas in this book. But it is the book that I wish had existed earlier. It attempts to take a multitude of writing advice scattered across books, blogs, videos, and podcasts and present it all in one synthesized toolbox of storytelling principles. Hopefully it can be of some use to you on your writing journey.

Who This Book is For (and Not For)

This book is for any and all creative writers, whether you're a screenwriter, a novelist, a short story writer, a flash fiction writer, a video game designer, or a comic book writer. We're all storytellers. We all strive to tell the most emotionally impactful stories we can. This is what unites us.

This book isn't for those who want a formulaic approach to storytelling, however. This book isn't for those who want a five-minute explanation of storytelling that can fit on an index card. This book isn't for those who want a beat sheet that will ostensibly fit all stories. Storytelling is an intricate craft. Any attempt to say that one story pattern can be used on all stories does a disservice to the creativity and skill of storytellers. For this reason, this book won't offer a precise, formulaic approach to crafting a story. If that's something you're looking for, this book may not be for you.

This book is also not for anyone who's too dogmatic in their storytelling beliefs. If you believe that a story can't succeed without an active main character, this book may not be for you. If you believe that *every* story must follow The Hero's Journey to a T, this book may not be for you. If you believe that a moment where the protagonist faces certain death is an absolute requirement of every story, this book may not be for you. If, on the other hand, you are willing to question existing beliefs about what makes a great story, this book may be for you.

While this book is written so that a newcomer to storytelling can understand it, it's not afraid to delve into advanced storytelling topics. If you're a beginner and would prefer a book aimed only at beginners, this book may not be for you.

If you're writing a story and you've got an open mind, this book is for you.

How This Book is Organized

This book is intended as a practical guide to writing a story. It's split into seven distinct stages.

The Idea Stage

We'll begin at the idea stage and explore how a story can start from a plot, a story world, a theme, or a character.

The Foundations of Story Structure

We'll learn the foundations of story structure and the organic flow of storytelling.

The Core Elements of Story

We'll take the initial spark of a story idea and flesh it out via the core elements of a story.

Vetting a Story Idea

We'll vet the story idea to ensure that any stumbling blocks are resolved.

The Beats of Story

We'll take our story's essential elements and structure them based on the beats of disruptions and morality arcs.

Dramatic Tools

We'll learn how to engage the audience with a collection of dramatic tools.

Dramatization and Scene Work

We'll bring the story structure to life through dramatization and scene work.

This book will generally alternate between the theoretical and the practical. We'll introduce a concept, explore a few examples, and then consider how we might use tools to put that concept into practice.

This book will primarily make use of examples from movies instead of books. The sole reason for this is that movies are generally more accessible and easier to consume than books. Using a movie as an example increases the likelihood that the reader will be familiar with the material. Movies and shows that are consistently used as examples in this book include *Star Wars, Breaking Bad, The Office,*

Frasier, The Godfather, Indiana Jones, Harry Potter, The Usual Suspects, Casablanca, Fight Club, The Sixth Sense, Jurassic Park, Die Hard, The Wizard of Oz, Avatar, The Silence of the Lambs, Good Will Hunting, Toy Story, Finding Nemo, The Incredibles, Ratatouille, Monsters, Inc., Up, Wall-E, Cars, The Graduate, Little Miss Sunshine, The Dark Knight, Titanic, The Little Mermaid, Hercules, The Nightmare Before Christmas, Shrek, The Shawshank Redemption, A Christmas Carol, American Beauty, No Country for Old Men, The Lives of Others, The Goonies, Forrest Gump, and *Four Weddings and a Funeral.*

If you're a seasoned writer, feel free to skip around and use this book as a reference manual.

1

TOOLS, NOT RULES

"There are no rules, but you break them at your peril."

— Peter Guber

When it comes to the craft of storytelling, we must shift our mindset from one of "rules" to one of "tools." There's no set of story laws that *must* be followed. There are, however, *effects* that we may strive for in our story.

Whether we want to surprise the audience, scare them, make them anticipate a future moment, or get them emotionally connected with a character, there are specific tools that we can use. Any effect in a story can be created with a tool.

As storytellers, we want to be intentional in our control of the audience's emotions and thoughts. We want to know when and *how* to craft the desired effect on the audience. We are the maestros and painters of emotion.

In this sense, there are no "rules" of storytelling. There are patterns and tools that create emotional and intellectual effects. Our job is to map out the emotional effects that we want to have on the audience and then to identify the tools that will give rise to those effects at the proper time.

We can, for instance, give our story a passive main character, but it'll have a particularly negative effect on our ability to keep the audience interested. If our story has a passive main character, we'll need to generate the story's forward momentum using a different story tool. Our storytelling tools are a collection of trade-offs.

To become better storytellers, we must learn the patterns and tools of story. We must learn the effects that those patterns and tools generate. And we must learn when to use those patterns and tools for maximum effect. We decide on the effect we want to have, we identify the tools that may help generate that effect, and then we apply them.

We must replace "rules" with "tools."

FIRST PRINCIPLES OF STORY

"Story as such can only have one merit: that of making the audience want to know what happens next. And conversely it can only have one fault: that of making the audience not want to know what happens next."

— E. M. FORSTER

Stories have two primary tasks:

1. Be interesting.
2. Be meaningful.

These two jobs correlate to the two foundational buckets of storytelling: drama and theme. Drama is responsible for keeping the audience interested and on the edge of their seats. Theme is responsible for changing the audience's perception of either themselves or of the world. Often theme is about exploring how one should live life.

The audience approaches each story with two demands: "Keep me interested. Change me." The journey and the destination. Compelling and life-changing.

Drama is where we engage the audience. Theme is where we change the audience. And in order to change, we must first engage. Throughout this book, we'll explore both dramatic tools and thematic tools.

.

PART I

THE BLUEPRINTS

STARTING WITH AN IDEA

Building a story is similar to building a home in some ways. It's a craft. It can be learned. And while not all homes are built the same way, there are certain principles that will maximize our chances of building a structure that will stand the test of time. We can put up the walls before we put up the wallpaper, for instance. We can put in the pipes before we bring in the furniture.

We're trying to avoid a situation where we begin painting the walls but realize it's in vain because the foundation is cracking under our feet.

Before we can build anything, of course, we need to know *what* we're building. This brings us to the start of our journey: the idea. We'll create the blueprints on which the story will be based.

Not all stories originate from the same spark. One story might start with an intriguing character idea, for instance. Another might start with a fascinating, new story world. Perhaps a story stems from an emotional theme that we want to explore. Or perhaps the story idea comes from a gut-wrenching plot twist.

Regardless of where our story starts, it'll eventually need the same core elements that any great story has. It needs a main character, something that happens to that main character (i.e. a plot), a place in which that something happens (i.e. a story world), and meaning that we draw from the character's journey (i.e. a theme).

We'll consider how a story might start from any one of these core elements. We'll then explore how we can take our kernel of an idea and fill in the other story elements so that we're left with a full story blueprint.

PLOTTING FROM DRAMATIC TENSION

Plot can be thought of as the sequence of events in a story. It's what *happens*. We might also think of it more broadly as a chain of cause and effect that's driven by one or more dramatic tools.

A dramatic tool is something that keeps the audience interested. It's something that generates narrative drive. We can define narrative drive as the audience's desire to know what happens next. Throughout this book, we'll explore a number of tools that generate narrative drive.

There are four primary dramatic tools that we'll use to craft and drive a plot: dramatic tension, dramatic irony, mystery, and convergence. Let's look at how each tool generates narrative drive to form the backbone of a story's plot. For each of these four dramatic tools, we'll first discuss how it works and then we'll look at how we might use it to craft a plot. Along the way, we'll also look at a few principles of drama that will help keep the audience engaged, not only throughout the overall plot but also throughout each scene.

Desire, Opposition, and Conflict

The most powerful technique to generate narrative drive is to give a character a goal. We want to see Marlin rescue Nemo. We want to see Woody get back to Andy. We want to see Sully get Boo back to her home. In all these instances, a character has an intense goal that drives the story forward.

As humans, we have a visceral understanding of goal seeking. When we accomplish a goal, our brain releases a reward chemical called dopamine. We also receive dopamine as we make progress toward our goals. This reward cycle, combined with our natural ability to empathize, is the basis for our inherent interest in the goal-seeking behavior of a character. For our purposes, we'll use the terms "goal" and "desire" interchangeably.

Desire is the fundamental building block of all drama.

Desire drives a story forward. A character wants something and takes action to get it. But desire only drives a story forward if a character has a *plan* to accomplish their goal. A goal without a plan is merely a longing and doesn't generate any dramatic tension in the story.

In *Finding Nemo*, Marlin plans to follow directions to P. Sherman, 42 Wallaby Way, Sydney, in order to rescue Nemo. In *Toy Story*, Woody plans to hitch a ride to Pizza Planet to be reunited with Andy. In *Monsters, Inc.*, Sully plans to find Boo's door to return her to the human world.

Plans tend to have one or more steps. Each step in the plan gives rise to a new goal to accomplish the step. For example, if a character wants to eat and their plan is to go to a restaurant, then their new goal is to go to a restaurant. In this way, goals can be hierarchical—each step of a plan can be said to be a sub-goal of the goal for which the plan was crafted.

Desire is such a powerful storytelling tool that we can often generate dramatic interest simply by showing the audience a character who's struggling desperately to attain something. The audience will stick around to see whether the character gets it.

While desire is the building block of drama, it doesn't create drama on its own. A desire must first be *opposed* before we reach compelling drama.

The state in which a desire is opposed is called conflict. In other words, conflict arises when desire meets opposition. Marlin is opposed by the sharks, the jellyfish field, the whale, and the ocean itself. Woody is opposed by Sid and by Buzz's desire to get back to his home planet. Sully is opposed by Randall and Mr. Waternoose.

When we hear people say, "Stories are driven by conflict," this is synonymous with saying, "Stories are driven by drama." Note that conflict can't exist without both a desire and an opposing force. This opposition can come in the form of an incidental obstacle (such as a moat that must be crossed) or, more interestingly, in the form of an opposing desire (such as an enemy knight who's pursuing the same treasure as the hero). This opposing desire can be external (originating from another character or being) or it can be internal (originating from within the same character). Opposition to a desire can also come in the form of a non-character force, such as society, an institution, technology, nature, or the supernatural.

Fundamentally we want to see someone struggle to get what they want. If we ever have trouble with maintaining audience interest, we should consider whether the story is lacking either desire or an opposing force to that desire.

All desires are fundamentally either a desire *for* change or a desire to *avoid* change. In this way, we might also then say that all desires are either a desire to attain (chase) or to avoid (escape).

Fear in Drama

Fear can be just as powerful a dramatic tool as desire. In fact, we can think of fear as the desire to avoid. In this sense, we can also give our character a strong fear and then force them to act on their desire to avoid rather than on any aspirational desire for change. We'll later discuss fear in depth as it relates to theme and character development. For drama, we'll keep in mind that characters can be driven either by aspiration or by fear.

> *Takeaway*: Drama requires both a forward force (desire) and an opposing force (opposition) in order to create conflict. Desire can be born of either aspiration or fear.

The Protagonist and the Antagonist

We call the character who desires "the protagonist." We call the oppositional force "the antagonist" or simply "the opponent." Note that from a dramatic perspective, the function of the protagonist (i.e. the one who desires) is neither inherently moral nor immoral. Likewise the function of the antagonist (i.e. the force that opposes a desire) is neither inherently moral nor immoral. It's for this reason that the protagonist need not necessarily be a hero, nor must the antagonist necessarily be a villain. In fact, the protagonist could be a villain and the antagonist could be a beacon of morality. We can roughly define a villain as one who's willing to use immoral methods to attain their goals.

In the first half of *Toy Story*, Buzz functions as a dramatic antagonist who Woody sees as standing in opposition to his desire to be the top toy—but Buzz is no villain. In *The Silence of the Lambs*, Hannibal Lecter is certainly a villain—but he doesn't actively oppose Clarice's goals and thus he isn't an antagonist.

While the terms "hero" and "villain" often denote morality, the terms "protagonist" and "antagonist" merely denote desire, not morality. The terms "protagonist" and "antagonist" are *dramatic* roles and not *thematic* roles.

We primarily use the term "protagonist" to denote the central character who pursues a goal over the course of a story. We can, however, also use the term "protagonist" to denote any character who pursues a goal at any level, including in a scene. In this way, the story's global antagonist might in fact be the protagonist of a particular scene if they drive the central goal in the scene.

Takeaway: The protagonist is the character who desires. The antagonist is the force that opposes the protagonist's desire. The protagonist isn't necessarily good, nor is the antagonist necessarily bad.

Structural Opposition of Desire

Dramatic situations are made most compelling when conflict exists as a structural opposition of goals. What does that mean exactly? It means that if one character gets what they want, the other character can't. It means that two characters want the same underlying thing and they can't both have it—even when it may not seem like they want the same thing on the surface.

For instance, let's say there's a police officer who wants to capture a criminal and a criminal who wants to escape. On the surface, these look like two different goals. And on the surface, that's true. But let's look deeper. What are the police officer and the criminal really fighting over? They're fighting over *control* of the freedom of the criminal.

What are the detective and the murderer really fighting over? They're fighting over *control* of the "truth" the public and the justice system will believe. In *Good Will Hunting*, Will and Professor Lambeau are both fighting over *control* of Will's future. In *The Dark Knight*, The Joker and Batman are fighting over *control* of the soul of Gotham.

When it comes to the control of something, there can only be one winner. Control is typically exclusive. In order for there to be an opposition of desires, of course, each character's vision of what to do once they win control must be different. If two characters agree about what to do once they get control, there's often no real conflict in who gets control. The two characters must have irreconcilable visions of the future of something.

We might also think of this as two characters who have clashing, irreconcilable agendas.

Of course, it's possible for two characters to have desires that are both mutually attainable. The two characters might only clash in their plans. This may not provide deep opposition, however, and can allow for the two characters to find a way to work together to both get what they want. This is generally bad for maintaining drama but can provide the opportunity for an interesting thematic lesson about cooperation.

In essence, a structural opposition of desires means that if one desire is attained, the other can't be. We want to apply this principle, not only to external conflict but to internal conflict as well. If a character has two goals, those goals should be structurally opposed. The character can't have both. If one internal desire wins, the other can't.

> *Takeaway*: Two characters are structurally opposed when they're vying for control of the same thing. Two goals are structurally opposed when they can't both be attained. This creates the deepest external and internal conflict.

Dramatic Tension and the Dramatic Question

The moment the fate of a goal becomes uncertain (typically at the moment when the desire meets opposition), a state of dramatic tension arises called a dramatic question. The dramatic question is essentially, "Will the protagonist get what they want?" Will the goal be attained?

Will Marlin find Nemo? Will Woody get back to Andy? Will Sully get Boo back home?

To generate dramatic tension, all we need to do is establish a character goal (which may be a desire to avoid) and then make the fate of that goal uncertain through the introduction of opposition. Dramatic tension is perhaps our most powerful tool to drive audience interest. It usually serves as the primary source of global tension over the course of a story.

It's important to note that the potential tension in a dramatic question is roughly proportional to our ability to concretely measure the exact moment of resolution of the goal. In other words, we need to be able to measure when a goal is attained or lost in order to feel tense about it. After all, how can we be tense about something we can't imagine ever being resolved?

As a general rule, the more concretely measurable the goal, the more dramatic tension we're likely to feel and thus the more narrative drive we're likely to generate.

Let's consider the goal "to be successful." It's not concretely measurable. Is success attained after the protagonist buys a car? Is it attained once they sell a particular number of units? We don't know unless the end point of success is explicitly defined (in which case the concrete metric of success becomes the new desire). The goal "to win the competition," on the other hand, *is* concretely measurable. We know definitively and without doubt whether the protagonist has attained or failed to attain this goal at any given moment. We can, of course, define in our story a clear metric of "success" and tie that success to a particular event such as buying a car or selling a certain number of units. We must ensure that the metric has been clearly communicated to the audience in order for them to be able to recognize opposition and feel tension about the desire's attainment.

It's also worth noting that the audience may not necessarily want the protagonist to achieve their goal. We might *want* the protagonist to fail. We might realize that a character has a self-destructive streak or that they're seeking a goal that won't get them any closer to filling their void (i.e. the emptiness within them). In these instances, we don't want the character to get what they want; we want the character to get what they *need* (typically a realization of the proper way to act in the world). We'll find that the tension between what a character wants (i.e. is consciously seeking) and what they actually *need* in order to become a better human being provides strong narrative drive. This technique of generating tension from what we *don't* want the protagonist to achieve can apply to any dramatic situation from the global story to a short scene.

> *Takeaway*: Dramatic tension is driven by the audience's desire to find out whether a character will get what they want. The "dramatic

question" is, "Will the character get what they want?" The success or failure of the dramatic question should be concretely measurable.

Stakes

The mere existence of a goal doesn't guarantee the audience's interest in seeing the goal attained (or foiled). This is where stakes come in. The stakes are what the protagonist stands to win or lose in the pursuit of their goal. As Pixar puts it, stakes are "the potential risks, impacts, and rewards" involved in a dramatic journey.

We can think of stakes as the consequences of either attaining or failing to attain a protagonist's goal. Stakes are responsible for answering the fundamental question, "Why do we care?" What does the protagonist stand to gain if they succeed? What does the protagonist stand to lose if they fail? What's important to the character?

Recall that a dramatic question is, "Will the protagonist get what they want?" This question implies an inherent set of stakes. The very thing that the protagonist desires is what's at stake. If a character has a desire to save their son from certain doom, the dramatic question is, "Will the protagonist be able to save their son?" and we implicitly understand that it's the son's life that's at stake.

With this in mind, we can view a dramatic question from both the perspective of desire (namely whether the protagonist will get what they want) and also from the perspective of stakes (namely whether the stakes will be won or lost). This allows us to view a dramatic situation from a desire-first perspective or a stakes-first perspective. They're two perspectives on the same thing.

Because of this organic relationship between desire and stakes, we can often raise a character's desire in order to raise the stakes and vice versa. When we feel that our story's stakes are too low, we may want to consider whether the character's desire can be deepened or strengthened. Have we fully explored just how much the character values the thing for which they're struggling? When a character's desire is too weak, we may want to consider whether we can offer or endanger something of true value to the character. Putting something of deep value at risk will tend to increase a character's desire.

We can think of stakes as things of value that are in question. This perspective allows us to get the most emotional impact out of the dramatic situation. The character has to care *deeply* about the stakes. So consider what the character holds dear. We must ensure that we're offering or threatening something of deep value to the character. Is it a relationship? Their physical safety? Their career? Their moral code? A piece of their identity?

When something of great value is offered to a character, they jump into action. When something of great value is threatened, they jump into action. In short, when things of great value are at stake, characters are motivated to make difficult decisions and take extraordinary (and sometimes desperate) actions.

Stakes are relative to each character. To one character, a particular pen may just be for scribbling down notes, but to another character that same pen may be the last artifact and memory of their beloved father. If that pen is teetering over a cliff ledge, we'll see categorically different reactions from each of these characters. Something can be high-stakes (i.e. high value) to one character but meaningless to another character. We must keep this in mind whenever we consider raising the stakes of a story. It's all relative. We don't always need "end of the world" stakes. We do, however, almost always want "end of the character's world" stakes.

We must keep in mind that stakes can extend beyond the physical. While we can certainly put a character's life at stake, we can also offer or threaten the emotional, social, mental, professional, romantic, moral, ethical, spiritual, etc. Instead of only putting a character's life in danger, we might also force them to risk their mental wellbeing, the love of their spouse, their career, their moral code, their religious beliefs, their identity, etc. These things can end up costing a character more than merely their life. They'll have to live the rest of their healthy life suffering the tortuous consequences of their failure.

Takeaway: Stakes are the things of value that are in question. When we define the stakes of a story, we're defining what's of value to a character. We offer or threaten things of value to put them at stake.

Manipulating Information

When writing a story we must remember that the audience and the characters are all stakeholders of information. In other words, when we consider who might know a piece of information, we must consider not only each individual character but also the audience itself. When it comes to information, we'll refer to each character as well as the audience itself as a "stakeholder" of information. In other words, each character and the audience itself has an interest in the information of the story.

When writing we must also remember that not everyone needs to know everything. In other words, the distribution of information can be unequal. In fact, we can often generate more dramatic interest in a situation by initially withholding information. The audience can know a piece of information that a character doesn't and vice versa. This means that a stakeholder can hold a superior or inferior position relative to another stakeholder when it comes to a piece of information.

When information is withheld, we can generate dramatic interest through the use of suspense, mystery, surprise, dramatic irony (which we'll explore soon), and dramatic tension.

Takeaway: The audience is a player in a story. The audience, like a character in the story, doesn't need to know everything all the time. We can withhold information to incite different emotions.

Suspense

Suspense is that feeling when the protagonist is hanging for dear life from the ledge. It's when the villain has a loaded gun aimed at the protagonist's loved one. It's when the bungee cord starts to snap.

Suspense arises when a stakeholder (typically the audience) wants to know the result of an uncertain, imminent outcome. In other words, a stakeholder feels suspense when someone wants something, it's uncertain whether they'll get it, and there's *urgency* behind the outcome. In short, suspense is a feeling that arises from *urgent* dramatic tension. Urgency is key.

To establish suspense, it's critical that whoever we want to feel suspense is able to envision the possible outcome (whether positive or negative). They must concretely know what failure looks like and what success looks like. Failure might be that the bungee cord snaps and success might be that it remains intact.

If the protagonist is walking down a dark alley in a bad neighborhood, we may feel tension but no suspense. We can't envision any *concrete* danger here. If, on the other hand, we see a man with a knife following the protagonist down the alley, we feel suspense. Everyone in the audience will be able to distinctly pinpoint the same possibility that the man with the knife might attack the protagonist. If the potential outcome can't be envisioned, then the audience may feel uneasiness or implicit tension but no suspense. Suspense requires that the audience be able to pinpoint the concrete danger in front of the protagonist.

Suspense requires that the final outcome be uncertain. If a particular outcome feels absolutely inevitable, we don't feel suspense. If we can see who's going to win a chess match, for instance, the suspense evaporates. We must see a raging duel between at least two opposing, possible outcomes in order to feel uncertainty. The likelihood of each possible outcome may fluctuate during this tug-of-war.

Suspense also requires that the reveal of the final outcome feel imminent. There must be some implicit or explicit deadline. Something must be actively threatening to cause a "failure" outcome. Without this threat, there's no feeling of suspense. The quickest way to generate suspense is to put a character's desire at risk (even a desire as simple as the desire to breathe), often through some sort of impending or approaching danger. There must be a sense of urgency.

Let's consider a scenario where we've got a rabbit stuck in a cage, trying desperately to reach a carrot that's just beyond his grasp. There's uncertainty about whether he'll get it (and we may indeed have strong feelings about whether we want him to get it), but there's no urgency and consequently no feeling of suspense. We can always introduce a feeling of urgency, however. Let's put the carrot teetering on the edge of a cliff, swaying back and forth in the wind, threatening to lose its balance with every stretch of the rabbit's paw. In this new scenario, we start to feel that the carrot may fall at any moment, most assuredly putting it out of the rabbit's grasp forever. The outcome is imminent. Now we feel suspense with every gust of wind. We can intensify the situation by first showing that the rabbit is starving (thus defining the value of the carrot and consequently the depth of the stakes).

Suspense is heightened by increasing the uncertainty of the envisioned outcome (sometimes by emphasizing just how bad the odds are or by actually making the odds worse) as well as by decreasing the perceived time remaining until the outcome is decided.

Urgency and ticking clocks can be used to great effect in heightening suspense, as we'll later learn. We want to emphasize that a precious resource is barreling toward a "trigger event" or a "trigger threshold." When that threshold is reached, an undesired outcome is likely to occur.

We can also use a "focus object" to heighten the feeling of suspense. A focus object is a physical object or symbol used as an indicator of how close we're getting to success or failure (i.e. how close we're getting to "the trigger event"). The focus object is a metric by which we can measure when the final outcome will occur. It might be a fraying rope, a rising carbon dioxide gauge, a timer, a decaying rose (as in *Beauty and the Beast*), or a potential victim of the opponent's desire, etc.

At its core, creating suspense is about putting a high-stakes goal at risk and threatening its imminent loss. It might be the desire to survive, the desire to conceal one's identity, the desire to prevent loss, the desire to regain something precious, etc. As we explored earlier, desire is relative and need only be personally important to the desirer in order to be high-stakes.

Suspense *doesn't* require that both the audience and a character have the same information. Consider a scenario where the audience knows that a character's drink is poisoned. The character goes to drink but is interrupted by a conversation, their lips still touching the glass. We wait in suspense as there's a tug-of-war between the drink and the conversation. The character isn't aware of their predicament but we in the audience sure are. We might also consider a bumbling protagonist who gets themselves into dangerous situations but lacks the self-awareness to know they're in danger. The audience feels suspense but the protagonist doesn't.

Remember that when it comes to information management, it's not just the audience that can feel suspense. Characters themselves can feel suspense, even if the audience doesn't (because the audience already knows the outcome, for instance).

Traditional suspense requires that the *audience* be aware of the threat to a goal.

> *Takeaway*: Suspense arises when a dramatic question is combined with uncertainty and urgency. At its core, creating suspense is about putting a high-stakes goal at risk and threatening its imminent loss.

Surprise

Surprise occurs when an expectation is subverted. Sometimes this subverted expectation is simply an expectation that things will remain as they are. If the protagonist is enjoying a Sunday drive with their partner and then out of nowhere is hit by a truck, that's surprise. We can also think of surprise as a reveal that a stakeholder (typically the audience) was lacking information of consequence.

A bomb going off in the middle of an otherwise calm, pleasant conversation is a surprise. Surprise necessitates that the stakeholder doesn't know they're missing information and thus, in this example, we can't know about the existence of the bomb.

Surprise can also occur as part of a suspenseful moment. Let's suppose we see a ticking timer on a bomb. We can imagine the outcome of the bomb exploding when the timer reaches zero and thus we feel suspense. If the timer reaches zero and the bomb does *not* explode, we're surprised. Our expectation was that the bomb was going to explode when the timer reached zero. That expectation was subverted.

We should never make story choices based solely on a desire to induce surprise in the audience. Surprise itself isn't always inherently satisfying.

We often hear that twists or reveals should be "surprising yet inevitable." For something to be a surprise means that it must subvert an expectation. For it to be inevitable, it must be apparent in retrospect how it could logically occur based on the story's chain of cause and effect. If an event or revelation isn't logical in retrospect, it's rarely worth consideration as a surprise. We'll explore this in more detail when we discuss story twists.

We must remember that it's not just the audience that can feel surprise. Characters themselves can feel surprise, even if the audience doesn't.

> *Takeaway*: A surprise is the subversion of an expectation. Surprises should generally be understandable in retrospect. In other words, their cause should be logical.

Promises

A promise is a contract with the audience that something will happen. Some promises are explicit, like in *Casablanca* when Captain Renault says to Rick, "Rick, there's going to be some excitement here tonight. We're going to make an arrest in your café." The audience now expects that there will be an arrest in the café. Other promises are implicit, such as a shadow that's moving toward the protagonist in an alley. There's an implicit promise that the shadow will become significant and perhaps clash with the protagonist.

We can think of a promise as a debt, which must be repaid with a "payoff." In this context, a promise is a "setup." A payoff is the fulfillment of a promise or the reveal of the significance of a setup. Each promise creates a contract that something will later become significant.

In his book *The Sequence Approach*, Paul Gulino breaks promises into two fundamental categories: telegraphing and dangling causes. He describes telegraphing as "pointing or advertising." We can telegraph by explicitly telling the audience that something *will* happen (often by way of a character promising it). We can telegraph by telling the audience what *must* happen (often through the use of a deadline of some sort). We can also telegraph by telling the audience what will *likely* happen (often through implying the significance of a story element by having a character meaningfully interact with it).

Gulino describes a dangling cause as a cause that doesn't have its effect until later. We can think of a dangling cause as a delayed effect. A character might order a hit on an enemy, for instance. The command is a cause, but it doesn't have an effect until it's carried out in a later scene.

In general, dangling causes attempt to predict or alter the future. We can raise dangling causes by including predictions, fortunes, omens, prophecies, premonitions, daydreams, assurances, threats, warnings, declarations of intent, demands, requests, orders, wishes, expressions of hope, assertions about the future, statements of desire, statements of worldview, statements about what can or should happen, and written or verbal promises in the traditional sense. Dangling causes raise a question about how the future will turn out.

Because promises raise questions, they also raise dramatic interest and create narrative drive. The audience wants to know what will happen. They want to see the promise fulfilled.

Takeaway: A promise is a contract with the audience that something will happen. Some promises explicitly tell the audience that an event will occur and others merely suggest that something may become significant through implication. Promises project into the future and thus create narrative drive.

Tension

There are two types of tension that are often conflated and used interchangeably. We'll make a distinction.

Explicit Tension

Explicit tension arises from delayed suspense. When the envisioned outcome feels uncertain, urgent, and imminent and yet the outcome still hasn't arrived, we feel explicit tension. The longer we can delay the outcome while still making it feel uncertain, imminent, and believable, the more tension we'll feel. The longer a rope strains and threatens to send a character falling to their doom, the more tension we feel from the suspense.

There's also a type of non-dramatic explicit tension that's not tied to a character desire. An example would be a cigarette ash that keeps growing but that the smoker refuses to flick. We know the ash will fall, but tension grows as the ash grows and the outcome is delayed.

Implicit Tension

Implicit tension arises when there's anticipation of some unknown outcome (often the anticipation of conflict). It's the feeling that "something bad might happen." Implicit tension is atmospheric tension. There's no explicit outcome in mind, but there may be *types* of outcomes envisioned. The stakeholder suspects that they're missing information about a potential outcome, but they don't know that for sure.

We can often create implicit tension through the use of promises. Recall that promises are created by projecting into the future. If a promise implies that something could go wrong in the future, this creates anticipation about the possibility of conflict in the future and thus creates implicit tension. If a boy says, "I'm worried Jim will beat me up on the first day of school," then the subsequent scene detailing the first day of school will have implicit tension even when Jim's not present.

How else might we create implicit tension? Here are a few methods:

- Put a character in proximity to danger.
- Throw a character into an unknown or unchartered situation or area (the unknown often implies danger).
- Put a character in a vulnerable situation or position where they're unable to defend themselves (such as in a shower).
- Have a character do something forbidden or frowned upon. This can be combined with the character trying to hide their forbidden or immoral actions.
- Linger on something that appears to have no significance (thus giving rise to tension based on an implicit promise). Be sure this promise is eventually paid off.
- Add a time limit even if we don't know what happens when the time expires (thus creating an unknown outcome).
- Show us something or someone that threatens to disturb the peace (especially the social calm). Psychopathic characters such as Anton Chigurh in *No Country for Old Men* or Travis Bickle in *Taxi Driver* are quite effective at creating tension.
- Give us a reason to believe we can't predict what will happen next (e.g. introduce chaos).

These elements can also be combined to further increase implicit tension.

As with all of our information management tools, it's not just the audience who can feel tension. A character might feel tension even if the audience doesn't. This can arise when the audience knows the nature of the situation but a character doesn't, giving rise to dramatic irony (which we'll soon explore).

> *Takeaway*: Explicit tension arises when a feeling of suspense is drawn out. Implicit tension arises when there's an atmospheric feeling that something bad may happen but we don't know what.

Plotting From a Dramatic Question

Most stories use dramatic tension (i.e. a dramatic question) to drive their plot. These stories follow a protagonist with an intense desire as they work toward their goal in the face of opposition. This is one reason that many writing guides insist that a story must have an active main character. This is absolutely true if our story's plot is driven by a dramatic question. It's not necessarily true if our plot is driven by something like dramatic irony, however. There are plenty of good stories with a passive main character. A passive main character does, however, sacrifice a great amount of narrative drive.

A plot driven by a character that intensely wants something (i.e. dramatic tension) is perhaps the most powerful plot for creating narrative drive and thus for keeping the audience interested. It's the core of drama. It's also the reason that most plots use a dramatic question to serve as their backbone. Marlin wants to find Nemo. Mr. Incredible wants to stop the bad guy and rescue his family. Indiana Jones wants to find the Ark.

Which character wants something intensely? That's the story's protagonist. Which character stands in their way (whether intentionally or unintentionally)? That's the story's antagonist. Note that there may be no specific character that stands in the protagonist's way (i.e. no antagonist). It may be the character themselves that sabotages their own desires.

We'll later explore how we can start a story idea with a character in order to craft an intriguing dramatic question and a heart-wrenching journey for our story.

Takeaway: To create a plot from a dramatic question, give a character a strong desire for something, give the character a plan to go after their goal, introduce opposition to that desire, define what will happen if the character fails to reach their goal, and push the urgency of the goal. Most plots are driven by a dramatic question.

4

PLOTTING FROM DRAMATIC IRONY

Dramatic irony is a specific type of information inequality where the audience has information that a character doesn't. The audience knows, for example, that the serial killer is in the basement but the protagonist doesn't. Dramatic irony maintains our interest as we wait to find out when one or more characters will learn what we already know.

The classic example of dramatic irony given by Hitchcock is of two people talking in a restaurant. It's revealed to the audience that there's a bomb under the table. The characters don't know this. The audience sits in suspense as we wait to find out if there's any way the characters will find out about the bomb before it goes off or if the bomb will be somehow diffused.

Consider that same scenario where one of the two characters knows about the existence of the bomb but doesn't reveal it to the other. Now we're in even more suspense, waiting to find out whether the one character will reveal it to the other. The otherwise normal conversation is dripping with subtextual meaning. Do they *want* the bomb to go off?!

Dramatic irony can arise when a dramatic situation makes use of knowledge the audience brings from outside of the story. For instance, a story may take place during a particular historical event. The audience knows the outcome of the event while the characters don't. An example is the movie *Titanic*.

We might also infuse a situation with a general dramatic irony by exploring an ordinary character who doesn't recognize their extraordinary situation (such as in *Forrest Gump*) or by exploring an extraordinary character who doesn't recognize their ordinary situation (such as Don Quixote). In either case, the audience sees that there's a gap between their understanding of the situation and the character's understanding.

Dramatic irony can be a powerful source of comedy, particularly in the form of misunderstandings, as we'll soon discuss.

Because the audience is in a state where they know more than a character, they tend to want to stick around to find out when the missing information will be revealed to the character. They also want to witness the subsequent reaction to the discovery of the information. In this way, dramatic irony naturally generates narrative drive.

Takeaway: Dramatic irony arises when the audience knows a piece of information that a character doesn't. The audience often wants to stick around to see the information revealed to the character.

Misunderstandings

Misunderstandings tend to play off of dramatic irony. The audience knows that two characters don't share the same information even when the characters act as if they do. Each character tends to then make incorrect assumptions about the other character's words, actions, and intentions.

Often each character is acting and interpreting the other in good-faith but can't understand how the other could hold their position given what they know. In comedy especially, the outrage or confusion over the other's position prevents a rational conversation to root out the source of the misunderstanding. Emotion and gut reaction trumps logic and rationality.

To fully exploit a misunderstanding, we must let the audience in on the differing perspectives (thus creating dramatic irony and narrative drive). Interest is derived from a character's actions based on the misunderstanding and also from the audience wanting to find out when the misunderstanding will be resolved.

Misunderstandings can be a ripe source of dramatic tension, irony, and comedy.

In *The Office* S09E03, Jim is talking to Pam in a back room and we can't hear their conversation. Darrell and Nelly are both watching them talk from outside the room. Nelly says to Darrell, "You know what this is all about?" (thinking the conversation is about Jim admitting to an affair). Darrell responds, "Yeah, you too, huh?" (thinking the conversation is about Jim revealing a new sports marketing job). She responds, "Yeah. [Looking at Jim] Go on. Spill it. Tell her all the gory details, you snake." Darrell responds, "Hey! He *deserves* this. And he said I could get in on it too."

> *Takeaway*: Misunderstandings arise when two characters don't share the same information but believe that they do. Each character acts in good-faith on the assumption that the other character shares the same set of facts. Misunderstandings often require that the audience understand the source of the differing perspectives.

How Does a Misunderstanding Arise?

A misunderstanding might arise when a character sees or hears what they *want* to hear or what they *fear* hearing. These emotional reactions tend to cut off any rational thought of scrutinizing the facts. This is a form of confirmation bias. A character who has an insecurity or vulnerability might be particularly prone to interpret dialogue or a situation as an attack on their insecurity. This might send the character into an emotional tailspin as all subsequent facts are seen as confirmation of the attack. This type of misunderstanding may persist because the character is too emotionally scared to communicate the existence of their insecurity or fear.

Some characters are also susceptible to wanting to interpret situations or dialogue as being in their interest (even when they're not). Let's say, for instance, that a man and a woman are sitting on a bench in the park. He's infatuated with her and is looking for any sign of reciprocation. As the sun's going down, she says, "It's getting awfully cold." He may interpret this as a sign that she wants his arm around her for warmth. What she's actually saying is that she's ready to go home.

Misunderstandings can also arise from the simple tendency for us to believe that which we want to believe. We also tend *not* to believe that which we don't want to believe. We put out of our mind those things that are uncomfortable to consider. We want to believe our heroes are here to help. We want to believe the villains are here to hurt. We believe that which is consistent with our current beliefs. We dismiss that which is inconsistent with our current beliefs. Misunderstandings can arise from failing to consider that something may go against that which we want to believe.

Misunderstandings can occur when one character makes the mistake of believing that they can read minds. Humans tend to do this. We believe that we can understand or in some cases even predict another's intention or reaction. We might also fail to ask for clarifying information and instead jump to conclusions based on ambiguous information. The feeling that we can read other's minds without asking for clarifying information is a potent source of misunderstandings.

The "availability heuristic" also causes us to assume that the current situation or current information relates to that which occurred most recently or that which is most readily accessible in our mind. In other words, we interpret information as being related to that which is most vivid to us or that which is "top of mind." In the previous example with *The Office*, Darrel believes the conversation between Jim and Pam is about Jim's new job opportunity because that's the last thing Darrel discussed with Jim. Nelly believes the conversation is about infidelity because that's what she discussed with Pam most recently.

Misunderstandings can also arise from fundamentally different value perspectives. In the movie *Big*, for instance, there's a scene where Susan is flirting with Josh. Josh, however, is just a 12-year-old boy inside and doesn't interpret the situation in a romantic context. It's a fundamental difference in perspective, resulting in a misunderstanding.

Misunderstandings can also arise from hearing partial information or from hearing information out of context. For instance, a character might hear that his love interest has had someone propose to her. He storms off in rage and depression before hearing that she said no. Or instead, he might overhear a conversation where his love interest is talking about getting married and it sounds like someone has proposed to her, but the context is really her fantasy about him one day proposing. He misunderstands the context and this creates a misunderstanding.

Misunderstandings can arise when one character lies to another, perhaps out of a desire to spare their feelings. In *Frasier* S06E22, Daphne is about to get married to Donny. Niles is in love with Daphne and Frasier and Martin want to spare Niles' feelings. They lie to him and tell him that Daphne's mother is dying. Niles talks to Daphne with the belief that her mother is dying while Daphne, of course, is speaking about the fact that she's getting married. Daphne says, "It's even better than I thought it would be. I can already picture the big day. Beautiful flowers everywhere! A sea of smiling faces! And I suppose everyone will want to have their picture taken with the lady of the hour." This line, of course, takes on a double meaning and makes Niles raise an eyebrow. Importantly all of Daphne's words can be rationally interpreted from either character's perspective.

To craft a misunderstanding, we might first decide on the perspective we want a character to have. What's the assumption we want them to make or the conclusion we want them to draw? Next we decide on what evidence would need to be presented to them in order to have them draw that conclusion (which might be different for each character). When presented with this evidence, the character should incorrectly jump to a conclusion, thus giving rise to a misunderstanding. We can then provide information that could be interpreted differently depending on one's perspective.

> *Takeaway*: Misunderstandings often arise from either confirmation bias or the availability heuristic. We hear what we desire to hear or what we fear hearing. We hear that which is on the top of our mind. The emotion that can accompany a misunderstanding sometimes blinds us and prevents any rational attempt to get to the bottom of a disagreement.

Secrets

Dramatic irony is all about secrets. The audience knows more than the characters and it's typically because at least one character is keeping a secret. A character holds a secret when they have a piece of information they don't want one or more other characters to know. When the audience is let in on a secret, they'll want to stick around to see the secret revealed (thus creating narrative drive). It's possible, however, that a secret is actually being kept *from the audience*, which allows for surprise rather than dramatic irony.

To maximize dramatic interest when it comes to a secret, let the audience know the secret or at least let them know that a secret exists. Once the audience is in on the secret, we can make use of suspense by introducing a threat that may lead to the intentional or accidental reveal of the secret. Some characters will go to desperate or comedic lengths to maintain a secret, sometimes seemingly acting out of character to those who are unaware of the existence of the secret.

In episode two of *Das Boot*, there's a scene where a German woman illegally meets with a French Resistance fighter. The Resistance fighter is picked up by the police, but the German woman escapes undetected. Later the German woman is brought in as a translator to interrogate the Resistance fighter she had illegally met. The police don't know that the Resistance fighter can point the finger at the German woman and identify her as a conspirator (a secret).

Now the German woman's duty is to interrogate this Resistance fighter, but at the same time she doesn't want the interrogation to be successful for fear of her secret being revealed. This creates a dramatic scene in which the secret keeper herself is given a task to reveal the secret. This also creates a strong inner conflict in the German woman.

> *Takeaway*: Secrets arise when a character has a piece of information they don't want one or more other characters to know.

How Are Secrets Revealed?

If a third party is in on the secret, the third party might be the source of the reveal (intentionally or accidentally). This might be a person who has a hard time keeping secrets for whatever reason (even when they know they should). In *The Office*, Kevin and Michael have a particularly hard time keeping secrets and are likely to accidentally reveal them. Dwight, on the other hand, is more likely to intentionally reveal a secret (perhaps feeling that it's his duty).

The secret might also be revealed by someone who's oblivious to the fact that the information is being kept secret. In *The Office* S09E10, Pam brought lice into the office and is keeping it a secret that she's the source. Later in the episode, she gets a speakerphone call from her mom who reveals that Pam's daughter is the source of the lice. The whole office hears.

Characters who are oblivious to the existence of a secret may also skirt around the edges of a secret or hint at it inadvertently. This can create tension around the reveal of the secret. In *The Office* S02E21, Michael is going through complaints and says, "The thing is, Angela, you are in here an awful lot. You have complained about everybody in the office, except Dwight, which is odd because everyone else has had run-ins with Dwight." The affair between Angela and Dwight is a secret.

A secret may be revealed when the evidence surrounding the secret becomes unavoidable. The secret may be deduced from circumstantial evidence (sometimes resulting in a feeling of betrayal by those from whom the secret was being hidden). Someone may also deduce that a secret exists but not know the details of the secret.

Secrets can, of course, be revealed by the secret keeper. The secret keeper may confess to the secret after no longer being able to maintain it due to some guilt, shame, or moral code. The secret keeper may feel they no longer have the ability to keep it a secret and that "it will come out sooner or later." The secret keeper may reveal it because it's no longer advantageous to keep (or its disclosure may provide an even greater advantage). The secret keeper may be coerced into revealing the secret (and thus feel that the price that must be paid to keep the secret doesn't outweigh the price of the reveal). The secret keeper may be manipulated or deceived into revealing the secret.

And, of course, the secret keeper may accidentally reveal the secret. The secret keeper may not even know that the information is a secret. In *Frasier* S05E09, Frasier grabs Roz's phone while Roz goes to get coffee. Frasier tells Roz's mom that Roz has been self-conscious about putting on some pregnancy pounds and that she should be mindful. Roz comes back and tells Frasier that she's been dreading telling her mom that she's pregnant.

The secret keeper may know that the information is secret but might believe that someone already knows the secret, sometimes due to a misunderstanding. In *Frasier* S05E03, Roz is pregnant and Frasier is the only one who knows. At a Halloween party, Daphne notes that Roz has a glow about her. Roz says she had kind of an accident but doesn't elaborate. Daphne assumes that Roz has been in a car accident. Later Daphne is speaking to Frasier in the terms of a car accident, but her phrases can also double as terms for an accidental pregnancy. Frasier assumes that Daphne knows about the pregnancy and confirms that Roz is pregnant in explicit terms. This episode is a masterful combination of both secrets and misunderstandings to generate dramatic interest.

The secret keeper may also believe they're revealing the secret to a particular audience when it's actually being revealed to a different audience. This is the case in *Frasier* S02E21 where Frasier thinks he's confronting Maris about her infidelity when it's actually Niles, Maris' husband, who's in the sensory deprivation tank. This is also the case in *Monsters, Inc.* and *Coco* where the villain reveals their true motivation and plan to the people that have already deduced it, but their speech is being transmitted or recorded. This is similar to a situation in which someone admits to their crimes among allies, but their confession is being recorded or monitored by some unseen entity. More broadly, this can occur when the secret keeper thinks they're talking to someone who already knows the secret, but they're actually talking to someone who doesn't know it yet (regardless of whether there's a misunderstanding). And finally, someone may overhear the secret keeper discussing the secret (either accidentally or intentionally through something like surveillance).

> *Takeaway*: A secret is revealed intentionally when the benefit of revealing it is greater than the benefit of keeping it. A secret may also be revealed unintentionally by either the secret keeper or by a third party.

Plotting From Dramatic Irony

Plots driven by dramatic irony are all about letting the audience in on a secret and then keeping important information from one or more other characters. Instead of asking what our character desires, we ask what they're trying to prevent or avoid. We ask what they fear. Then we ensure that each scene threatens that fear over and over. A plot rooted in dramatic irony is one alternative to having a character with a strong, aspirational desire.

We might imagine a plot where a detective is tracking a serial killer. In this plot, however, we let the audience (but not the detective) know who the serial killer is. Now anytime the detective interacts with the serial killer as part of their investigative process, the scene is brimming with tension.

Another powerful use of dramatic irony is to give a character a secret that they're trying desperately to keep. The character's goal isn't an aspirational one for which they must make a plan. Instead it's a desire to avoid discovery and every interaction becomes a threat to that desire. This is one way to inject interest into a story with a passive main character. *The Graduate* uses this technique as Ben tries to keep secret an affair with Mrs. Robinson.

Plots driven by dramatic irony tend to have passive main characters due to the fact that those characters are often trying to hide or avoid something (rather than trying to pursue something). In order to counteract the lack of narrative drive that comes from a passive main character, we must ensure that the stakes of the story are especially high. If a character is keeping a secret, there need to be intensely negative consequences to the reveal of that secret. If a character is avoiding a fear, that fear must be deep and absolutely terrifying.

Which character is trying to keep a secret, avoid a fear, or prevent something from happening? That's the story's protagonist. Which character is trying to uncover the secret, force the protagonist to confront a fear, or cause something unwanted to happen (either unwittingly or unwittingly)? That's the story's antagonist. It's worth noting that the story's antagonistic force may be a community rather than a single character. This is the case in *Lars and the Real Girl*.

Takeaway: A plot rooted in dramatic irony should let the audience in on a secret and then play with the natural drama and comedy that arises from misunderstandings, a character's struggle with the dilemma of the secret, and threats to reveal the secret.

5

PLOTTING FROM MYSTERY

Mystery is the realm of missing information. A mystery arises when someone wants to know something that they believe is knowable (in contrast to suspense where an outcome has not yet occurred and thus isn't yet knowable).

Mystery is rooted in a desire to uncover *existing* information (even if the existing information is about a future event). It's a bit tautological, but if a question is answerable, then its answer exists in the present. While questions such as, "Who will kill him?", "Where will the meeting take place?", and "When will her death occur?" are all about future events, the asker (if not being rhetorical) is presuming that their answers are all currently knowable in the present reality. The time and location of future crimes, for instance, are knowable within the story world of *Minority Report*. Contrast this with suspense where the outcome in question isn't knowable in the story world because it hasn't yet occurred.

A mystery is fundamentally about an outstanding question. And the desire to answer that question can range in intensity from a mild curiosity to a burning necessity. A mystery driven by a light curiosity might be called "passive." A mystery driven by an intense desire that *requires* an answer might be called "active." The tools we use to create an "active" mystery are slightly different than those we use to create a "passive" mystery. We'll explore both.

When we withhold information from a stakeholder, whether the information is mildly or intensely desired, we've created an implicit promise that the information will be revealed at some point. This promise generates a mystery as well as narrative drive. Generally the audience will want to stick around to discover the missing information.

Note that mysteries are subjective. A character may be missing information while the audience isn't (thus creating dramatic irony).

> *Takeaway*: A mystery is an open question that has an answer in the present. Contrast this with suspense, which is driven by an open question that isn't yet answerable because its answer hasn't yet occurred.

How to Create a Passive Mystery

Creating a passive mystery (i.e. one driven by curiosity) is essentially about making a stakeholder (often the audience) realize that they have only partial information. This piques the curiosity of the stakeholder and creates a puzzle for them to solve. Perhaps the best way to do this is to start a situation in medias res ("in the middle of things") without context. This invites the stakeholder to stick around and seek context so that they can better understand the situation.

The first *Harry Potter* movie opens with this technique of starting in medias res. The idea is to show a character either in the midst of a disruption to their life or in the midst of executing on a plan. Here's the opening conversation between Professor McGonagall and Albus Dumbledore:

"Are the rumors true, Albus?"

"I'm afraid so, professor. The good and the bad."

"And the boy?"

"Hagrid is bringing him."

"Do you think it wise to trust Hagrid with something as important as this?"

"Ah, professor. I would trust Hagrid with my life."

Notice how this conversation begins and ends with no context. We're not told what the rumors are. We're not told who the boy is. We're not told who Hagrid is, nor why McGonagall may not trust him with something important. This simple conversation raises a number of questions and thus mysteries that the audience will want to uncover.

We can also often create a mystery by revealing unusual, unexpected, or contradictory information. This can include unusual, unexpected, or contradictory behavior as well. As we'll later explore, we can upend a schema or archetype in order to create something unusual. Contradictory information in particular often calls out for resolution in the mind.

Additionally we can create a mystery by presenting obscured, veiled, or clouded information. A character might say, "There are only two sources I trust—and one of them is my cat." Let the audience know about the existence of the whole and then only reveal a portion of it.

This is the technique used in *Casablanca* when we're first introduced to Rick. First we hear people speaking highly of a "Rick," but we haven't yet seen him. Then once we do finally see him signing a check, we're not shown his face. This obscuring of the face creates a mystery. Who is Rick and what does he look like?

This technique is also used in Hitchcock's *Notorious* when agent Devlin is first introduced. Agent Devlin is seated facing away from the camera. We see his silhouette but can't see his face. This technique is also used in the opening of *The Godfather*. In each instance, we're often intrigued by the missing information and want to stick around a bit longer to uncover the identity of this mystery person.

And finally, we can raise a mystery by explicitly establishing that information is missing. One way to do this is to show that someone is seeking information that they need in order to get what they want. Another way is to have characters ask explicit questions such as in the opening of *Arrival* when reporters are asking questions about the vessels. "If this is some sort of peaceful first contact, why send twelve? Why not just one?"

We can also use promises to create implicit questions about what will happen. We'll later explore techniques to raise questions that the audience will be invited to answer in their imagination.

Passive mysteries can be raised quickly and thus are an ideal tool for piquing the audience's interest in the very beginning of a story. Unlike active mysteries, passive mysteries require little or no context. We're just playing off a spark of curiosity. This appeal to curiosity allows us to invite the audience into the story where we can later raise more active mysteries.

> *Takeaway*: A passive mystery can be created by starting a situation in medias res; by introducing unusual, unexpected, or contradictory information; by presenting obscured, veiled, or clouded information; or by having a character ask an explicit question.

How to Create an Active Mystery

An active mystery consists of a lack of information that a character believes they *need* in order to accomplish another goal. These are the mysteries that drive story plots.

To create an active mystery, we first incite a strong desire in a character via a disruption (i.e. a problem or an opportunity). We then hide or remove information that's necessary to attain that desire. A mystery has now been created and the character must now embark on a search for the missing information. Let's look at an example.

Let's say that our story begins with a protagonist whose loved one is murdered. This incites in the protagonist a desire to seek revenge. From here, we hide important information from the protagonist by concealing the identity of the killer. In order to seek revenge, the protagonist must now set out to uncover the identity of the murderer.

We might also imagine a story that begins with a protagonist whose neighborhood is in danger of being demolished. They learn of the existence of a treasure. From here, we hide important information from the protagonist by concealing the location of the treasure. In order to find the treasure and save the neighborhood, the protagonist will need to seek clues about where it might be hidden. This is essentially *The Goonies* but with a mystery twist.

Because active mysteries are driven by a desire, they're a type of dramatic tension and thus create a dramatic question. The audience wonders, "Will the protagonist get the information they need?" An active mystery generates a much stronger narrative drive than a passive mystery.

> *Takeaway:* An active mystery can be created by inciting a strong desire in a character via a problem or opportunity and then hiding information necessary to attain that desire. An active mystery raises a dramatic question.

Plotting From Mystery

A plot driven by mystery is all about the reveal of disruptive information. When writing a plot founded on mystery, we want to ensure that we have enough hidden information to allow us to keep the story moving forward with powerful revelations that shake the audience's understanding of what's going on.

Mystery plots tend to be driven by a protagonist's desire to uncover the mystery. In this way a mystery can typically be seen as a subset of dramatic tension. These stories often follow a detective on a journey to get to the truth. Examples include *Chinatown, The Maltese Falcon, Zodiac, The Da Vinci Code,* and *Mystic River.*

Which character is trying to hide information? That's the antagonist. Which character is trying to uncover information? That's the protagonist. And if the story's point of view character is the one trying to hide information, then we've got a "crime" story. In a crime story, the protagonist (typically the criminal) is the one trying to hide information and the antagonist (typically the police force) is the one trying to uncover the information. This might be considered a subset of dramatic irony if the audience is in on the information that the protagonist is trying to hide.

When determining the story's antagonist, consider *why* a character may be trying to hide information. A character may try to hide something because their actions are illegal or immoral. They may fear the social consequences of the information becoming public. The character may also be hiding information as part of a plan that requires deception or manipulation. In this case, it's in the character's interest to mask the truth in order to get something else that they want.

Takeaway: To craft a plot from a mystery, determine what's hidden, who's hiding it, why they're hiding it, and what happens if it's revealed (i.e. the stakes for the one doing the hiding). Then send a protagonist on a journey (willingly or unwillingly) to unravel the mystery.

6

PLOTTING FROM CONVERGENCE
PROMISE AS PLOT

Engaging plots (and dramatic situations in general) are driven by one thing: directionality. No matter which dramatic tool we use as the backbone of our plot, the key is to give the audience a sense of direction. We want them anticipating a particular point in the future.

Each dramatic tool we've discussed thus far *implies* a specific future moment in the audience's mind. A dramatic question implies the moment that the protagonist will either successfully attain their goal or fail to attain their goal. Dramatic irony implies the moment that hidden information will be revealed to a character. Mystery implies the moment that the missing information is discovered or revealed.

Our last dramatic tool promises the significance of a future moment. By signaling that there's an important event in the story's future (i.e. by making a promise), we're asking the audience to stick around until that moment. This future event is typically promised in the form of either a ticking clock or convergence.

Urgency and Ticking Clocks

The deadline for that dreaded presentation is approaching. The protagonist has only two minutes until the enemy arrives. The timer on the bomb is ticking down. These are all examples of urgency and they're all fundamentally driven by time.

Urgency requires the explicit or implicit threat (or promise) of something undesired (or desired) happening once a deadline is reached. In other words, the audience needs to know (or at least be able to envision) what might happen once a deadline is reached. This tends to result in suspense since it often creates an uncertain, unknown, and imminent outcome. We might alternatively create tension and mystery by introducing a deadline but not letting the stakeholder know what will happen once the deadline is reached.

Urgency consists of either an explicit or implicit deadline defined by a resource (time, distance, carbon monoxide level, blood remaining, number of champagne bottles remaining, etc.) moving toward a trigger threshold. When the resource reaches the threshold, the deadline is triggered (i.e. the "trigger event" is reached) and the imminent outcome occurs. The resource might be decreasing toward an expiration level or might be increasing toward a level of toxicity.

The moment that a deadline is reached and the trigger event occurs, we have essentially "forced the stakes." We've forced a decision as to whether the stakes of the situation will be won or lost. Time's up.

The deadline resource can either be measured explicitly or implicitly. Often the resource is simply time and is measured by some sort of countdown timer. When the timer reaches zero, the deadline is triggered and the outcome occurs. We can use resources other than time to create urgency, of course. *Apollo 13* uses a gauge to measure the carbon dioxide level in the air. If the carbon dioxide level reaches a certain level of toxicity, it's the end for the crew. *Beauty and the Beast* uses a rose to measure the time remaining until the curse is permanent.

While the resource can be measured explicitly through the use of a measurement device, the resource can also be measured implicitly through dramatization. We simply dramatize the movement of the resource toward or away from the trigger threshold, without the use of an explicit measurement device. We might imagine a man with a knife approaching an unsuspecting character, for instance, or a raft getting closer and closer to a waterfall (where the resource here is distance).

In *Star Wars*, the trigger event is the moment that the Death Star becomes operational. The moment it's up and running, the Rebellion will have essentially run out of time, thus allowing the destruction of entire planets and even the rebel base itself. The resource here is time and the measurement device is a series of updates about how close the Death Star is to operational.

Urgency requires a constant or increasing movement of the resource toward the threshold. If the resource is holding steady or moving away from the trigger threshold, there's little or no urgency. Fundamentally we must feel like some sort of outcome is likely to occur in the relatively near future.

To heighten urgency, we generally want to allow the uncertain outcome to run as close to the deadline (i.e. the trigger event) as possible. As we get up to those final moments before the trigger event, we may want to make the final outcome unknown for as long as we can get away with. We want the audience to desperately wonder, "Were they able to meet the deadline? Did the trigger event occur or not?" This allows us to stretch the dramatic tension.

To most effectively use urgency, ensure that high stakes have been defined. Urgency coupled with high stakes results in a feeling of intense pressure for the protagonist (and the audience). The higher the urgency, the more the audience is driven by the question, "*When will it happen?*"

This tool is sometimes simply referred to as a "ticking clock." Ticking clocks can be set on the global story level, but they can also be used within each scene. Here's the fundamental question: Why is at least one character running out of time? It might be because they're late for a bus, because their favorite show is on, because someone might discover them, or because the sun's going down. Whether explicit or implicit, add a ticking clock to heighten drama.

Introducing urgency is a surefire way of heightening any dramatic situation.

> *Takeaway*: Urgency is created when a resource (typically time) is hurtling toward a trigger threshold (typically a deadline). This urgency can be heightened by getting as close to the trigger threshold as possible. Urgency is a critical piece of heightening a dramatic situation.

Convergence

The ticking clock is actually a piece of a broader principle that we'll call convergence. The core idea here is that we can put two elements on a crash course and provide continual updates as their distance closes. The closer the elements get, the more explicit tension we feel as we anticipate their collision.

This principle isn't limited to just time. We can use it in space as well. We can, for instance, use convergence to create anticipation by setting two characters on a path to the same location. We can then use parallel perspectives to switch back and forth between them and watch as they get closer and closer.

It's also possible to use convergence where only one of the elements is in motion. For example, Dante's Inferno explores a spiraling journey into the depths of Hell, converging at a final point, the ninth circle. A map can give us a clear understanding and feeling of inevitability as the character barrels toward a final destination. This feeling of inevitability is a powerful tool for making the audience want to stick around to get to that final moment of convergence.

Like our other dramatic tools, convergence can be used on both the scene level and the global story level in the form of ticking clocks or physical collisions. Convergence tends to create dramatic interest as we anticipate the point of collision and wonder what will happen when the elements meet.

Takeaway: Convergence is the realization that two elements are on an inevitable crash course. It creates a feeling of anticipation and thus interest. Urgency is a type of convergence where a resource is hurtling toward a threshold.

Plotting From Convergence

A plot driven by convergence is all about focusing on the existence (and typically threat) of a specific future moment in time. We often want to continually remind the audience of the approaching event (thus reminding them of the stakes of the story and emphasizing the ticking clock).

A convergence plot may focus on a character's desire to avoid a looming threat, a desire to prepare to face it, or a desire to reach it. When this is the case, this type of plot is a subset of dramatic tension but adds an element of anticipation by focusing on an explicit moment in the future. *Armageddon* is an example of this type of plot.

The future event may exist merely to raise a mystery about what will happen in between the current moment and the anticipated event. It also sets a time boundary for the story. This is the case in *American Beauty*.

If the future moment is bad, who wants to stop it? That's the story's protagonist. Who's trying to make it happen? That's the story's antagonist. If the future moment is good, of course, then the protagonist is the one trying to make it happen and the antagonist is the one trying to stop it.

Takeaway: To plot from convergence, introduce a deadline, ticking clock, impending collision, or looming threat. The key is to explicitly focus on the significance of a future event.

Reviewing Plotting

This has been a brief introduction to various tools that drive story plots, but it's not where our exploration of plotting ends. Throughout this book, we'll look at story structure, beats, and plotting in detail so don't be concerned if you haven't yet figured out the plot for your story yet. We'll also soon find that many plots arise organically from character.

And finally, while we've explored four main categories from which plot may arise, most stories are driven by a character who wants something and struggles to get it. A story's plot in and of itself need not be especially unique.

7

STARTING FROM A STORY WORLD

We can think of a story world as the culture, time, and physical space in which a story takes place. But perhaps more importantly, a story world is also the set of rules that governs what *can* and *can't* happen over the course of the story. Failing to properly define the rules upfront can lead to audience frustration when a solution comes from "out of nowhere" or a character is able to access some power or technology, for instance, that hasn't been referenced or defined.

In our story creation process, we might more broadly think of a "world" as a collection of concepts that go together. In other words, we'll consider a "world" to be any collection of concepts that are thematically cohesive. For instance, we might say that *Finding Nemo* explores the "world of fish." *The Incredibles* explores the "world of superheroes." *Up* explores the "world of explorers" or the "world of adventurers."

One powerful method for creating a story world is to use a metaphor. We take a familiar concept from a "world" (i.e. a thematically cohesive collection of concepts) and then we consider how it might be expressed within some other "world." In effect, we're asking, "What is [x] in terms of [y]?"

For instance, let's say we've identified that we're interested in the "world of psychics." We might then identify a séance as being a part of the "world of psychics." Let's take that concept and apply it to another world. We might then ask, "What is a séance in the world of fish?" What would that look like? We might imagine a clairvoyant fish looking into an oyster pearl, as a fortune teller does. An audience of fish are all sitting on their sponge chairs around a table of coral. An anglerfish provides the candlelight.

Of course, let's also note that a séance in the world of fish looks different than fish in the world of a séance. One takes the tropes and activities of a séance and expresses them as fish would understand them and the other takes the tropes and activities of fish and expresses them as those individuals in a séance would understand them.

We might consider *Harry Potter* as the "world of school" expressed in terms of the "world of wizards." Or in other words, what does school look like in the wizarding world? It looks like Hogwarts.

Star Wars shows us the "world of dogfighting" in the "world of space," which ends up looking like TIE Fighter battles. It also shows us the world (or culture) of Samurai in the "world of space," which ends up looking like the Jedi and the Sith.

The story world doesn't need to be one of fantasy or sci-fi. Recall that a "world" is simply a collection of thematically cohesive concepts. A story might explore the world of the FBI and serial killers (as in *The Silence of the Lambs*). It might explore the world of boxing in Philadelphia (as in *Rocky*). It might explore the world of space missions (as in *Apollo 13*). It might be the world of coliseums and gladiators (as in *The Gladiator*). The key is that we pick a distinct collection of thematically cohesive concepts that we can then explore and potentially consider expressing in different terms.

> *Takeaway*: To begin creating a world, consider selecting a thematically cohesive collection of concepts. These concepts can then be expressed in the terms of a different world altogether. *Harry Potter*, for instance, explores the world of school within the world of wizards.

Research and Development of Story World

Once we've chosen a basic set of thematically cohesive concepts that we'd like to explore (i.e. a "world"), it's time to expand that world through research and development.

While Pixar has the resources to bring in experts and travel to different locations around the world, sometimes we're not able to go to these lengths for our own stories. A deep dive on Wikipedia, however, is often a suitable substitute. Pixar covers the walls with images and notes. We might consider keeping our own virtual room of images and notes after extensive use of image searching to ignite the imagination.

While researching, we want to jot down anything that sparks our interest. When it comes to story world, we're in the realm of the unfamiliar and consequently we want to capture the feeling of wonder and fascination. More than anything, we want to pursue that which fascinates us about the world. That's our guiding light in this research process.

When doing research on a story world, take particular note of a few things. First list any interesting settings and locations. Take note of any unique relationships between the occupants (people, animals, plants, or objects) and their surroundings. Research any rituals, activities, processes, ceremonies, festivals, celebrations, or gatherings. How do these gatherings relate to the setting and location? Take note of the culture of the world more generally. How does the world organize itself? What are the power dynamics? Does the world have any heroes? What are the value systems of the world's communities? What are the varied worldviews of the occupants?

Next look for categories of beings in the world. The world of wizards is filled with magic users, non-magic users, creatures, witches, warlocks, necromancers, psychics, fairies, griffins, dragons, carnivorous plants, etc. We should also expand this list to consider occupations that might appear in the world. What might a police officer, detective, chef, civil engineer, investigative reporter, artist, athlete, and surgeon look like within the world of wizards?

Take special note of any objects that are particularly important to the world. Are there any objects that are symbolic of larger or deeper ideas or values? What objects are used on a day-to-day basis? What objects are revered? We're really looking for anything that a character might manipulate or interact with. In this sense, the object doesn't necessarily need to be mobile.

Finally note any value systems, philosophies, worldviews, mantras, or deeply held beliefs in this world. What does the culture of this world value above all else? With what is the world obsessed? Who does the world revere? What do they think is the correct way to live life? What does the world fear? What does the world look down upon? What does the world shame or guilt? Are there any societal rules about what must be done or about what is forbidden? In *Monsters, Inc.*, for instance, there's a societal rule that monsters can't come into contact with a human child. We can then take these value systems and determine some of the basic desires and fears of characters in the world.

Remember, when it comes to exploring a story world, we want to prioritize that which sparks our imagination. We should pursue that which evokes awe above all else.

Takeaway: We can explore a story world by assembling images and ideas that spark the imagination. We then want to ask questions about the world's value system. We should pursue that which fascinates us above all else.

8

STARTING FROM THEME

Where a story world is based almost entirely on the unfamiliar and fascinating, theme is based almost entirely on the familiar and resonant. While we generally want to shun that which came before us when it comes to story world, we want to revere that which came before us when it comes to theme. Common themes and dilemmas about the best way to live life appear to be deeply ingrained in humans. These constant thematic struggles have occurred for time immemorial and it doesn't appear that these dilemmas will be definitively solved anytime soon. If our goal is to create a deep connection with the audience on an emotional level, we can give ourselves a head start by learning from the themes of the past and incorporating them into our own stories.

Before we consider how we can begin crafting our story from a theme, let's explore the principles of theme in story.

First Principles of Theme

Theme is responsible for changing the audience's perception of either themselves or of the world. Theme is the protein of story. Without it, the audience leaves a story empty, subsiding on the momentary sugar-high of drama. To leave them full and satisfied, we need to make sure the candy of drama is filled with the protein of theme.

Theme allows us to explore different emotions than those invoked by drama. We move from the world of surprise, suspense, hope, and fear to the world of nostalgia, clarity, purpose, significance, triumph, and heartache. What tools can we use to evoke these emotions? How do we infuse our stories with meaning in such a way that they have the ability to change the audience's perception of either themselves or of the world?

Just as no single molecule of water is wet, no single thematic tool will provide us with the emotional impact we need. Wetness is an emergent property of water molecules taken together. In the same way, the emotional impact of theme is an emergent property of a number of thematic story elements used in harmony.

We'll explore several thematic tools to help us capture these emotions and to infuse our stories with meaning.

What is Theme?

We often see stories explore topics such as "love," "war," "corruption," or "loss." Some people refer to these concepts as "themes." But for our purposes, these aren't themes—they're theme topics. Let's define theme in more detail.

Adam Skelter says, "Themes are generally claims about how the world works." We might also say that themes are claims about how the world *should* work. A theme is the storyteller's moral vision. It's the answer to a question about the right way to live one's life. When crafting a story, we'll consider theme to be a *specific* observation about how the world works or about how one should live in this world.

Michael Hauge suggests we phrase a story's theme as, "In order to ___, you must ___." It's a piece of advice to the audience. He offers the example that "In order to recover from deep grief, you must honor the past by living in the present." Of course, any piece of advice implies that there's an alternate route that one *could* take (otherwise the advice itself would be unnecessary). Instead of honoring the past by living in the present, for instance, we could memorialize the past by actively bringing it with us in the present. In the movie *Up*, Carl initially honors the past by holding on to it and eventually learns that he needs to form new relationships and live his new life to the fullest in order to truly honor the past.

> *Takeaway*: A theme is a specific message about how one should act in the world in order to live one's best life.

The Dilemma Pair

Because theme can be phrased as a piece of advice, we can always consider the opposite of the advice. This means that we can think of theme as one half of two opposing ways of living life—two opposing value systems. We'll refer to these two opposing approaches collectively as a dilemma pair, a thematic opposition, or thematic conflict. Each theme, then, is merely one side of a dilemma pair.

Each side of a dilemma pair is a value system. It's a set of beliefs about what makes a good and fulfilling life.

A few common dilemma pairs are faith versus reason (do we put our trust in faith or do we put our trust in reason?), the individual versus the community (do we prioritize the individual or the community?), means versus ends (do the ends justify the means? Are there lines we should never cross?), and duty versus love (do we forsake our duty to pursue true love and passion?). Let's more closely consider the dilemma pair of duty versus love. One side of this dilemma might argue, "In order to live a fulfilling life, one must always prioritize one's duties and responsibilities over love." The other side might argue, "In order to live a fulfilling life, one must pursue true love even if it means forsaking one's duties."

We must keep in mind that these are legitimate dilemmas. Both sides of the opposition have merit. We must resist the urge to say that one side is always right and one side is always wrong. Let's consider a dilemma pair that seems like it would have a clear answer: means versus ends. The central dilemma here is whether the ends always justify the means or whether there are some lines (means) that shouldn't be crossed. This is one of the central dilemmas between good and evil—between the heroes and the villains. Heroes often believe that one should not stoop to immorality in order to win. Villains, on the other hand, tend to believe that the goal always justifies the tactics, whether or not the tactics are moral.

Our initial instinct might be to say that the correct way to live life is to avoid immoral means. But let's consider a few scenarios. Would you steal in order to save your family? Would you kill someone already on death row in order to save the life of a loved one? Would you commit a crime if you knew your family would be killed if you refused? What tactics should society allow to extract information when millions of lives are in imminent danger? These dilemmas might cause us to think critically about our thoughts on ends versus means. The point here is to highlight that we as storytellers must do our best to consider all sides of a dilemma—not just the one we think is correct.

One way to open our minds to both sides of a thematic dilemma is to reframe our questions. We want to change our mindset from considering *whether* something is permissible to considering *when* something is permissible. Instead of asking, "Is it ever okay to kill someone?", we might instead ask, "Under what circumstances is it okay to kill someone?" Instead of asking, "Is it ever okay to torture?", we might instead ask, "Under what circumstances is it okay to torture?" This asks us to stretch our minds and perhaps consider unusual or extreme circumstances that involve things of intense value for the dilemma's participants.

Some dilemma pairs can be subsets of others. We might consider that duty (community) versus love (individual) is a subset of the dilemma pair community versus individual. We can also take a dilemma such as duty versus love and consider more specific dilemmas such as country versus family, career vs relationship, and obligation versus passion.

Takeaway: A dilemma pair consists of a theme on one side (i.e. a piece of advice) and the anti-theme on the other side (i.e. the opposite piece of advice). Legitimate arguments can be made on both sides of a thematic dilemma.

Conveying Theme

Now that we've defined theme, the next logical question is: How is theme most effectively communicated to the audience? To start, we can say how it's most *ineffectively* communicated: through sermonizing and preaching. There are few things that turn an audience off faster than a character that preaches to the audience about how they're living their life wrong and about how they should change.

We'll need to change our mindset when it comes to delivering a message to the audience. Our goal isn't to explicitly communicate a theme but rather to *explore* a dilemma pair. It's only by comparing a piece of advice to its opposition that we (and the audience) can know a theme's true meaning. The audience doesn't want to be told what to think—they genuinely want to explore alternatives and come to their own conclusion. This is the opportunity we must give them.

Just as the question, "How do we generate dramatic interest?" was our driving question for drama, "How is a thematic dilemma pair best explored?" will be our driving question for theme. We'll go over several thematic patterns that we can use to explore a dilemma pair.

Takeaway: The best way to "deliver a message" in a story is to explore all sides of a thematic opposition without sermonizing or preaching.

The Great Decision Moment

The argument for one side of a dilemma pair can perhaps best be expressed through dramatizing a decision. If we want to argue that duty is more important than love, we need to show the audience a definitive moment when a character is forced to make the great decision between duty and love. Powerful stories tend to have a Great

Decision moment where a character must take everything they've learned over the course of the story and decide between one of two value systems. This is the ultimate moment where the storyteller makes their argument about the best way to live life (often by rewarding the protagonist for the correct decision or punishing them for the incorrect decision). This is the climax.

In *Casablanca*, Rick must ultimately decide between helping the Resistance by losing the love of his life, Ilsa, or taking Ilsa for himself and potentially dooming the Allied cause (love versus duty). In *Star Wars*, Luke's climactic decision moment is when he's in the trench of the Death Star. He must decide whether to use his guidance computer or turn it off and use the force as his final attack. In this moment, Luke is making a choice in the thematic battle between faith (the force) and reason (technology). In *The Lord of the Rings*, Frodo must decide whether to keep the ring for himself or cast it into the fires of Mount Doom—essentially deciding between personal power (individual) and societal wellbeing (community).

Perhaps the most important requirement of The Great Decision Moment is that it must actually be a choice. The protagonist can't be forced to choose one side or the other—they must make the decision of their own volition. If Frodo has no choice in whether to cast the ring into the fires, then we don't have a real decision and thus the thematic conflict is merely a façade.

Secondarily the audience shouldn't know which side the protagonist will choose. There should be true uncertainty. If we know what the answer will be, there's effectively no dilemma and consequently what was supposed to be the most climactic moment becomes boring.

To heighten uncertainty on a thematic level, we must ensure that we've used the story to thoroughly explore both sides of the thematic opposition. We've got to make the arguments that each side of the dilemma would make in good faith. What are the arguments for destroying the ring and what are the arguments against? Even if we as storytellers don't believe in the "opposing" side, we must present and explore its point of view in good faith. We've got to pull the protagonist in both directions.

And finally, this Great Decision must be the moment with the highest stakes in the story. The character must have everything to gain and everything to lose. Here the stakes aren't just physical or even emotional, they're philosophical. They also tend to be tied closely to the character's identity. This moment, after all, will be the moment that defines who this character *is* based on the thematic choice they make. We are, in this moment, quite literally *defining* character.

As the audience, we become emotionally invested in these difficult decision moments. These dilemmas tend to be fascinating—we wonder if we would have made the same choice in that situation.

We must remember that this Great Decision isn't just a dilemma about whether to get on the plane with Ilsa, or whether to use a guidance computer to destroy the Death Star, or whether to throw the ring into the fire. It's an internal dilemma where both choices pull on the character (sometimes to pursue and sometimes to avoid). There's a devil and an angel on the protagonist's shoulder. It's a philosophical battle between two value systems. It's the ultimate climactic moment when the opposition inherent in the dilemma pair comes to a head. The individual and the community face off. Faith and reason face off. Duty and love face off. It's the moment when the protagonist plants their flag in the ground and declares through action which side of the thematic opposition they've chosen. It's the last and most important decision the character will make in the story.

Let's now consider a few of the possible journeys that a character might take to arrive at their choice in The Great Decision.

Takeaway: The best way to explore a thematic opposition is to force a character to confront a great decision between two value systems. The character must take action to demonstrate their commitment to one value system over another.

Value System Exploration

Recall that our guiding question in the thematic realm is, "How is a dilemma pair best explored?" To explore a dilemma pair, we've got to set up and explore an opposition of value systems. The next question then becomes, "How might a thematic opposition be embodied and dramatized?"

In the realm of theme, relativity is king. Duty is made meaningful only by comparing it to love. Selfishness is made meaningful only by comparing it to selflessness. A thematic argument is made meaningful only when it's juxtaposed with its counter argument, creating a thematic opposition. It's often only through comparison that we understand something's true value. This will be a central principle for not only exploring value systems but also for heightening emotion in our stories.

There are two primary methods of dramatizing a thematic opposition and they're both rooted in relativity and comparison. The first method is to juxtapose the thematic choice of a character at one point in their life with the thematic choice of the same character at a different point in their life. By comparing the difference in thematic choices over time, we highlight the character's change. This change is often called a character's arc.

Alternatively we might juxtapose a character with a community (i.e. with other characters), thereby setting up a societal opposition of values. This allows us to compare two value systems side by side and see their effects. These are archetypal patterns, of course, and we can also explore theme through the use of multiple character arcs rather than simply one. We'll take a look at each technique individually, but first we've got to discuss morality.

> **Takeaway:** A thematic opposition is often explored by comparing a character to a community or by comparing a character's choices at one time to their choices at a later time (i.e. a character arc).

Morality in Dilemma Pairs

Morality is about defining which actions are "right" and which are "wrong" when dealing with other people. In other words, morality is about how to act properly in human relationships. That which is immoral is said to hurt others, by definition.

Certain dilemma pairs more readily imply that one value system is moral while the other is immoral. For instance, in the thematic opposition of personal power versus societal wellbeing, it's fairly clear that societal wellbeing is the more moral choice of the two. Likewise in the thematic opposition between means and ends, valuing the means is the more moral choice of the two. Other dilemma pairs such as faith versus reason aren't as clear in their morality. Is it more important to value faith or to value reason? And what about duty versus love?

Of course, the morality of these dilemma pairs can vary by society. One society may see "duty" as the clear moral winner in duty versus love. One society may view the individual as more important than the community while another may view the community as superior. Perhaps our most unappreciated power as storytellers is that we influence which side of a thematic opposition is considered moral by society. This may be why Plato is believed to have said, "Those who tell the stories rule society."

> *Takeaway*: Morality is about how to act properly in human relationships. It's about defining which actions are "right" and which are "wrong."

Character Arc (Value System Change)

A character arc is the transition of a character from initially embodying one value system to later embodying a different value system. This is an internal transformation.

Character arcs are often about the shift of a character from moral weakness to moral strength or from moral strength to moral weakness (i.e. immorality). These are morality arcs. There are two broad character arc types: the positive character arc and the negative character arc.

The positive arc shows us a character who starts with some personality trait that causes negative moral action—or what John Truby calls a "moral weakness." This character is one we might call a "flawed character." The key here is that we must show how the moral weakness (often in the form of a personality trait or behavior) causes action that negatively affects *others* (remember morality is about our relationships with *others*). The character then learns to overcome this moral weakness over the course of their arc, resulting in moral strength. We might also call this the "rise arc" or in some cases the "redemption arc."

We can also imagine a character who starts with a moral weakness but fails to overcome their moral weakness. This is a flawed character who never learns what they need to learn. If we go this route, we often want to make it abundantly clear that they *should have* learned a moral lesson (typically by making it clear to the audience that their moral weakness is the source of their problems). This allows the audience to learn the lesson even if the character doesn't.

The negative arc, on the other hand, shows us a character who starts as a relatively moral person. Over the course of the arc, the character makes decisions that compromise their morality. They give in to temptation. The character becomes morally corrupted. This results in a new moral weakness that negatively affects others. We might also call this the "fall arc" or the "corruption arc."

The moral weakness is the character's embodiment of a negative value system. A state of moral strength is the character's embodiment of a positive value system.

Of course, we can also imagine a character arc that isn't strictly from the moral to the immoral or from the immoral to the moral. Perhaps a character starts out valuing duty and arcs to valuing love or vice versa. Perhaps a character starts out valuing reason and arcs to valuing faith or vice versa. This type of arc isn't as much about overcoming a moral weakness as it is about changing one's beliefs (i.e. value systems).

We can also explore a character who starts the story without any entrenched belief. This character may then be influenced by characters on both sides of the central dilemma pair. This is the case with Luke in *Star Wars*. He doesn't start the story with any clear preference for faith or technology. His battle tactics in the trench run on the Death Star dramatize that he's chosen the side of faith over technology. This character doesn't go from moral weakness to moral strength but rather from no clear belief to belief.

> *Takeaway*: A character arc consists of a character shifting from one value system to another. A positive arc consists of a character going from moral weakness to moral strength. A negative arc consists of a character going from moral strength to moral weakness.

Societal Value Opposition

We've discussed exploring thematic opposition by showing a single character arc from one value system to the opposing value system. We can also explore a thematic opposition by juxtaposing two communities where each community embodies one of the value systems.

The *Star Wars* story world sets up two primary communities: the Rebel Alliance and the Empire. The Rebellion embodies the value system of societal freedom, democracy, and means over ends. The Empire, on the other hand, embodies the value system of personal power, autocracy, and ends over means. In this opposition, the Rebel Alliance is more closely aligned to moral action (the "light side") while the Empire is more closely aligned to immoral action (the "dark side").

Star Wars takes this a step further and sets up an additional thematic opposition within these larger communities. The secondary opposition is between the force users (most often Jedi or Sith) and the non-force users or technologists. The force users embody the value system of faith while the technologists embody the value system of technology or reason.

This secondary opposition allows the *Star Wars* universe to explore not just means versus ends but also faith versus technology. Additionally the faith versus technology opposition isn't divided along the same lines as means versus ends. For instance, Han Solo values both freedom and technology. Obi-Wan values freedom and faith. Grand Moff Tarkin values power and technology. And Darth Vader values power and faith. Just because one is a force user doesn't necessarily make one moral or immoral. And likewise, just because one is a technologist doesn't necessarily make one moral or immoral.

The inclusion of two central dilemmas allows a multi-dimensional opposition of value systems. This also allows Luke Skywalker to be a character of both moral strength and hope when it comes to the dilemma of ends versus means (and autocracy vs freedom) and at the same time be influenced in the dilemma of faith versus technology.

This multi-dimensional opposition also potentially allows us to explore a dilemma pair in a less biased way. The audience can't infer, for instance, that just because only the good guys hold the faith value system that faith is the "correct" answer. Likewise the audience can't infer that just because the bad guys hold the faith value system that faith is the "incorrect" answer. There are both morally good and morally bad characters on both sides of the dilemma pair. This helps us assess each side of the dilemma pair of faith versus technology on merit.

Takeaway: We can explore a dilemma pair by exploring the actions of two or more communities that each embody one side of the thematic opposition.

Character Versus Community

Another way to explore a thematic opposition is to juxtapose a single character with a community. As with character arcs, this pattern often consists of exploring a dilemma pair that implies a morality. Typically there's a moral character juxtaposed with an immoral community or an immoral character juxtaposed with a moral community.

The key with this pattern is that, unlike with a character arc, this character won't change. We explore both sides of the thematic opposition by showing the character's morality in conflict with the community's.

If the character is moral, then their thematic goal is to persist in their moral strength in the face of the community's immoral influence. This moral character is sometimes called a traveling angel. If the character is immoral, on the other hand, then it's the community that must persist in its moral strength in the face of the character's immoral influence. This immoral character is sometimes called a traveling devil.

We call the character "innocent" when they're moral and steadfast in the face of an immoral community. Luke Skywalker is an innocent character who spreads his moral strength throughout society. In *Little Miss Sunshine*, Olive is an innocent character who starts the story already believing in herself but must remain steadfast in the face of opposition from her father and the pageant community at large. The innocent character tends to embody a value system that stands in opposition to the community's value system.

We could alternatively have an anti-hero character who begins the story living in immorality and remains steadfast in their immorality even when presented with opportunities to be moral. Of course, it's also possible that both the character and the community are immoral as is the case with Lou and the community of nightcrawling in the movie *Nightcrawler*.

> *Takeaway*: We can explore a dilemma pair by giving one value system to a character and the opposing value system to a community.

Community Arcs

We'll find that a community can take on many of the storytelling functions of a character. Communities, for instance, can arc in a similar way to how characters arc. This is often the case when an innocent character spreads their influence to the community at large and causes a societal change. We might consider this to be the case in *Little Miss Sunshine* when Olive influences the value system of her family. In order for a community to arc, of course, one or more characters who represent the community must change.

Dramatizing a Value System

Of course, we can't just have a character wear a sign to indicate their value system at any point in time. We've got to dramatize it. So how do we dramatize that a character embodies a value system?

We dramatize a character's value system by dramatizing choice. This can't be just any choice, however. A character's value system is defined only when a *high-stakes* choice is made. In other words, there must be potential negative consequences to the dilemma. A choice with no consequence proves nothing. It's meaningless. Anyone can make a decision when they lose nothing by choosing incorrectly. It's only when a thing of value might be lost that a choice reveals a character's value system. Actions speak where words deceive. What one truly believes is only revealed when something of value is on the line.

Another way to look at this is that values are demonstrated based on what we're willing to risk in order to defend or champion those values. Of course, a character doesn't actually have to lose in order to demonstrate their value system—they just need to be *willing* to risk that which they value.

This principle is at the root of The Great Decision Moment. It's the moment when we dramatize the character's definitive choice of value system.

Action under pressure is what *defines* a character. Character, in the most basic sense, is defined by the actions that one takes in response to a dilemma. Decision creates character.

> *Takeaway*: To dramatize that a character embodies a value system, show them choosing one value system over another in a high-stakes decision. Character is defined by choices made under pressure.

Making a Thematic Argument

Once we've set up a thematic opposition and explored both sides of a central dilemma pair, we have to consider how we're going to argue which side of the theme is the correct one. To make this thematic argument, we either reward or punish the decision made at The Great Decision Moment.

We can endorse a value system by rewarding an affirmative choice of that value system. We can endorse a value system by rewarding a character who remains steadfast in that value system, especially in the face of temptation. We can also endorse a value system by punishing the inability or unwillingness to either choose or remain steadfast in that value system.

In most cases we will want to reward the moral value system and punish the immoral value system. We can, however, provide the audience a feeling of injustice, hopelessness, or meaninglessness by rewarding an immoral value system or punishing the adoption of a moral value system.

The next question is, "How do we reward and punish?" One technique to reward a character is to give them what they want. That is, we can allow the character to attain their desire. However rewards can be given in a way the character didn't expect. Instead of giving a character what they wanted, we can give the character what they need in order to live a more fulfilling life. In other words, we have the character overcome their moral weakness and then show how their relationships begin to flourish. The key is to show the positive effect on the character's relationships. This is the heart of morality. To punish, we show damage to a character's relationships, which then propagates to their mental wellbeing.

> *Takeaway*: To make an argument about which side of a thematic opposition is "correct," reward the adoption of the moral value system and punish the adoption of the immoral value system.

Crafting From Theme

To start a story from theme, we want to consider which thematic dilemma pair may best suit the message we're trying to convey in our story. We'll then ground the chosen dilemma pair in the context of the story world. Let's explore a few of the most common dilemma pairs. This is by no means a comprehensive list, but it's a good start.

Individual Versus Community

Which is more important, the individual or the community? Is the individual worth sacrificing for the community? Is it worth sacrificing the community to save an individual? Do we prioritize ourselves or our relationships? We can also conceive of the "community" as the species, herd, tribe, social group, family, mission, or cause. Do we sacrifice an individual for the cause? Do we sacrifice someone to keep an important secret?

In *The Imitation Game*, the group has cracked the Enigma Code, but they can't let on that they've cracked the code. If they stop a ship from being sunk (saving those on board), the enemy might know they've cracked the code, which will endanger more lives in the future. Do they save the ship or sacrifice them to keep the secret? This dilemma is also one of interventionism vs isolationism—do we have a moral obligation to help others when we're in a position to?

Faith Versus Reason

Should we live primarily by faith or by reason? This dilemma also comes in the form of faith versus technology (which is the primary thematic drive of *Star Wars*). We might also see a form of emotion versus logic, feeling versus thinking, brain versus heart, and trust versus proof. Which principle should guide our decisions and actions?

Love Versus Duty

Should we prioritize love and our relationships or our duty and obligations? We might see this dilemma as a form of individual versus community where love is about the individual and duty is about the community. This is the primary dilemma in Hitchcock's *Notorious*. It might also be seen as love versus career, which is the form it takes in *Monsters, Inc.* We could see it as love versus patriotism, which is the form it takes in *Casablanca*. Should we value our relationships over society? Or do we sacrifice society for our relationships? Should we value romance over family? This is the dilemma of *Romeo and Juliet*.

Attachment Versus Detachment

Is it better to commit oneself and risk loss or to stay detached and ensure no loss? In other words, is it better to commit and risk failure or stay out of it and guarantee no failure (but also no success)? Is it better to have loved and lost or better to have never loved at all? Is it better to have hope and potentially be let down or better to be pessimistic (and thus have no expectations) and never be let down? The movie *Up* explores a subset of this dilemma by asking the question of whether it's best to honor the past by living in the present (detach) or to memorialize the past by actively bringing it with us in the present (attach). Carl must eventually learn that in order to recover from deep grief, he must honor the past by living in the present.

Ends Versus Means

Does "might make right" (valuing the ends) or does "right make might" (valuing the means)? Does the reward justify any strategy to attain it? Or are there some goals that must be forsaken if they can only be reached by immoral means? Do the means justify the ends if we're saving people? Can we torture, for instance, in order to save a large number of people? Do we make a deal with evil in order to catch evil? This is the question explored in *The Silence of the Lambs*— do we appease one killer to catch another? Do we need to play evil's game in order to beat evil? Is it worth going to any means necessary to defeat evil? What if you can't beat evil except by being evil?

Power Versus Morality

This dilemma is a form of ends versus means. In *Star Wars*, the dilemma between dark and light is "the power of the dark side" versus "the morality of the light side." We might also think of this dilemma as a form of individual versus community. Do we take power for ourselves or do we protect the morality and wellbeing of society? This is one of the dilemmas in *The Lord of the Rings*. If we don't destroy the thing that provides personal power, are we allowing the opportunity for the thing to be used malevolently in someone else's hands? If we allow consolidation of power for the good, will it eventually be used for evil? Do we avoid all consolidation of power with this in mind? Can some good things only be done with enough consolidated power?

Easy Versus Right

This dilemma is a form of ends versus means. Do we pursue that which is easy or that which is right? The easy way tends to be comfortable and quick but immoral. The right way tends to be difficult and slow but moral. Another form is moral versus practical. Sometimes that which we think is right isn't that which we think will actually work. Do we forgo our principles and values for that which we desire now? Do we sacrifice freedom for security? Do we lie (easy) or tell the truth (right)?

Justice Versus Legality

This dilemma is a form of ends versus means. Do we follow the law if it means the bad guy will get away? Do we take the law into our own hands and use extrajudicial tactics if it means capturing the bad guy? Can we work outside of the law to avenge our loved ones? Do the ends of defeating a greater evil justify any means? What tactics are permissible (or required) to bring bad guys to justice? Do we break the law in order to get justice? Is what's legal always just? Is what's just always legal?

Knowledge Versus Ignorance

Is it better to know (and face the implications, stress, and responsibility of knowledge) or is it better to stay in the dark (and face a potentially unpleasant surprise)? Would we want to know when we're going to die? Would we want to know when the world will end? Would we rather remain ignorant and blissful or would we rather know and be faced with the potentially weighty knowledge and implications? Would we forget the past if we could? How much would that be worth to us? This is one of the dilemmas in *Eternal Sunshine of the Spotless Mind*.

Interventionism Versus Isolationism

What's our moral responsibility to address an injustice? Do we have a moral obligation to help others when we're in a position to help? What if getting involved might put us in danger? This is explored in the movie *Schindler's List* where Oskar Schindler *could* walk away and ignore the atrocities around him but he *chooses* not to. This is also the case in *The Imitation Game* when the group has cracked the Enigma Code. They're faced with the dilemma of whether to help a ship and potentially reveal that they've cracked the code or let the ship be attacked.

Another form of this dilemma is: Do we prioritize justice or peace? Do we ignore and/or appease that which is evil in the hope that it'll go away? Or do we fight (and risk our lives) in order to quash it? This is one of the dilemmas in *Harry Potter*. Do we continue to believe in (or at least tolerate) something we know to be unjust/corrupt in order to maintain peace? Or do we instigate violence or disruption for the hope of something better in the future? Do we maintain order under the current totalitarian tyranny? Or do we overthrow tyranny for what will surely result in chaos? Do we appease someone who wants something in order to keep them at bay? Or do we confront them, possibly resulting in war or conflict?

Life Versus Death

What actions are permissible in order to survive? What would we be willing to do to survive? Would we cut off our arm? Would we betray others? Would we betray ourselves? Would we betray our values? Would we betray our religion, relationships, etc.? Is it permissible to break the law to survive? Is it better to live enslaved or to die? Is it better to be tortured and live or to prefer death over torture? How do we summon the strength to continue on through such torture? It is, perhaps, the ultimate dilemma: to be or not to be?

Gratitude Versus Ambition

Is happiness derived from appreciating what we already have? Or is happiness derived from having and chasing a goal? Is the grass actually greener on the other side? Is there harm in going to the other side to check?

Short-Term Versus Long-Term

Do we enjoy life in the moment by spending our resources, relaxing, and having fun or do we conserve, prepare, work hard now, sacrifice now, and plan for the future? Are we ever guaranteed tomorrow? Should we live life as if it'll never come? What kind of life is tomorrow if it does arrive and we haven't prepared for it? This is the thematic dilemma in *The Three Little Pigs*. How would our decisions change if we knew how long we had left to live?

Nature Versus Nurture

What defines family? Who's considered a true member of the family? Can one be a family member if one doesn't have the family's blood? Are we products of our environment and culture or of our genetics?

Progress Versus Tradition

Do we move forward with industry, progress, and innovation at the cost of jobs? Do we move forward with industry at the cost of nature? Do we move forward with progress at the cost of our culture, history, and heritage?

> *Takeaway*: A story's theme is rooted in one or more timeless dilemmas. Exploring one or more of these dilemma pairs provides a story with a strong sense of familiarity.

Find the Boundaries of Theme

There are some dilemma pairs that may seem to have clear answers to a person of moral character. Do the ends always justify the means? Is torture okay? Is killing the innocent ever justified? Our first instinct may be to say, "Of course not!" Unfortunately that's not a helpful perspective when exploring both sides of a thematic opposition. Recall that we can reframe these thematic dilemmas in a way that forces us to consider the other side of the dilemma. Instead of asking, "Is it ever okay to kill someone?", we might instead ask, "Under what circumstances is it okay to kill someone?" This perspective can allow us to explore the grey areas of a thematic opposition where the choice becomes less clear.

We may want to ask ourselves, "In what scenarios is this justified? Under what scenario can be this be rationalized?" From a personal perspective, we may ask what would need to happen for us to do something immoral. Would a loved one need to be in imminent danger? It can be fruitful to ask ourselves thematic questions that force answers beyond a "yes" or a "no."

Want Versus Need

There's one dilemma into which most others can fit comfortably: the dilemma between that which one wants and that which one needs in order to live a better life. What we *want* is often easy, comfortable, short-term, self-centered, and ends-oriented. What we *need* to do is often difficult, uncomfortable, long-term, other-centered, and means-oriented. It's seldom easy to do what we *should* do. One of the greatest challenges of life may be doing what we know we *should* do when it's most uncomfortable, terrifying, and sometimes personally disadvantageous. This is perhaps the ultimate character dilemma.

Grounding Theme in Story World

After we've chosen a dilemma to be at the heart of our story, we need to ground that dilemma in the story world or culture. In other words, we need to represent the various possible approaches to the dilemma through various characters and communities.

Crafting From Dilemma

There are a few ways to ground a theme in a story world. The first technique is to start with our dilemma pair and express it in terms of the story world. Let's say that our story world is the "world of the savanna" and that we've chosen the dilemma "individual versus community." We next want to consider how this thematic opposition might be expressed in terms of the story world. First of all, what are the "terms" of the story world? They're the salient properties and prominent features of the world. It's the stuff we flesh out when exploring a story world. In the savanna, prominent features might be elephants, cheetahs, giraffes, lions, gazelles, the sun, the oasis, drought, wildfire, famine, hunting, poaching, the food chain, predators, the herd, etc.

We previously discussed how a single character might express both sides of the dilemma pair at different times, resulting in a character arc. We also discussed how a character might spread their worldview throughout a community, resulting in a community arc.

Who or what might represent each side of the dilemma? Female cheetahs hunt alone so we might say that they represent the side of the individual. Lion packs, on the other hand, hunt in groups and thus they might represent the side of the community. We might focus on a young cheetah cub with her hungry mother cheetah. She sees in the distance a pride of lions feasting and wonders why her mom doesn't hunt with other cheetahs. This sets us up with an innocent character who's born into a society that prioritizes the individual but wants to spread the value and benefit of the community. We might alternatively consider a lion cub who doesn't see the point in having to deal with the foolish hunting plans of others and goes off on her own to hunt. This potentially sets us up with a flawed character who must learn the value of working with others.

This technique of expressing the dilemma directly can be a bit over-simplified or "on the nose." One way to make the dilemma feel a bit more realistic is to further specify it. We can explore the value system of each side of the thematic opposition. For instance, what might the individual value? Self-reliance, self-governance, an enterprising spirit, chasing one's dreams, making one's own decisions, resilience, ambition, and reward. What might the community value? Helping others, sacrifice, protecting others, unity, sharing, altruism, laws, responsibility, and contribution. We might then create a dilemma between these sub-values. For instance, we could explore the dilemma of protecting oneself versus sacrificing and protecting others—all within the world of the savanna. This new dilemma becomes a subset of the larger dilemma between individual versus community.

We should also remember that "community" can be replaced with mission, cause, family, relationships, team, etc. One possible dilemma could be whether one should give up on one's dreams in service of helping the cause/mission of the herd, for instance.

> *Takeaway*: We can take a dilemma pair and express it in a story world by contrasting communities and/or showing a character change from one side of the thematic opposition to the other. We can also explore a subset of a dilemma in order to make it less "on the nose."

Crafting From Worldview and Belief

Recall that we originally explored how a story's theme can generally be considered a piece of advice (i.e. the side of the dilemma pair that the storyteller is arguing). It might come in the form "In order to ___, you must ___" or "In order to live the best life, one should ___" or "The most important thing in life is___." One method by which we can ground a theme is to first choose the advice we want to convey (i.e. the way we think people *should* act in the world) and then determine the opposition to that advice afterward.

We might start with the thought, "In order to live a more fulfilled life, one should have and raise children." The opposition to this advice might be that one can live a fulfilled life by prioritizing other dreams without children. We might then create a character who doesn't initially believe this statement (as is the case with Dr. Grant in *Jurassic Park*). In the world of *Jurassic Park*, this thematic opposition is explored by forcing Dr. Grant to metaphorically adopt and take care of children while running from dinosaurs.

Consider what makes a whole, individuated, healthy person. Consider what helps someone grow into their full potential. From this, we can explore advice that can be opposed by either a character or a community. The opposing character or community may then learn the value of the advice through a series of dilemmas.

We might consider this method as one of crafting a worldview or statement of belief. We want to consider what belief a character or community might have within the story world. The belief might be about how the world works or about how it *should* work. We can then craft an opposing worldview or statement of belief. In our world of the savanna, the lions might view the world as consisting of only winners and losers. In the terms of the story world, this might be the view that the world is made up of those who are predators and those who are prey (an individualistic mindset). The elephants, on the other hand, might view the world as consisting of those who are selfish and those who are selfless (favoring the community). In the terms of the story world, the elephants might see the world as consisting of those who help the herd and those who endanger the herd. The elephants might believe, for example, that one's value is derived from one's ability to help others.

Examples of other worldviews might be, "You've got to look out for yourself because no one else will." "You've got to take that which you want—nothing will be given to you." "We've got to serve others in order to maintain stability." "The social hierarchy exists to protect us." Consider how natural, opposing worldviews might arise from these statements.

We can also try to identify the natural worldviews that might arise from occupational value systems in the story world. If the giraffes are scouts, lookouts, or guards, they might believe the most important way to approach life is, "If you suspect something, say something" (while a thematic opposition might note the propensity for a boy who cried wolf situation).

It can also be helpful to pore over the universal truths held in proverbs, adages, and aphorisms in order to spark ideas for character worldviews and beliefs. From there, consider why someone might reasonably or unreasonably reject the worldview, thus creating a thematic opposition.

Of course, it's important to consider that if a character or community is going to change their worldview or belief, they need not always flip to the polar opposite belief. It's possible that two opposing characters (or communities) actually come to some sort of compromise where the "truth" is somewhere in the middle. And, of course, one character could realize the value of the middle way while another fails to have any realization whatsoever.

> *Takeaway*: Theme can naturally arise in a story world by giving a character or community a strong worldview about how the world works or how it should work. We can then also explore characters or communities that hold the opposite worldview.

Crafting From Decision

Another method by which we can ground a theme in a story world is to first start by imagining The Great Decision Moment. With what dilemma will the protagonist be faced at the story's climax? By exploring a concrete decision in the story world, we can uncover the thematic argument represented by each side of the dilemma.

This decision moment is one in which a character (or community) is forced to decide between two value systems—often that which they want and that which they need. Rick wants Ilsa, but he must value duty over love and prioritize the cause of freedom over himself. Marlin wants to protect Nemo, but he must demonstrate his trust in Nemo's ability to take care of himself. In *Little Miss Sunshine*, Olive must decide between allowing others to judge her as a "winner" or "loser" versus defining herself as a winner through her own self-expression. In *Toy Story 2*, Woody must decide between his old family and his new family. What might a character *want* to do? And how might they be faced with an alternative that they morally *should* do?

In the world of the savanna, an elephant might be forced to decide between saving their lion best friend and saving the elephant herd. A lion might need to choose between fulfilling their duty to the pride as a predator and their inner call to protect other animals.

Sometimes choosing the thing they know they *should* choose gets the character what they want in the end—and sometimes it doesn't (as in *Casablanca*). And sometimes choosing the thing they want over the thing they need causes the character to lose both.

Of course, our story doesn't necessarily need to have a flawed protagonist that's faced with this Great Decision. In fact, it can be the community at large that must make the decision (with a surrogate character representing the community). A community might be forced into a decision point where beliefs must be settled. In *Rata- touille*, Anton Ego is the representative of high-brow food society who will decide whether "anyone can cook" (i.e. whether Remy the rat can cook). We might think of this as a sort of "want versus need" dilemma for society itself. A community may want to maintain its dominant value system, but it might morally "need" to shift from its moral weak- ness to a value system that embodies moral strength. In this context, the high-brow food society believes that not anyone can cook while Remy represents the thematic argument that anyone can cook. This theme might be abstracted to the dilemma between whether power belongs in the hands of the many or in the hands of the few.

To brainstorm potential "want versus need" dilemmas for a char- acter, we can first consider from what in the story world a character might derive their value. A lion might derive their value from their role as a predator, for instance. Forcing a lion to choose between their identity and some greater moral value can result in a dilemma. As we'll learn, characters often derive their value from their void (typi- cally an obsession, lie, or ghost). It may be helpful to first fully flesh out a character and then come back to approaching theme from a want versus need perspective. We can then force the character to choose between the thing from which they derive their value and some moral need.

> *Takeaway*: Theme can be inserted into a story world by first starting with the climax of the story. What Great Decision must the

protagonist make? How will each side of the decision represent one side of the thematic opposition? How will it be a choice between want and need?

Crafting From Obsession, Desire, and Fear

One final method we might use when grounding a theme in a story world is to consider what the world, community, or culture is obsessed with or afraid of. What does each character desire and fear? How might these desires and fears be representative of a particular value system? What does the story world itself fear most? What does the culture shame or guilt? What are the implications of the community's value system? In *Monsters, Inc.*, the society fears human children and consequently a scaring career would be valued over a bond with a human child. In *The Nightmare Before Christmas*, the society values the ability to scare. Consequently, Jack Skellington is revered as a hero. He's a cultural icon of their value system.

The story world of *Up* is obsessed with the value of adventure. One of the questions that arises from the story is, "What is adventure really?" Is adventure a fantastical journey to faraway and unknown places? Or is adventure about the everyday experiences we have with our loved ones? We can choose a subject on which to base a value system and then consider the differing worldviews or beliefs about that subject.

> *Takeaway*: We can define the theme of a story by first considering the desires and fears of the story world communities. We can then consider how these desires and fears may be indicative of deeper value systems that may represent worldviews.

Adding Thematic Dimensions

Thus far, we've primarily considered a thematic opposition between two polar opposite worldviews. Real arguments about the right way to live life, however, are often gray and complex. They rarely boil down to two distinct, opposite views. We want to allow a multi-faceted and multi-dimensional exploration of our story's theme.

To do this, we consider how we might give characters nuanced worldviews when it comes to the central thematic dilemma. Perhaps a character believes that both the individual and the community have value under different circumstances. Perhaps a character rejects the dilemma itself and doesn't believe that either side is valuable. Perhaps a character agrees with a particular value system but gives it a low priority. Perhaps a character values the individual but only under certain conditions—they approach the value system conditionally.

We previously discussed how *Star Wars* explores two separate thematic dilemmas: faith versus technology and means versus ends. Because "means versus ends" is often a battle between good and evil, it allows the story world to explore the "faith versus technology" dilemma from the perspective of both good and evil. There are both moral and immoral characters on both sides of the debate. This creates a multi-dimensional thematic opposition.

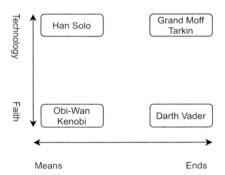

Takeaway: Real arguments about the best way to live life are often nuanced. They contain more than two polar opposite worldviews. We can deepen our story's thematic dilemma by providing more than two viewpoints.

9

STARTING FROM CHARACTER

Character is how we bring theme to life. As Adam Skelter says, "Though we need to make them believable, [characters] are not human beings. They are complex emotional constructions that represent thematic values." Because character is the physical embodiment of theme, we must be able to create compelling and thematic characters in order to properly dramatize a theme.

Let's explore a few techniques for creating compelling, thematic, multi-dimensional characters.

The Void and the Spine

The "void" is the source of all character energy. It's a lack at the center of a character. It's a hole that a character is always trying desperately to fill. Just like a desire, a void drives action. Unlike a desire, however, a void is often subconscious rather than conscious.

We can think of a character's void as an emptiness. Characters with voids also tend to have strong character spines. A character's spine is the drive to fill (or in some cases validate) their emptiness. As Andrew Stanton puts it, the spine is "an inner motor—a dominant, unconscious goal that they're striving for—an itch that they can't scratch." The character is always working, whether they know it or not, to attempt to fill their void.

The void is the emptiness inside. The spine is the drive to fill that emptiness. Stanton offers a few examples of character spines. Michael Corleone's spine is to please his father. Wall-E's is to find the beauty. In *Finding Nemo*, Marlin's is to prevent harm. These characters all take action to attempt to fill an emptiness within themselves—whether from a place of curiosity, wonder, fascination, love, hope, fear, hatred, jealousy, romanticism, or insecurity.

This emptiness of the void doesn't need to be associated with any sort of negative emotion. It can simply be an aspiration for more. In these cases, we can think of the void as an obsession. It often manifests as a longing for something that can't ever quite be attained. It's typically a feeling that something's missing.

A void can generally be categorized as either an emptiness that grows out of aspiration or as an emptiness that grows out of fear. The line, of course, is rarely clear-cut and most voids are some mixture of both aspiration and fear. Generally we might say that flawed characters have voids that grow out of fear while innocent characters have voids that grow out of aspiration. Marlin's drive to prevent harm grows out of a fear of losing his family. Wall-E's drive to find the beauty is one of aspiration.

How are voids created? We will consider three dominant patterns: trauma, obsession, and misbelief. These patterns aren't mutually exclusive and a single character may have a void that arises from any combination of these patterns.

Takeaway: Deep characters typically have an emptiness within them called a void. The drive to fill a character's void is known as their spine. A void usually arises from a trauma, misbelief, and/or obsession.

Trauma and the Ghost

When a character undergoes some sort of trauma, whether in a single event or over time, that trauma tends to create a void within the character. In these instances, the character typically doesn't know how to healthily deal with the emptiness within them. Instead of trying to properly mend the void, the character might instead try to hide it, compensate for it, rationalize it, justify it, project it on to others, validate its existence, prevent it from ever happening again, prevent it from happening to others, or more generally try to address it via unhealthy behavior, among other techniques. In effect, the character will use coping mechanisms to try to deal with their void. While they often simply want to ignore the void, what they need to do in order to live a better life is to learn to address it, heal it properly, and let it go.

In *Finding Nemo*, Marlin's trauma occurs when a barracuda attacks his family, killing all but one of his children, Nemo. This trauma creates a void within Marlin. His coping mechanism is to attempt to prevent the trauma from ever happening again by becoming overly protective and co-dependent. His spine is to prevent harm. This drive is taken too far, resulting in a moral weakness of over-dependence, which negatively affects his relationships. What Marlin *needs* is to learn to trust his son and to allow others to live independent lives.

In *Good Will Hunting*, Will was abused in his childhood. He attempts to cope with his void by detaching, putting up a façade, becoming aggressive, and lashing out at others. These coping mechanisms result in immoral behavior, which negatively affects Will's relationships (particularly with his love interest, Skylar). What Will needs is to realize that the abuse was not his fault and that he can drop his façade and let others into his life.

We can think of these characters as having a ghost from the past that continues to haunt them to this day. This ghost is the source of their void. It's often some past event or experience that the character can't let go of. It's often a trauma or a loss of some kind. A character with a ghost might falsely believe that they've dealt with it and that it's no longer a problem. It's rare, however, that a character has dealt with their ghost in such a way that they're free from it without first having had a meaningful self-revelation.

The ghost might sometimes manifest as a character's "inner demons." It's the thing that won't let go of the character. In *Casablanca*, Rick's ghost is Ilsa and the traumatic moment in Paris when he was abandoned. In *Finding Nemo*, Marlin's ghost is the barracuda attack. In *Up*, Ellie is Carl's metaphorical ghost. Not all characters have ghosts, but to attempt to identify the ghost, ask, "What happened in the character's past that they can't let go of?"

When it comes to these traumas, there's what actually happened (i.e. reality) and then there's what the character *believes* happened. There's the entity that's *actually* responsible for the event and then there's the entity that the character *blames* for the event (often them-selves). Much of the time, the character constructs a lie in order to rationalize the trauma. This lie might be centered on what caused the event or who's responsible. Sometimes the true nature of who's actu-ally responsible might be hidden from the character, which can lead them to create false beliefs. A character might have survivor's guilt for living through a trauma that their loved ones didn't. This can result in symptoms of post-traumatic stress disorder for the character.

Revealing a Character's Ghost

A character's ghost can be revealed through either dramatization or dialogue. In other words, we can either show it (such as in *Finding Nemo* and *Twister*) or we can have a character recount the traumas of their ghost (such as in *Good Will Hunting* and *Jaws*). While general writing advice tells us to prefer showing over telling, that's not always the case when revealing a character's ghost. Hearing about a past trauma in a character's own words can convey the emotional weight of the trauma and trigger the imagination in a way that showing never could. Additionally some past traumas may be too horrific to show the audience and would be better conveyed through words.

One of the decisions we must make in our story is *when* to reveal a character's ghost. Given that ghost events tend to be traumatic, revealing a character's ghost early is a powerful way to show undeserved misfortune and thus to establish empathy. On the other hand, if we keep the ghost event a mystery and reveal it later in the story, we can maintain an air of mystery about the character's past. This can make the character more intriguing.

By revealing the ghost early, we sacrifice mystery. But by keeping the ghost hidden, we sacrifice a powerful method for establishing empathy. It's a trade-off between empathy and mystery. If we can find an alternative way to establish empathy for the character (such as with a humanistic virtue or an admirable trait), then we may want to keep the ghost hidden and take advantage of mystery (such as with Rick in *Casablanca*). If the character has no redeeming qualities, we'll likely want to reveal their backstory and take advantage of the empathy (such as with Marlin in *Finding Nemo*).

Characters with ghosts are often trying desperately to avoid confronting their past directly. It's often only by accepting themselves and realizing that the trauma was not their fault that a character can begin to heal.

> *Takeaway*: A ghost is some traumatic event or experience from the past that haunts a character to the present day. The character typically creates coping mechanisms to attempt to mask their ghost without directly addressing it. The character must learn to acknowledge their ghost, heal it properly, and let it go. The ghost may be revealed through dramatization or dialogue.

Lie or Misbelief

Some voids are created by a misbelief. In her book *Creating Character Arcs*, K.M. Weiland calls this misbelief a "lie" that the character believes. This lie is often the source of either immoral action (sometimes resulting from a feeling of inadequacy or a feeling that the world should be different than it is) or a drive for more. In other words, the lie tends to be the source of either a deep fear or an obsession (or both).

A particularly powerful type of lie is one that makes a value judgment about one's life or identity. A character who believes this type of lie tends to believe that they're only valuable if some condition is met. They tend to believe that their value is defined by some outside person, object, or idea. For instance, Woody believes he's only valuable if he's Andy's favorite toy. Buzz believes he's only valuable if he's a space ranger. Marlin believes he's only valuable as a family man. Mr. Incredible believes he's only valuable in his capacity as a superhero.

A lie might be about one's limitations. It might be an insecurity. It might be a judgment about what one deserves and what one doesn't deserve. Shrek believes he doesn't deserve love because of his ugliness as an ogre.

A lie might be some belief about how the world works or how the world *should* work. We can think of this as a worldview. It might be a belief about what kind of behavior makes a person fulfilled or worthy in the world. It might be a belief about how others act in the world. It might be a belief about how others *should* act. A strong worldview tends to put a character squarely on one side of the story's thematic opposition. A character with a strong lie or worldview may have something they feel they need to prove—whether to themselves or to the world.

Some lies arise as a way for a character to rationalize their trauma or ghost event. Perhaps they believe that they're not worthy of love. Perhaps they believe that the world isn't worthy of being loved. These lies are the only way for the character to reconcile their life with their past trauma.

A lie doesn't necessarily need an explanation for how it came about. In *Toy Story*, it's never explained why Woody believes he's only valuable when he's Andy's favorite toy. Mr. Potato Head tells us that Woody has "been Andy's favorite since kindergarten." These misbeliefs and lies can form simply out of a feeling that things have always been this way so they must continue to always be this way (due to status quo bias). Perhaps the lie arose not in a single moment but over a long period of time. Some lies are culturally ingrained in us. Perhaps the lie was instilled into the character from their subculture. Some lies arise from incorrect assumptions.

> *Takeaway*: A character void can arise from a misbelief or "lie." A lie may be about one's value, one's limitations, or one's identity. A character may also have a lie about how the world works or how the world *should* work. We can call this a worldview.

Obsession

Some characters simply have an obsession. It's just built into these characters that they're not satisfied unless they're fully immersed in their obsession. Anything less leaves these characters feeling an emptiness inside.

There are two primary ways we can use the obsession for narrative drive. The first method is that we can give the character a concrete desire that's driven by an attempt to fulfill the obsession. This is the case in *Little Miss Sunshine* when Olive wants to win the Little Miss Sunshine pageant to fulfill her obsession of becoming a beauty queen and "winning" in the eyes of her father.

The second method of generating narrative drive through the obsession is to take away the obsession, triggering a deprival super-reaction syndrome. This is done in *Toy Story* when Woody's place as top toy is taken away. We find this in *Finding Nemo* when Nemo is taken away from Marlin. This is also done in *Up* when Ellie is taken away from Carl. We can then watch the character cope with the loss of their obsession. We can optionally give the character an opportunity to win back their obsession. This is done in *The Incredibles* when Mr. Incredible is given the opportunity to be a superhero again.

The obsession can also be thought of as some sort of longing. Luke Skywalker longs for adventure. Almost all '90s Disney characters long to find a world they've never known. Ariel longs to be on land. Belle longs for "more than this provincial life." Jack Skellington feels an emptiness in his bones. Obsession is about intense desire buried inside. To give a character an obsession, we give them a deep, burning desire in their soul.

This obsession model of the void is fairly flexible in that both flawed and innocent characters can often be viewed through the lens of having an obsession. Michael Scott's obsession is to be liked, loved, and admired (at the same time as having a deep fear of being lonely). Wall-E's obsession is to find the beauty. In *Cars*, Lightning McQueen's obsession is winning. Clarice Starling's obsession is to become an upstanding and accepted member of the FBI.

A character's obsession can also be intrinsically linked to their ghost or worldview. A character may, for instance, be obsessed with avenging or somehow "righting" their ghost event. A character may also be obsessed with proving their lie or worldview.

> *Takeaway*: A character void can arise from an obsession. These characters aren't satisfied until they're living fully immersed in their obsession. This obsession may also take the form of a longing for something more.

Individuation

Many characters must come to learn that their worth isn't defined by some outside person, object, status, role, idea, or past event. They need to learn that their value isn't derived from their drive to fill their void (i.e. their spine).

These characters derive their value from what we might call a "comfort concept." The comfort concept is a security blanket. It makes a character feel safe and it helps them maintain their façade. The character often believes the lie, "I am only important insofar as I can have my comfort concept." Characters generally respond with deprival super-reaction syndrome to any attempts to threaten or take away their comfort concept.

These characters tend to use the comfort concept as an emotional shield to create a façade (i.e. a false identity) so that they don't ever need to confront their void. In other words, the façade is a coping mechanism to help the character avoid experiencing the pain of confronting their ghost, confronting the falsity of their lie, or losing their obsession. It's all about avoidance.

The façade is constructed around the comfort concept and is the character's safe space. Until the character learns that they're valuable without their comfort concept, they'll continually want to hide behind their façade and they'll desperately resist any attempt to break it.

Mr. Incredible must learn that his value isn't derived solely from his role as a superhero. Marlin must learn that his value isn't derived solely from his ability to take care of Nemo and prevent harm. Woody must learn that his value isn't derived from his position as top toy. Clarice Starling must learn that her value isn't derived from being accepted by the FBI's boys club.

These characters must often learn to let go. When the character is able to recognize their own worth apart from anyone or anything else, they can become whole and individuated. It's at this moment that the character grows and is able to connect with others in a healthy way. Characters must learn not to seek their value through others but rather to find their value within themselves.

Takeaway: A character with a void must learn that their worth isn't defined by some outside person, object, status, role, idea, or past event. They must learn that their value can be found within themselves and not others. This often requires a character to drop their façade and accept themselves.

Worldview

Some characters have a strong worldview or philosophy. They have strong feelings about the way the world works or about how it *should* work. In other words, they tend to have strong beliefs about the "right" (or most effective) way to live life. The worldview might be about how relationships work, about how power is attained, about how "good" and "evil" work, about how to get the most out of life, about how to be successful, about what it means to be happy, etc.

Where a lie is often a personal belief about oneself, a worldview tends to be a more generalized belief about others. The worldview itself can be a character's lie or it might organically grow from the lie. For instance, if a character's lie is, "I'm not worthy of being loved," then perhaps their worldview becomes, "Only happy people are worthy of being loved."

A personal misbelief about oneself (i.e. a lie) can grow into a worldview, which creates immoral behavior, resulting in a moral weakness. One's thoughts about oneself can be projected on to others in a negative way, even if one isn't consciously aware that these thoughts are subconsciously targeted at oneself. One's hatred of a certain group or culture, for instance, may be targeted at the existence of some element of that group or culture within oneself.

We may know a character's worldview but not ever learn the experience or lie from which it stems. In *Little Miss Sunshine*, Richard is the thematic antagonist (i.e. opponent) and has the worldview that "there are winners and there are losers."

Worldviews can sometimes take the form of prejudices. They might be assumptions or generalizations about how people act, for instance.

The worldview, like the lie, may have come about based on a previous experience. But it might also have simply been instilled into the character by their culture, community, family, friend group, media, etc. It might also be something the character simply assumes based on their circumstance (such as Woody believing he *must* always be the top toy because he always *has been* the top toy).

A worldview tends to be a character's explicit take on the thematic opposition. Not all worldviews must be incorrect, of course. An innocent character or a thematic mentor, for instance, may have a worldview that aligns with the moral side of the thematic opposition.

Victoria Schwab also thinks of the character's worldview as a mantra. She offers an example mantra, "If a thing is worth having, it's worth taking." She then makes her characters break their mantra over the course of the story. This is a helpful model for producing both thematic and dramatic interest.

> *Takeaway*: A worldview is a belief about the way the world works or about the way the world should work. Where a lie is a personal belief about oneself, a worldview is typically a generalized belief about others.

The Character Engine

We learned in our exploration of plot and drama that desire is the rocket fuel of narrative drive. Character is the embodiment of that narrative rocket fuel. Behind every compelling character is an engine. This character engine produces action. And that desire-backed action (or reaction) is often the source of plot. In this way, character drives plot. To start our story with a character, we'll first craft a compelling character engine.

A character engine has at its nucleus a void. A void is an emotional emptiness that the character can't ever seem to fill or ignore. What's missing deep in the character's soul? Recall that this void typically arises from a ghost (i.e. something in the past that haunts the character to the present day), a lie (a misbelief), or an obsession. The void might also arise from any combination or mixture of these elements. Characters are often trying to conceal (a trauma), affirm (a lie), or fill (an obsession). It's worth noting that a character might take all of these approaches at the same time and attempt to address their void by concealing, affirming, and filling (as in the case of Marlin in *Finding Nemo* who tries to conceal his past trauma, affirm his lie that the world is dangerous, and fulfill his obsession to protect others). In other words, the character is trying to deal with that emptiness inside of them. Sometimes the emptiness is born out of a negative emptiness and sometimes it's born out of an aspiration for more.

Once this core is defined, we can move to the character's spine. We'll later define this in more detail but for now we just need to know that a character spine is an inner motor that constantly pushes the character to try to deal with their emptiness. It's the character's never-ending drive to conceal, affirm, and/or fulfill their void. The spine is the basic action that the character takes to attempt to deal with their void. Deep in their soul, what does the character constantly try to *do*? Wall-E searches for beauty. Woody protects his relationship with Andy. Michael Corleone tries to please his father. Marlin tries to prevent harm. This spine is the deepest source of character action and it continuously drives the character to fill, conceal, and/or affirm the emptiness within them. This is the heart of the character engine and the source of a character's deep, inner motivation.

The void is the emptiness. The spine is the drive to deal with that emptiness.

> *Takeaway*: Characters are driven to action as they work to conceal, affirm, or fill their void. The action that a character repeatedly takes to address their void is their spine. This unending drive is the source of plot.

Façade

Recall that a character may develop a façade (i.e. a false identity) in an attempt to conceal, affirm, or fill their void. This façade typically arises as a result of experiencing a deep pain. The character vows to never experience that pain again. This results in the construction of a shell. They hide their true self from others and often from themselves. It's armor. It's crafted in order to present a very particular image to the world about who the character is. It's a lie.

This façade is one form of coping with the existence of a character's void. It's to prevent others from seeing the void. A character with a façade must gradually learn to drop this false identity and embrace their true "essence," as Michael Hauge would say. The character must learn that they can open up and trust others. They must learn to define themselves, not in terms of outside people, objects, roles, or ideas but rather to define themselves as a whole individual. They must become individuated.

> *Takeaway*: Some characters develop a false identity called a façade in order to conceal their void and to prevent ever having to experience the pain from their past again. These characters must learn to drop their façade and accept their true "essence."

Moral Weakness

Some characters have one or more moral weaknesses. A moral weakness is some behavior that negatively impacts those around the character. Moral weaknesses are often the result of coping mechanisms and an attempt to maintain one's façade.

Characters use coping mechanisms to help them deal with their voids (particularly if the void arises from a ghost or trauma). Sometimes these coping mechanisms exist to prevent others from seeing a character's void. If a character's void is born out of a lie or misbelief, a character might act immorally in order to maintain or validate the lie. If a character's void is born of an obsession, it's possible that the character acts immorally in the pursuit of that obsession (essentially valuing the obsession over their relationships). If the void is born out of a past trauma or ghost, the character may act immorally in an attempt to avoid pain and to prevent others from getting too close.

If we want to give our character a moral weakness, we *must* dramatize *how* the character's behavior is negatively impacting others.

Need

A character with a weakness tends to also have a "need." A need is something that a character must do or learn in order to live a happier, healthier, more fulfilled life. If a character has a moral weakness, then the need is often clear: fix the root of the thing that's causing the immoral behavior. A character often needs to address their void in order to live a more fulfilled life. They need to learn to live in their essence and drop their façade. They might need to learn to confront their trauma or ghost. They might need to learn that their past doesn't define them and that their identity is separate from their trauma. They might need to learn a healthy way to attain their obsession or perhaps they need to learn that they don't have to attain their obsession in order to be valuable. They might need to learn that their lie is indeed false and that they can live a healthy life without it. In short, a character typically needs to do the thing that scares them most.

Spine

A character's spine, like their moral weakness, is often subconscious. Characters often don't realize that they're driven by one central, basic action. This spine does, however, tend to result in concrete desires throughout the story. Characters are seldom aware that these conscious desires are subconscious attempts to conceal, validate, or fill their void. Of course, sometimes these desires are also *conscious* attempts to fill their voids, particularly with characters who are driven by obsessions. There's typically one central, concrete, external desire that spans the length of the story.

Not all external goals are aspirational. Some characters desire to return their life to the status quo. This typically occurs when a character's lie is threatened or some element of their ghost reappears. Some characters desire merely to avoid having to confront their void (as in the case of Will in *Good Will Hunting*).

Many characters have a fear associated with their void. A character with a ghost or past trauma may fear that they'll be forced to confront their trauma or that others will see their trauma. A character with a lie may fear the thing implicit in the lie or that their lie will be revealed to be false. A character with an obsession may fear that they will never fill their void or that the thing they love most will be taken away from them.

A character engine consists of these elements: a void, a spine, a moral weakness, a need, a desire, and a fear.

Character From Theme

Character is an expression of theme and plot is an expression of character. In this way, character isn't separate from our story's theme. If the character doesn't embody the theme, we either need to change the character or change the theme. They must be congruent.

Theme is expressed through character action. Because the character engine dictates how a character will act, we want to ensure that the character's action will in some way address the theme. For instance, if we want our theme to be about faith versus reason, then selfishness isn't the most optimal moral weakness for our protagonist. Instead we might consider a character whose obsession with evidence and validation prevents them from living a life of trust. In this instance, a character's initial weakness, lie, or obsession might express one side of the thematic opposition and their self-revelation might express the opposite side. Of course, we can also *discover* our story's theme based on our character's engine and the actions that a character would take based on their void.

A Character's Life Experience

We've explored how a story's theme is defined by a central dilemma pair. There's an additional technique to express a story's theme that we've only mentioned briefly.

Recall that theme is about exploring what we should do to get the most out of life. In order to argue the best way to live life, it's often valuable to dramatize the emotional experience of living. And, of course, sometimes we want to demonstrate how *not* to live life. To this end, we must see a character undergoing a *significant* life experience.

We often hear about a character entering a new or "special world" at the inciting incident of a story. We usually associate this entrance with a literal geographic change and the introduction of new story rules, new characters, and new settings. That, however, is simply the new *external* story world. The inciting incident also pushes the protagonist into a new *internal* world. This internal world is the new world of emotion and the life experience. In this way, the character is pushed into a fundamentally new life experience on an internal level and will be forced to deal with the emotional challenges. The character enters a new *stage* of their life.

This life experience is the simple, emotional journey that a character takes over the course of a story. It's a snapshot of the human condition. It's often about a relationship (with another character or with oneself). Examples include becoming a parent, searching for one's identity, pursuing one's passion, facing one's great fear, losing a loved one, mourning, being abandoned, falling in love, cheating, getting married, getting divorced, being hunted, being dethroned, and attaining the crown.

Exploring a life experience is a powerful tool for exploring a story's theme. We can make a thematic argument about the best way to live life by showing how a character uses or rejects a value system in response to a challenging life experience.

The key here is to remember that fiction is metaphor. The goal isn't to exactly recount all of the specific moments of a life experience directly in a story (although this is one possible route). The goal is instead to explore the *emotions* that arise from this life experience. If the life experience is betrayal, each story beat should in some way address the emotions that arise (from all sides) in relation to betrayal —from the perspective of both the betrayer and the betrayed. There's no reason to be heavy-handed with metaphor—it's an imprecise tool. It's symbolic. Remember that elements of the story need only be representative of the life experience, not literal. As admitted by Pixar writers, *Monsters, Inc.* is about becoming a father. Note, though, that while Boo functions as Sully's metaphorical child, Boo isn't literally Sully's child.

A strong argument can also be made that *Jurassic Park* is about the life experience of becoming a father (for Dr. Grant). Lex Murphy and Tim Murphy are John Hammond's grandchildren who fall under the care of Dr. Grant after things go terribly wrong in the park. Through the external story beats, Dr. Grant undergoes the internal journey of exploring what it's like to become a father.

Ensuring that the protagonist is undergoing some sort of fundamentally new life experience creates an emotional throughline for the story. Of course, this life experience should be organically tied to the story's Great Decision. In *Monsters, Inc.*, Sully is exploring the decision of family versus career in the context of becoming a father. This is an organic dilemma that arises from becoming a new father.

We'll notice two common threads in life experiences: most of these experiences involve relationships and they all evoke emotional responses in their participants. These are key ingredients for a life experience worth exploring. On a thematic level, the audience wants to explore the various ways one might deal with this type of life experience and how those different approaches have different effects. The key is that these experiences should be both life-changing and fundamentally *new* to the character (which is something important to keep in mind for sequels).

This life experience shouldn't just be an arbitrary event we've added to the character's life. It must be deeply tied to the character's void by eventually forcing the character to confront that void. This confrontation often occurs gradually throughout the story in the form of implicit threats to the character's emptiness and reminders of their great fear. The confrontation of the void might then come to a climax at The Great Decision Moment where the character is implicitly asked to dramatize how to best deal with the life experience (by choosing the side of the thematic opposition that should be used to best address the emotions of the life experience) and thus how to best live life.

Each life experience tends to have in it a core conflict. The character *wants* to respond to the life experience in one way, but they *need* to respond to it in another way. In *Up*, Carl's life experience is the loss of his wife, Ellie. He wants to respond to this experience by holding tightly to her memory. He wants to do the things they never got to do together. He needs, however, to respond to the experience by forming new relationships. He needs to honor Ellie by living a full life and having new adventures with others.

The character is offered the choice to either remain comfortable and entrenched in their void (i.e. do what's easy) or to confront their void and get what they need in order to live a more fulfilled life (i.e. do what's right). The organic consequences of the life experience should force this decision.

To brainstorm a life experience for our character, we might ask, "What life experience would strike at the heart of the character's void by forcing them to eventually confront the fact that they have an emptiness?" Or perhaps more simply: What experience would force the character to face their deepest fears? What experience would force the character to confront the question of what it means to be happy?

The life experience should directly challenge the value system of the protagonist. In *Monsters, Inc.*, Sully is a company man who values career. He's forced to confront the prospect of being a father who values love over career. In *Jurassic Park*, Dr. Grant's lie is that kids aren't worth taking care of. He's confronted with needing to take care of kids, directly challenging his lie. In *Finding Nemo*, Marlin's spine is to prevent harm and his obsession is to take care of his son. His life experience is the loss of his son, directly challenging his value system of dependence and harm prevention. We generally want to either threaten their value system or put them face-to-face with the opposing value system.

The life experience must also organically climax in The Great Decision Moment. We want to choose a life experience that will force an exploration of the thematic opposition, resulting in a choice between the central dilemma pair. Combine a familiar life experience with the story's Great Decision and you've got the ingredients for an emotional gut punch. The key is in organically connecting them and exploring the *emotions* that arise from both elements. Remember, fiction is metaphor. We don't need to get literal with these elements. Story is about an exploration of these aspects of theme, not a literal recounting of them.

Here are few shortcuts to creating a life experience that will force the protagonist to face the opposing value system:

- Take away the character's comfort concept (i.e. the thing by which they define themselves).
- What would the character most fear learning?
- What would upend the character's identity?
- What would most threaten the character's role?
- What experience would likely cause the character to change?
- What would highlight the emptiness inside of the character?

Alternatively give the character the opportunity to get what they think they want, only to later demonstrate that it's not what they thought. These experiences will tend to force the character to deal with the dilemma between what they want and what they need.

These life experiences ask us implicit questions about the best way to live life under certain circumstances. In *Casablanca*, we're asked, "What do we do when an old love returns?" In *Up*, we're asked, "How do we handle the loss of a loved one?" In *Finding Nemo*, we're asked, "How do we handle the loss of a child?" In *Toy Story*, we're asked, "How do we handle emotional and physical abandonment?" By exploring these questions and situations, we learn the tools for living life. Some stories don't have this emotional layer or life experience and they tend to ring hollow.

To explore life experiences and elements of the human condition, consider exploring aphorisms, adages, and proverbs.

Takeaway: A life experience is a simple, emotional journey that a character takes over the course of a story. It's a snapshot of the human condition. We generally want to explore a life experience that will best force a character to change.

Plot From Character

We've now covered a number of dramatic tools that can serve as the basis of a story's plot. We've also explored the engine that drives a story's character. Perhaps one of the most effective ways to create an organic story idea is to create a plot that arises naturally from a character engine.

Before we look at how plot can arise organically from character, we first need to look at another dramatic tool: the disruption.

Disruptions

Narrative drive is generated when the audience witnesses significant change. The central idea behind using a disruption to create narrative drive is that we're inherently interested in change and inherently uninterested in that which remains the same. If a story doesn't ever "turn" in a new direction, it becomes boring.

These moments of change occur when a story value shifts from one value to another. A story value is, quite simply, some form of good or bad. It's happy or sad. It's alive or dead. It's rich or poor. It's hope or despair. It's success or failure. It's a quality of human experience. In the context of a story, it's essentially a measurement of how things are going, whether broadly or for a specific character or community.

For instance, one character may be experiencing success (a "success" value) while another character is experiencing failure (a "failure" value). At this same time, the audience may be experiencing hopelessness (a "hopelessness" value). As a story progresses, these story values can (and should) change. Characters go from success to failure and from rags to riches. Audiences go from hopelessness to joy and from happiness to sadness. It's the nature of stories and of story values to change.

We can think of these moments of disruption as "turning points." They're when a story value goes from one value to another. Often we can get the most dramatic interest from a change in a story value's polarity—from a negative situation turning into a positive one or from a positive situation turning into a negative one. A hopeful situation might turn to a hopeless situation. A moment of fear might turn to a moment of desire.

Of course, a story value doesn't *need* to shift its polarity in order to generate dramatic interest. A character might go from content to enthusiastic after a turning point. Or fear might turn to anger. The key is that the change must be significant. That is, the change must be indisputably *noticeable* to the audience. Going from content to slightly more content doesn't generate dramatic interest.

When the polarity of a story value *does* shift from either negative to positive or positive to negative, the turning point (i.e. disruption) might also be referred to as a "turnaround" or a "reversal."

So how do we spark a turning point that shifts a story value and generates dramatic interest? We do it via a disruption. A disruption is simply when something unexpected and consequential happens. It's consequential as defined by the fact that it alters a story value. A disruption is the arrival of either an opportunity or a problem. It's either a revelation (i.e. the reveal of new information, sometimes via discovery) or an action. It might introduce chaos by significantly altering reality (i.e. peripeteia) or it might introduce order by revealing the truth (i.e. anagnorisis). A disruption might also be the combination of both chaos and order, which typically results from a "twist" such as when Oedipus Rex realizes he's killed his father and married his mother. When recounting a story, a disruption is when "something happens."

Although a disruption is necessarily unexpected, it doesn't need to be random or coincidental. In fact, it's often better when a disruption is *caused*. Disruptions are perhaps most impactful when they're caused by characters. A character might decide to reveal a secret, for instance. This might create a disruption in the life of the character to whom the secret is being revealed. A character might take a step too far and do something unforgiveable (such as in *The Office* S04E13 when Jan throws a Dundie at Michael's TV, bringing an end to the dinner party). An antagonist might take a decisive action that causes the protagonist to appear to fail in the pursuit of their goal. The point of a disruption is that it changes a story value and turns the story in a new direction.

We can often heighten the drama of a disruption by intensifying the story value before the shift. In other words, if a disruption is going to make a character sad, we want to first ensure the character is happy (rather than merely neutral). If a disruption is going to make a character happy, we want to first ensure the character is sad (rather than merely neutral). We make the lows lower and the highs higher in order to highlight the impact of the disruption. In *Marriage Story*, for instance, Nicole is going to serve Charlie divorce papers. That's the negative disruption. To heighten the impact of this disruption, we first hear that Charlie has won a MacArthur Grant. The negative impact of the divorce papers now stands in stark contrast to the initial joy of the award.

These moments necessarily provide new information and generally make us want to know what will happen next. Disruptions are also sometimes known as "impetuses" or "inciting incidents." They often incite new desires in those they affect. Sometimes the desire is to fix or avoid the problem raised by the disruption and other times it's to pursue the opportunity or question raised by the disruption. We'll later explore a plotting tool we'll call "the disruption cycle."

In *Toy Story*, the arrival of Buzz Lightyear is a disruption. It's a problem for Woody and incites the desire to get rid of Buzz. Andy leaving Woody and Buzz at the gas station is a disruption. It's a problem and incites in Woody and Buzz the desire to get back to Andy. The discovery that Buzz's helmet can magnify the sun and spark a fuse is a disruption in the form of a revelation. It's an opportunity and incites a desire in Woody to use the helmet to light Buzz's rocket.

In *Finding Nemo*, Nemo being taken is a disruption. It's a problem and incites in Marlin a desire to rescue Nemo. Bruce the shark getting a whiff of blood and going from friend to killer is a disruption. It's a problem and incites in Marlin and Dory the desire to escape.

In *The Incredibles*, superheroes being banned is a disruption. It's a problem and incites in Mr. Incredible the desire to become a super-hero again. Mr. Incredible being offered a superhero job is a disruption. It's an opportunity that incites in him a desire to accept the job and reclaim his identity as a superhero.

Disruptions are a story's source of change. They shift the current situation from one emotion to another. Sometimes problems can later turn out to be opportunities. Oftentimes opportunities later turn out to be problems.

We can craft disruptions around the emotion we want to convey. If we want to create a feeling of fear, we can craft a disruption that threatens a character's desire to avoid. A character might spot the antagonist walking into the room, for instance. If we want to create a feeling of hope, we can craft a disruption that offers a possible solution to a problem. In *Toy Story*, for instance, Woody realizes that Buzz's helmet can magnify the sun and spark their rocket. His despair turns into hope as the two have finally figured out a way back to Andy. Alternating between disruptions of fear and hope can keep the audience on a wild ride.

Disruptions are the foundation of story structure. As we'll discover, the event that ends act one is a disruption that incites a desire that often lasts until the end of act two. The end of act two also ends with its own disruption that's often a tragic problem. Disruptions are also the backbone of the scene. Each scene climaxes with a turning point that often shifts the polarity of the scene from one story value to another.

Peter Russell talks about how these disruptions can create a zig-zag between good news and bad news to generate dramatic interest. He offers the example, "Good news! I'm giving you twenty bucks! Bad news, I'm slapping you!" We can use this zig-zag rhythm to keep the audience interested in what's coming next.

Because a disruption is either a problem or an opportunity, it'll often create a desire in the affected character to either return to a state of equilibrium (i.e. solve the problem) or to pursue the opportunity. Recall that a desire raises an implicit dramatic question—will the character get what they want? For this reason, disruptions create narrative drive.

Creating a disruption is often as simple as considering how something unexpectedly good might happen or how something unexpectedly bad might happen.

> *Takeaway*: A disruption is when something unexpected and consequential happens. It's a problem or opportunity that alters a story value and turns the story in a new direction. A disruption can be either a revelation (i.e. the reveal of new information, sometimes via discovery) or an action. A disruption incites in a character a new desire and thus serves as an inciting incident.

Disrupting a Character

A character is fundamentally driven by their void. They're driven to avoid the pain of their past, to pursue their obsession at all costs, and to hold on to their lie or worldview in the face of opposition.

To create a plot that arises organically from our story's character, we need only disrupt their void. We introduce a problem or an opportunity that's tied directly to that deep emptiness within the character.

If a character has an unfulfilled obsession, we present an opportunity for them to pursue it (as with Jack in *The Nightmare Before Christmas*). If they already have an obsession, we threaten it or take it away (as with Woody in *Toy Story*).

If a character has a ghost from the past, we have one or more other characters persistently attempt to bring it out (such as Sean in *Good Will Hunting* or Hannibal Lecter in *The Silence of the Lambs*). Or we create a situation that forces the character to confront their ghost in the present day. If the ghost is associated with a person, we may even reintroduce that person into the character's life (such as Ilsa in *Casablanca*).

If a character has a strong worldview or lie, we force the character to confront opposition to their worldview. We threaten their lie with new facts. Or we might introduce an opportunity for the character to prove that their worldview is correct, once and for all (as with the Joker in *The Dark Knight*).

As we continue to fill in the details of our story, we'll learn that disrupting a character's void stands at the heart of an organic story.

Stage I Wrap-up

Thus far, we've discussed the four pillars of story: plot, story world, theme, and character. We considered different techniques for starting a story from each of these pillars. And while any pillar can be a good place to start, we must eventually consider them all as we bring life to a full story. Next we'll consider some of the core elements of story structure and how basic stories work.

PART II

POUR THE FOUNDATION

A BRIEF INTRODUCTION TO STORY STRUCTURE

Now that we've got the blueprints for our story, it's time to pour the foundation. We'll learn the layout that will serve as the base of our story.

10

QUESTIONS AND DISRUPTIONS

Questions and Answers

The events of a story are all building up to one climactic moment of heightened drama and theme: The Great Decision Moment. It's the climax. It's the philosophical battle. It's the *reason* we watch the movie or read the book. It's the surprising and inevitable answer to all of the events of the story.

The climax of a story is the beginning of the conclusion of a story's events. It's an answer to the questions that have been asked over the course of the story. In the beginning of the story is an event called the inciting incident. This event kicks off the story and begins to raise the story's primary questions. This basic question-answer form is the basis of story structure.

This question-answer structure makes up not just the global story but also each unit of story from the scene, to the sequence, to the act. The inciting incident asks a dramatic (and/or thematic) question about whether the character will get what they want (or need) and the climax typically answers the question.

These questions are often either dramatic or thematic. Recall that the basic dramatic question centers around whether a protagonist will attain their desire. This gives rise to dramatic tension. The inciting incident, then, is the event that "incites" a desire in the protagonist and thus raises a dramatic question about whether they'll attain that desire.

Where a dramatic question is about whether a character will accomplish their goal, a thematic question is about which side of the dilemma pair will win the thematic opposition. This thematic question might take the more specific form of asking whether the hero will learn the lesson they need to learn in order to live a better life. The question then gives rise to a general thematic tension. A thematic question may take longer to blossom in a story and tends to only come to full fruition in the latter half of the story. The Great Decision Moment is the climax that provides the much desired answers to the story's dramatic and thematic questions.

> *Takeaway*: Story structure consists of a basic question and answer form. The inciting incident asks a dramatic (and/or thematic) question and the climax typically provides an answer.

The Disruption and the Turning Point

Jack finds the beanstalk. The Big Bad Wolf arrives. Nemo is kidnapped. Buzz knocks Woody out of his spot.

A story doesn't start until "something happens." That "something" is a disruption. It's either a problem or an opportunity. It's either an action/event or a revelation. Every disruption is a bit of fuel added to the narrative rocket engine. A disruption is an upheaval. It's the creation of an imbalance. It's an impetus. It's an inciting incident. It's a provocation. It's a destabilization. It's where something changes.

We might think of a disruption as an event that begins with words like "then suddenly..." or "until one day..." or "then something happened..." or "until finally..." It's something that's necessarily unexpected.

We can say that any disruption worthy of its name gives rise to a new desire. If a disruption doesn't give rise to a new desire in at least one character, we might say that it's had no meaningful effect (and thus is ineffective). Because of this, we can say that a disruption gives rise to a dramatic question: Will the new desire be attained?

With this in mind, we can say that every disruption is an inciting incident. And likewise, a story's inciting incident is a disruption. It *incites* a desire and it asks a dramatic question (namely will the protagonist attain this new desire?). It's the start of story structure. It initiates a new narrative unit (a scene, sequel, act, etc.).

A disruption can also be called a turning point. A turning point "turns" the story. It takes the story moment from one feeling to another. It might take the story from hope to fear, or from sadness to happiness, from happiness to jubilance, from sadness to depression, or just more generally from bad to good or from good to bad. In other words, the audience feels that things just got better or worse—but they definitely changed in a noticeable way.

A disruption can often be categorized as either an action/event or a revelation. A revelation is the reveal of information to a stakeholder. Of course, some actions and events eventually lead to revelations.

Takeaway: Every narrative unit starts with a disruption in the form of an inciting incident. This disruption gives rise to a new desire, which then serves as the basis for the dramatic question of the narrative unit. Narrative units also frequently end with a disruption.

The Least Important Becomes Most Important

"At the start of a good movie, the thing that seems most important is actually least important and the thing that seems the least important is actually the most important."

— SETH ROGEN PARAPHRASING ROBERT TOWNE

The events of a story are kicked off and solidified with a disruption that incites a dramatic question of whether the protagonist will get what they want. Will Marlin find Nemo? Will Carl make it to Paradise Falls? Will Woody get back home to Andy and regain his position as top toy? This is what the story *appears* to be about. In the beginning of a story, it's the most important question. But lurking behind that dramatic question is a budding thematic question about the best way to live life.

As the story progresses, the dramatic question starts to take a backseat to the deeper thematic question. The most pressing question now becomes: Will Marlin learn to trust others? Will Carl learn that forming new relationships is the best way to honor Ellie? Will Woody learn that the best thing he can do to love Andy is to share his love? That which initially seemed the least important is revealed to be the most important.

This phenomenon of the least important question growing into the most important question is the core feeling we want to create. Throughout the story, we want to continually give new meaning to existing questions in such a way that they take on new depth. We want to upend questions and give them new significance. The only way we can grow the thematic question into the star of the show is by exploring it from multiple perspectives. And in order to do that, we've got to buy ourselves time using our dramatic tools (often by continually raising the stakes and generating tension).

Story structure can help us bring out what is most important while maintaining the audience's attention. Structure can help us explore a thematic opposition in a dramatically interesting way. That's the power of great story structure.

Takeaway: At the beginning of a story, the story appears to be about the dramatic question. We later find out that it's really about the underlying thematic question. Story structure can help us bring the thematic question to the forefront while we maintain the audience's attention.

11

STRUCTURE OVERVIEW

The Organic Logic of Storytelling

Story artist Emma Coats shared a list of twenty-two guidelines she learned while working at Pixar. Number four contains a set of simple steps that we might consider an organic logic of story. These steps form the basis of a simple narrative. Let's review the steps and see what we can learn.

> *Once upon a time...*
> *And every day...*
> *Until one day...*
> *And because of this...*
> *And because of this...*
> *Until finally...*
> *And ever since that day...*

Let's fill in the gaps with a prototypical story. Once upon a time, we find a character in a story world. And every day, the character lives their normal life in their normal world. Until one day, something unexpected happens and the character is swept off to a literal or metaphorical new world. And because of this, the character wants to return home. And because of this, the character faces new conflicts and obstacles in their journey to get back home. Until finally, the character engages in a climactic battle where they're forced to change, allowing them to return home. And ever since that day, the character has lived as a changed person.

This is perhaps the most natural form of a story. We might tell our stories in this structure when we're coming up with them on the spot. We start with a character (equilibrium). Something happens to them that causes them to get into trouble (inciting incident). Finally they've got to confront their fears and face the trouble (climax). It's only then that things can go back to normal (resolution).

This template provides a solid starting point for story structure. Let's take note of two steps in particular: "Until one day..." and "Until finally..." "Until one day..." is the story's inciting incident. It's the central disruption that kicks off the events of the story and initiates the dramatic question. The "Until finally..." step is the climactic Great Decision Moment of the story that brings the journey to an end. It's the climax. It's the answer to the dramatic question (and thematic question) raised at the inciting incident.

Let's also take note that between the inciting incident's question and the climax's answer, the journey is connected by "because of this..." In other words, each step is *causally* connected. The next step of the story doesn't just *happen*, it's *caused*. This is a foundational principle of story structure that we'll need to keep in mind. Later we'll explore practical tools for creating this chain of cause and effect.

Takeaway: The organic logic of storytelling starts with a disruption in the form of an inciting incident and comes to a close with a climax. Questions are asked and answered. All events in between these disruptions are causally related.

The Global Turning Point (Crisis)

Stories often have a particularly impactful moment between the inciting incident's question and the climax's answer. This moment is the story's global disruption (i.e. turning point), also sometimes known as the crisis point. Recall that all disruptions raise questions. So what question does this global disruption raise? This global turning point is typically responsible for bringing the thematic question from the background to the foreground—from the implicit to the explicit. It's responsible for taking what once seemed like the least important part of the story and making it clearly the most important part. Once the thematic opposition is made prominent in the audience's mind, it's driven home at The Great Decision Moment (i.e. the climax) with a grand act of thematic choice.

Let's expand the organic structure by inserting this global disruption before the climax. We'll refer to this disruption as "Until suddenly..." in our structure.

> *Once upon a time...*
> *And every day...*
> *Until one day...*
>
> *And because of this...*
> *And because of this...*
> *Until suddenly...*
>
> *And because of this...*
> *Until finally...*
> *And ever since that day...*

The traditional advice regarding the crisis point is that it should consist of some kind of great loss for the protagonist. It's sometimes called the "all is lost" moment. It's traditionally where something happens to the protagonist that appears to make their central desire impossible to complete successfully. It's where Woody and Buzz are hopelessly stuck in Sid's house. It's where Syndrome has captured the entire Incredibles family. It appears that the protagonist has officially lost. It's shortly after this point that the protagonist often realizes some thematic lesson, which they'll take with them to the climax in order to attain their desire. This moment of realization is called the self-revelation.

We must be careful not to limit ourselves when it comes to this turning point, however. To consider our options at the crisis, we've first got to consider the *purpose* of this global turning point. The purpose is to bring the thematic question center stage so that it overshadows everything else. We want the audience fully thinking about what's *actually* most important (i.e. the thematic lesson to be learned from the story). The traditional way of doing this is ostensibly taking away what the protagonist wants so that they're forced to learn a lesson.

But we might also, for instance, consider *giving* the protagonist what they want. Perhaps the protagonist then realizes that the thing they wanted so badly is a hollow victory. They come to understand what really matters in life. This is the case in *Up* where Carl gets his house to Paradise Falls but realizes it's meaningless without Ellie. Or perhaps the protagonist doesn't get what they want, but they realize that it's not actually worth chasing anyway. This is what happens with Woody in *Toy Story* when he realizes he can share Andy's love with Buzz. In this way, the crisis point isn't only constrained to an "all is lost" moment of defeat.

It's at this crisis point that we need to raise the story to the next level. We need to take the story beyond simply "Will the character accomplish their goal?" It must become "Will the character learn what they need to learn? Will the character be able to make amends for their past injustices? Will the character get what they *need*?" These are the questions we take into The Great Decision Moment of the climax. We start to fully realize what the story is *actually* about. The thing that was least important has now become most important. We then barrel straight toward the climax with the thematic opposition clearly in mind.

> *Takeaway*: At about the three-quarters mark of a story is an event known as the "crisis point." This is a global turning point that brings the thematic question from the background to the foreground in a clear way. It typically consists of a moment of great loss for the protagonist. The crisis is often followed by the protagonist's self-revelation about the proper way to live life. The protagonist must bring this revelation with them to the climax where they'll be forced to make a consequential thematic choice at The Great Decision Moment.

Three-act Structure

Now that we've added the global turning point to our organic structure, notice that we've got two disruptions—the inciting incident and the global turning point (i.e. the crisis point). When we split the story at these points, we can think of the story as consisting of three parts: the time before the turning points, the time between the turning points, and the time after the turning points. Or in other words, we have the time before the dramatic question (act one), the time where the dramatic question is typically most prominent (act two), and the time where the thematic question is typically most prominent (act three).

In the traditional three-act structure, the inciting incident can typically be thought of as two pieces. The first piece functions as a disruption that thrusts the character into a metaphorical (and sometimes literal) new world but provides them with little to no direction as to what to do. This first piece is called "the inciting incident" and often occurs at about the 10% mark of the story. The second piece of the inciting incident might be called the "dramatic question moment" (and is also known as "plot point one", the "lock-in" moment, or the predicament). It's at this moment that the protagonist solidifies their central goal (which is typically to deal with the initial disruption). This dramatic question moment occurs at about the 25% mark of the story. We'll later see that in some stories the inciting incident and the dramatic question moment are one and the same.

The first part of the three-act structure is act one. Act one consists of about 25% of the story and ends at the "dramatic question moment." This moment gives rise to the story's central dramatic question and main dramatic tension. The second part is act two, which consists of about 50% of the story and ends at the global turning point (i.e. the crisis point) at the 75% mark. The third part is act three, which consists of about 25% of the story and contains the climax as well as the resolution of the story.

Act 1   Act 2   Act 3

While we'll see this structure referenced as three separate acts, we'll often see it functionally *treated* as *four* separate acts. It's easy to see where the additional split might occur. Act two is twice as long as either of the other acts and can be divided at the midpoint.

Act 1   Act 2a   Act 2b   Act 3

Takeaway: The traditional three-act structure consists of 25% of the story before the clear dramatic question, 50% of the story between the dramatic question and the crisis point, and 25% of the story after the crisis point. The inciting incident can often be thought of as two moments: the moment that sends the protagonist into a new world and the moment that gives rise to a new desire and raises a clear dramatic question. The first piece is called "the inciting incident" and the second piece is called "the dramatic question moment."

The Midpoint

Well-structured stories tend to have a particularly important moment right in their dead center. It's appropriately called "the midpoint" and it cuts the classic act two into two parts: act 2a and act 2b, leaving us with a four-act structure. (We could number each act sequentially, but the three-act structure is so solidified in the writing community that maintaining a common three-act nomenclature allows us to communicate effectively with other writers).

Like the global turning point (i.e. the crisis point), the midpoint is also a disruption. Its function in the story is to be "the moment of first truth." In other words, the midpoint is the point at which we *first* get a glimpse of the thematic question. It's often where the protagonist gets a glimpse of what their life *could* be like if they learned their lesson. Or it's where we get our first glimpse at what a community *could* be like if it adopted the proper side of the thematic dilemma. If the story is one of a protagonist becoming corrupted, the midpoint might be the moment in which the protagonist faces and, for the first time, gives in to real temptation. If the story follows a character who becomes disillusioned, the midpoint might be the moment where the character begins to truly lose hope for the first time. In essence, the midpoint tends to be a short, temporary preview of the story's final thematic outcome.

In effect, the midpoint is the moment where we start to suspect that maybe there's more to the story than just the dramatic question. We start to see that perhaps there's a thematic question coursing through the depths of the story. From the midpoint to the crisis, the theme will start to bubble up as the protagonist often begins to realize that the problem they actually face is deeper than they had initially anticipated.

The midpoint has other special properties as well. It's the moment in time around which story elements are mirrored. For instance, if a story element appears at the 10% mark of the story, we may want to consider bringing it back at the 90% mark. Likewise that which appeared at the 25% mark should probably be brought back around the 75% mark. We call this "mirroring around the midpoint." It's also called "chiastic structure" or "ring composition." It's the natural symmetry of a well-structured story.

We'll explore the midpoint in more detail later.

> *Takeaway*: The midpoint of a story cuts the traditional act two into two pieces: act 2a and act 2b. This functionally leaves us with a four-act structure. The midpoint is the moment where the theme begins to come to the forefront of a story. The midpoint is also the moment in time around which story elements should be mirrored.

The Life Experience

In his video "Endings: The Good, the Bad, and the Insanely Great," Michael Arndt argues that great stories have three sets of stakes: the external, the internal, and the philosophical.

Recall that stakes are the consequences (risks, rewards, and implications) of the pursuit of a desire. Three sets of stakes, then, also implies three separate questions that a story must address. We've explored the dramatic question (the external spine) and the thematic question (the philosophical spine). Now let's take a look at the emotional question (the internal spine). This is the simple, emotional journey of the story.

In order to learn how to live life properly, we must *dramatize* the challenges of living life. In other words, we can get a powerful emotional throughline in our story by exploring some significant stage of life. This life experience can be thought of as the internal, metaphorical journey that a character takes in response to a significant change in their life. It's a fundamentally new stage in the character's life. One might say that this emotional throughline is the *reason* for writing the story.

The life experience is a slice of the human condition. It's that nebulous element that people talk about when they say "write what you know" and "tell a story only you can tell" or "tell a story you're specially designed to tell." It contains the positive and negative aspects of what it means to be human—whether that be birth, friendship, love, divorce, death, or an identity crisis. A character might find themselves wearing the crown for the first time. They might find themselves becoming a parent. They might find themselves as an outcast for the first time. They might realize that they don't know who they are. This is the element that makes one's writing "authentic." This is what it means to "tell your own story" and to be "vulnerable."

Pete Doctor of Pixar notes, "What you're trying to do, when you tell a story, is to write about an event in your life that made you feel some particular way. And what you're trying to do, when you tell a story, is to get the audience to have that same feeling." We're trying to explore and share the emotions of the human condition. We're trying to follow a character's emotional journey as they respond to a life-changing situation. We'll later explore how we can ensure that our story has an impactful life experience. For now, it's just important that we understand that a life experience is a powerful tool for exploring a story's theme.

> *Takeaway*: The life experience of a character is a slice of the human condition. It explores the emotional journey of a character as they undergo a fundamentally new stage in their life. It's a powerful tool for exploring a story's theme.

Promise as the Foundation of Story Structure

Story isn't reality. Story is a hyper-reality. It shows only that which is important. It shows only that which is *significant*. This is the basis of the core promise that every storyteller makes with their audience: "What I show you will be significant."

Story is founded on the principle of promise. Recall that a promise is a contract that something will happen. With each story element that's introduced, the storyteller has made an implicit promise that the element will become significant. To be significant is to serve a purpose (i.e. to have an impact, effect, or consequence).

This implicit contract gives rise to the most basic form of story structure: setups and payoffs. This structure tells us that every story element of significance must have been set up or foreshadowed. It also says that every story element of seemingly no significance must eventually payoff with significance.

A setup is the foreshadowing of the future significance of a story element. It's a promise that an element will eventually become significant. A payoff is the moment when a story element that was previously set up (i.e. foreshadowed) is now revealed to be significant. A callback is when a story element reappears that has already revealed its significance. In the ideal structure, any element of significance must have been set up and any element of non-significance must eventually become significant.

Anton Chekhov famously wrote, "One must never place a loaded rifle on the stage if it isn't going to go off. It's wrong to make promises you don't mean to keep." This principle that every element of a story must have dramatic significance is called "Chekhov's Gun." It tells us that if a gun appears in act one, it must go off by act three. In other words, story elements must have significance. Chekhov also wrote, "Remove everything that has no relevance to the story." Fiction is silently selective. Readers assume that what we omit isn't significant and that what we include has significance.

The first half of a story is responsible for making promises and the second half of a story is responsible for paying them off. Here we again see the basic structure of question and answer. We'll find this symmetry between setups and payoffs to be an important guide as we structure our stories.

Takeaway: Any element included in a story must eventually be significant in some way. A setup is a promise (often implicit) that an element will eventually become significant. A payoff is when an element that has already been set up reveals its significance. The principle that every story element must have significance is called "Chekhov's Gun."

Stage II Wrap-up

We've now explored some of the simplest ideas and mechanics behind story structure and how basic stories work. Next we'll take this foundation and consider a few of the elements that can bring a story idea to life.

PART III

PUTTING UP THE FRAMING

EXPANDING THE STORY IDEA

Now that we've poured the foundation of our story, it's time to put up the framing. We'll put in the studs and lay the pipe. In essence, it's time to establish the skeleton on which the rest of the story will hang. We've explored a few methods for crafting a story idea from plot, story world, theme, and character. It's now time to take the initial story idea and turn it into a framework.

12

STARTING FROM THE END

We'll start crafting our story from the end. By knowing where we'll end up, we take the guessing out of where to start.

Thematic Strategy

Because the events of a story spring from its theme, we'll begin the process of crafting our story by considering the strategies we'll use to explore our story's theme. The core question here is, "How is the story's theme best explored?"

The first strategy is to ensure that our story contains thematic opposition. Recall that we can best explore a theme by ensuring that our story includes both arguments *for* and *against* the theme. We want to see opposing approaches to life. The most effective way to make these arguments is to give a character (or community) a deeply held belief or worldview that's staunchly entrenched in one side of the story's thematic dilemma. When a character or community holds strongly to a value system (i.e. a worldview), we see the evidence of their beliefs through the actions they take to champion or defend their value system in the face of opposition. Do they sacrifice their loved one or the future of the community? Their value system and beliefs are demonstrated by the decisions they make under pressure.

If our story's theme is about the merits of love versus duty, for example, then we want to be sure that each side of the theme is argued (explicitly or implicitly) by at least one character or community. We might have one character who believes love is more important than duty and another who believes that duty is more important than love. This is how theme comes to life on the page—through an opposition of worldviews. How far is each character willing to go to defend their approach to life?

Another thematic strategy is to include a character (or community) who transforms from one value system to the other via a character arc. A character might be redeemed by switching value systems. They might be corrupted by switching value systems. A character might come to doubt their value system. A character might need to persist in their value system against a domineering community. We have to also consider whether the character will be rewarded or punished for their transformation. And, of course, we might see a character who *should* change their value system but fails to learn a lesson.

Theme can also be explored by including dilemmas between opposing approaches to life. We want to set up scenarios where a character or community is continually forced to decide between one way of life and an opposing way of life. Do they defend the individual or the community? Do they defend faith or reason? We force them to make a choice and to deal with the consequences of that choice. Additionally we want our story's conflict to grow out of an opposition of these value systems. We want every scene to be a battle, literally or symbolically, between our story's value systems.

And finally, recall that a theme can also be explored by following a character as they face a fundamentally new stage of life. This life experience is a piece of the human condition such as birth, death, marriage, divorce, becoming a parent, an identity crisis, etc. This experience is often the exploration of some type of relationship. It might be the relationship between a parent and a child, the relationship between two lovers, the relationship between a group and a follower, or even one's relationship with oneself. Where possible, we want to detail the life experience and its key relationship at every level of our story, from the scene to the global structure.

Will our story focus on two dueling approaches to life? Will it show a character as they arc from one belief to another? Will it explore impossible moral dilemmas? These thematic strategies should be kept in mind as we craft the details of our story.

> *Takeaway*: We want to explore a theme by setting up scenarios where a character or community is continually forced to decide between one way of life and an opposing way of life. We can also explore theme by putting a character through the emotions of a life experience.

The Great Decision

The next step in crafting our story is to define The Great Decision. Recall that The Great Decision is a thematic choice (often a moral choice) that a character (or community) must make between two value systems. This final choice is where the character demonstrates through action any lesson they may have learned (or failed to learn) over the course of the story. It's often a choice between what the character wants and what they need. This is also often the moment where the character argues the story's theme through action. This Great Decision Moment is the philosophical and thematic climax of the story. It typically occurs as part of the story's external climax.

We explored this element in our discussion of theme so we won't belabor it here. By taking the time to define the final choice that a character will make, we can more clearly see how they'll need to make a different and often opposite choice at the beginning of the story (assuming we want to use a character arc to explore and express the story's theme). This is the final thematic choice that the central character will make.

Self-revelation

The self-revelation is the moment when the character has a key insight into themselves to which they had previously been blind. The character typically realizes how their behavior has been negatively affecting others. They realize that their behavior and moral flaw has been the root of their problems. They come to terms with their ghost and trauma from the past. They accept that their lie was in fact a lie. They drop their façade. They become individuated by realizing that their value isn't derived from something or someone outside of themselves. The character learns what's truly valuable in life. They have a growth experience.

It's at this moment that the character consciously learns their lesson. They fully understand what they need to do to live a more fulfilled life. What the character needs fully overshadows what they want. We may think of this as the moment when a character's dramatic desire is replaced by a higher, thematic desire.

While the character realizes the error of their ways at the self-revelation moment, it's typically not until The Great Decision Moment that they demonstrate through action that they've learned their lesson.

We must first clearly define what it is that the character comes to realize about themselves and about the most fulfilling way to live life. We must then determine how their lesson will contribute to their choice in The Great Decision Moment.

Life Experience

Recall that a character's life experience is a simple, emotional journey that a character takes over the course of a story. It can be thought of as the internal, metaphorical journey that a character takes in response to a significant change in their life. It's often about a relationship (with another character or with themselves).

The key to defining the life experience of a character is to determine what sort of human experience will directly challenge the character's beliefs or comfort zone. Through this challenge and direct confrontation, the character must either remain steadfast in their beliefs or change (for better or worse).

Consider also an experience that will force the character to challenge their identity. We want as much as possible to force the character to question themselves and their way of life. This is one powerful pattern for exploring theme and character change.

When we create an experience that challenges a character's belief or value system, we're trying to push them to decide between their current value system and a new value system. This tends to result in the climactic Great Decision Moment where the character must make a final choice and demonstrate their change, resistance to change, or inability to change.

The life experience is a powerful way of forcing a character to confront their void. That's what we're trying to do here. Different life experiences will affect different characters. For some, the arrival of a new child may force a particular character to confront their void. For others, the arrival of an opportunity for power will force them to confront it. We're trying to push the character to confront their void no matter how much they may want to run away, refuse to acknowledge its existence, or try to fill it in unhealthy ways. We must continually remind the character that there's something missing in their life and we won't leave them alone until they confront it. That's the purpose of the life experience.

> *Takeaway*: The key to defining a character's life experience is often to determine what sort of experience will directly challenge the character's beliefs or comfort zone. We want to force them to confront their void.

13

ELEMENTS OF THE CHARACTER'S JOURNEY

Central Story Disruption

There's one central disruption in a story that kicks off the main chain of cause and effect. We'll call it the "impetus" or "initial disruption." It's also sometimes called the "inciting incident" or "catalyst" and it typically occurs around the 10% mark of the story. All events after this disruption are but an inevitable ripple from the initial splash. It's the butterfly effect and this central disruption is the flap of the wings.

Generally we want this disruption to be tailor-made for our story's character. It should be crafted specifically to force the character to acknowledge their void. It's the first attack. Sometimes this means dangling something of value in front of the character to make them think there may finally be a path to filling their void. Sometimes it means threatening a worldview or lie that the character holds dear (such as the belief that they're only valuable if some condition is met). Sometimes it means bringing back some ghost or trauma from their past or trying to get them to confront a ghost from their past. And sometimes, it means threatening or taking away something of great personal value to the character—essentially creating an emptiness within the character that they'll be driven to fill.

Recall that a disruption is either a problem or an opportunity and it's almost always something unexpected. This central disruption is either the main "story problem" (which often turns out to be an opportunity in retrospect) or the main "story opportunity" (which often turns out to be a problem in retrospect). It's the first time the storyteller says, "Until one day, something happened..."

> *Takeaway*: The central story disruption is the story's inciting incident. It's the first disruption that begins the process of forcing the character to confront their void.

The Initial Opportunity

Most opportunities come with a catch. In Pixar's *Onward*, for instance, Ian and Barley get an opportunity to bring their father back to life for twenty-four hours by casting a spell. The catch is that they mess up the spell to bring him back, and only his lower half makes it back to life. This leads to the desire to get back the other half of their father. In *The Little Mermaid*, Ariel is given the opportunity to be a human, but the catch is that she has to kiss the prince in three days or she'll be Ursula's forever. In *Big*, Josh gets to be "big," but the catch is that he'll be an adult in an adult world and no one will take care of him. He'll have to fend for himself. Sometimes the catch is some sort of upfront payment that the character will need to make in order to pursue the opportunity (such as Ariel sacrificing her voice). As Ursula puts it, "You can't get something for nothing, you know."

When an opportunity has a catch, the catch is particularly impactful when the character is ill-suited to deal with it. In *The Little Mermaid*, Ariel not only has to kiss Prince Eric, but she also can't talk. In *Big*, Josh isn't only an adult, but he's also still a kid inside so he apparently has no skills or knowledge to deal with the adult world.

If the initial disruption is an opportunity, it might be the immediate granting of something of great value to the character. When this is the case, the opportunity often comes with an immediate catch. We find this in the movie *Big*, for example, where Josh is granted his wish but not in the way he thought. Dealing with the catch then tends to become the character's central desire. We also find this in Pixar's *Onward*.

The initial disruption might also be an offer or opportunity that requires a task to be completed before it's fulfilled. We find this in the movie *Avatar* where Jake Sully is offered a chance to regain control of his legs but only if he successfully infiltrates the Na'vi. We also find this in *The Goonies* when the discovery of the treasure map essentially presents a solution to Mikey's problems but only if the treasure is found. The pursuit and attainment of the opportunity tends to become the story's central desire.

The initial disruption might also be the appearance of an object of desire that the protagonist thinks will fill their void. In other words, the protagonist thinks that the attainment of something will cure their feeling that something's missing. In these cases, the character often initially has no concrete plan to attain their object of desire. In *The Little Mermaid*, Ariel rescues and falls in love with Eric who represents the human world for which she longs. She vows to be with him (but initially has no concrete plan to do so). In *The Nightmare Before Christmas*, Jack discovers Christmas Town and his eyes are opened to a whole new opportunity for a holiday (but initially he has no idea how to concretely incorporate it). It's typically not until the dramatic question moment that the character formulates a concrete plan to attain their desire. We see this in *The Nightmare Before Christmas* when Jack has a eureka moment. The plan might also be offered or assigned to the character in the form of an opportunity. We see this when Ariel makes a deal with Ursula to become a human.

For any opportunity, we have to first show the reason that the character will be particularly predisposed to jump at the opportunity—especially if it has a cost. This means we've got to show the character's desire before the opportunity arrives. We have to see how much Mr. Incredible loves being a superhero before he's given the opportunity to become one again. We have to see how much Ariel wants to become a human and how she's fallen in love with Prince Eric before she gets the opportunity to be one. We have to see how much Josh from *Big* wants to be big before he's given the opportunity. We have to see how Jack has an emptiness deep in his bones before he discovers Christmas Town. This helps us establish the stakes in the pursuit of the opportunity.

> *Takeaway*: If the central story disruption is an opportunity, it'll typically come with a catch. Before we present a character with an opportunity, we must first demonstrate how much they value the thing offered.

The Initial Problem

The initial disruption may create a clear problem in the character's life. This can often be accomplished by threatening or removing something of great value to the character. We might think of this as threatening a character's obsession, façade, comfort concept, world-view, or lie. This is the case in *Finding Nemo* when Marlin's son is taken. The disruption strikes directly at Marlin's identity as a family man. We also see this in *The Incredibles* when superheroes are banned. Mr. Incredible believes he's only valuable as a superhero and thus the ban strikes directly at his identity. This is also the case in *Shrek* when the fairy tale creatures arrive and threaten Shrek's façade. Shrek wants to keep everyone away because he doesn't believe he's worthy of being loved. We force him to confront his lie by forcing him on a journey where he'll find love.

The initial problem may not directly strike at a character's void, but instead it may trigger the chain of events that will lead to the character being forced to confront their void. We find this in *Good Will Hunting* where Will's arrest (i.e. the initial disruption) leads to a deal where he must undergo therapy in order to defer prosecution. The therapy itself is what will force Will to confront his past.

We might also consider bringing back a character's ghost in order to force them to confront their void. We find this in *Casablanca* when Ilsa walks into Rick's saloon. This disruption forces Rick to confront his past heartbreak and wrestle with the thematic opposition of love versus duty.

As with all disruptions, we want the initial problem to force the character to respond in some way. If the character can ignore the problem, it's not an effective disruption to their life.

Takeaway: We can strike at a character's void by threatening or removing something of great value to the character.

The Initial Revelation

The initial disruption may also be something that's a mix of both a problem and an opportunity. This might come in the form of a discovery that shakes a character's identity or worldview. It might alternatively come in the form of an inner calling that arises within the character. The disruption might cause the character to question what they know about themselves, their loved ones, or the world. The key here is that the disruption needs to drive the character to action.

We find this disruption in Disney's *Hercules* where an outcast Hercules has an inner calling to find out more about where he came from. Hercules, of course, later receives an opportunity from Zeus to regain his godhood. This type of disruption also occurs in *Elf* when Buddy finds out that he's not an elf. He's got a human father in New York. We also find this in *Hamlet* when the ghost of Hamlet's father reveals that he was murdered by Hamlet's uncle.

The character might see the discovery as a problem in that their identity or reality has been shaken, but they may also see it as an opportunity to uncover the truth or to right some wrong. The general response to this type of revelation will be to embark on a journey of search, discovery, or revenge. We want to be sure we've got plenty of revelations in this type of story.

The Disruption and the Desire

The central disruption may or may not immediately incite the central desire of the protagonist. In *Ratatouille*, the journey to the sewers and the arrival in Paris doesn't incite any desire in Remy except to find food. In *Finding Nemo*, on the other hand, the loss of Nemo immediately incites the central desire in Marlin to find and rescue Nemo. In *Monsters, Inc.*, the arrival of Boo immediately incites in Sully a desire to return her to the human world (driven most prominently by Monstropolis' ban on human children). In *The Goonies*, the discovery of the treasure map incites the desire to find its treasure in order to save the neighborhood. In the pilot episode of *The Mandalorian*, the opportunity for a high-value bounty acts as both the initial disruption and as the immediate start of the protagonist's central desire for the episode.

Whether this initial disruption immediately incites the central desire or not, it always kicks off the chain of cause and effect. And in this way, this initial disruption will eventually *lead* to the protagonist's central desire.

The protagonist may directly or indirectly cause the disruption (as in the case of *Ratatouille* when Remy's snooping in the old woman's house leads to him being flushed into the sewers of Paris). The protagonist may discover a piece of information that creates a problem or presents an opportunity (as in the case of *The Goonies* when Mikey discovers a map to buried treasure). The disruption may be incidental and have nothing to do with the character's actions (as in the case of *Toy Story* when Buzz Lightyear appears "from out of the sky").

> *Takeaway*: The initial disruption may or may not immediately incite the central desire of the protagonist.

Initial Disruption Possibilities

Here are a few powerful possibilities when choosing an initial disruption for our characters:

- Take away or threaten their obsession (as in the case of *Toy Story* and *Finding Nemo*).
- Provide an opportunity for the character to pursue their long-time obsession or dangle the chance in front of them (as in the case of Jack in *The Nightmare Before Christmas*, Olive in *Little Miss Sunshine*, Ariel in *The Little Mermaid*, Luke in *Star Wars*, and Clarice in *The Silence of the Lambs* when she's given the opportunity to prove herself within the FBI by capturing Buffalo Bill).
- Introduce an opportunity to fix an existing problem (as is the case in *Avatar* with Jake Sully being offered spinal surgery or in *The Goonies* when Mikey finds a map to buried treasure).
- Reintroduce the character's ghost into their life (as with Rick in *Casablanca*).
- Introduce a challenge to the character's value system (as is the case in *Monsters, Inc.* when Boo falls into Sully's care).
- Introduce a challenge to their lie or worldview (as is the case in *Jurassic Park* when Dr. Grant must care for two children).
- Introduce a challenge to their façade (as is the case in *Shrek* when the fairy tale creatures encroach on his façade of solitude).
- Introduce an opportunity to prove or validate their lie.
- Reveal something about their identity (as in the case of *Hercules* where he finds out he's part god).
- Trigger a life experience that breaks the camel's back and makes it clear that the protagonist can't continue with their life as it is (as is the case with Walter White's cancer diagnosis in *Breaking Bad*).

In some stories, this initial disruption can be seen as the opponent's first attack (particularly when opposition is embodied in a physical antagonist). When this is the case, consider how the antagonist might initiate their plan. This enactment of the antagonist's plan often creates a problem for the protagonist, thus kicking off the chain of cause and effect. This is the case in *Die Hard*. It might also create a trap for the protagonist in the form of an opportunity or temptation. This opportunity might present itself as some sort of deal or offer by the antagonist to the protagonist (as in the case of *Collateral* when Vincent offers Max money for a night of chauffeuring).

There are many instances where the initial story disruption takes the character into a new physical world, but it's not necessary to force a geographic change on the character. The initial story disruption does, however, always take the character into a new *metaphorical* world. It kicks off the character's central life experience, which will often force them to challenge their beliefs or value system.

> *Takeaway*: The initial disruption should either threaten or offer something of great value to a character.

Desire / Want

Many stories have a protagonist with one central, external desire that lasts from the end of act one (i.e. the dramatic question moment) to either the end of act two (i.e. the crisis point) or the climax (i.e. The Great Decision Moment). The key to this desire is that it must be concretely measurable. In other words, the audience should always definitively know whether the protagonist has attained their desire at any point in time. It's only by making the desire concretely measurable that we can use it to generate narrative drive.

This central desire often arises at a moment called the "dramatic question moment" (also known as "plot point one" or the "lock-in" moment). This moment is a disruption. It can often be thought of as a *type* of inciting incident in the sense that it *incites* the central desire and thus the story's central dramatic question of whether the protagonist will get what they want. This dramatic question moment typically occurs at the end of act one or around the 25% mark. In stories that are driven by a dramatic question, this event is responsible for establishing the main dramatic tension of the story.

Desire From the Void

We discussed how the story's initial disruption should be crafted to force the character to acknowledge their void in some way. If the character has a deep-seated desire for something, the initial disruption may dangle it in front of them (either by offering a concrete form of the deep-seated desire or by presenting some sort of opportunity). If the character values something (especially if they're using their attachment to it as an emotional shield in order to avoid confronting the emptiness within them), the initial disruption may take that thing of value away from the character. It's the point of first attack on the character's void.

The dramatic question moment can be thought of as the event that incites the character's desire to respond or react to the impetus (i.e. to the initial disruption). If the impetus threatens the character's void or façade, the dramatic question moment may be the moment that the character discovers a plan to return to equilibrium or to remove the threat. If the impetus takes something of value from the character, the dramatic question moment may be the moment that the character is presented with an opportunity to get it back. If the impetus dangles some object of desire that the character thinks will fill their void, the dramatic question moment might be the moment that the character discovers or crafts a concrete plan to get it. Where the impetus is the first push on the character's void, the dramatic question moment is the first clear response.

It can be helpful to think of the dramatic question moment as the moment that a concrete plan begins to take shape. It gives rise to the central dramatic question of whether the character will get what they want. It's also known as the "lock-in" moment because it's the moment that the character has fully committed to the journey ahead of them. The character begins to see a clear method by which they could either get what they've always wanted or return things to the way they've always been. It's the birth of a clear, specific plan to fill, validate, or conceal their void.

Takeaway: The dramatic question moment can typically be thought of as the event that incites the character's desire to respond or react to the impetus (i.e. to the initial disruption). It's the moment that a concrete plan begins to take shape.

Desire From False Belief

Recall that a thematic dilemma can often be distilled down to a struggle between what a character *wants* to do and what they *need* to do. Since the "need" is typically the correct approach to life, the "want" is typically some misguided or misplaced (although often easy or comfortable) approach to life. In this way, a character's central desire can often be seen as a futile attempt to address their void. It's an understandable but misguided reaction to the initial disruption.

The central desire may be the protagonist's attempt to solve their problem (or pursue their opportunity) through the use of their façade and coping mechanisms (which often includes their moral flaw or lie). In this way, the pursuit of the central desire may itself be a coping mechanism to attempt to deal with the character's void in an unhealthy way. Sometimes the whole journey could have been avoided if they had just learned their lesson from the beginning (but, of course, they needed to go on the journey to learn the lesson).

It can sometimes be helpful to think of the character as starting the story with a false belief about what will bring them happiness. They may believe, "If I just do [x], or attain [y], or become [z], I'll be happy and fulfilled." Shrek believes that if he can just get the fairy tale creatures off his land, he'll be happy. In *Legally Blonde*, Elle believes that if she can just get her boyfriend back, she'll be happy. Woody believes that if he can just get rid of Buzz, he'll be happy. In *Up*, Carl believes that if he can just get his house to Paradise Falls, he'll be happy. Mr. Incredible believes that if he can just become a superhero again, he'll be happy. Of course, this belief is almost never true. The character must often learn that true fulfillment comes from deriving value from oneself and connecting to others in a healthy way. A character might believe that "If I go out on a journey, I'll experience true adventure," but the reality is that "True adventure comes from those you love." A character might believe, "If I escape, I'll be free," when the reality is, "True freedom comes from within." Breaking down the false belief often requires a change in perception, occurring at the self-revelation moment.

A character often *thinks* that their desire will get them what they need in life. They think that it'll fill the emptiness within them. We know, of course, that it seldom does. The central desire tends to be focused on chasing what's outside (the wrong approach to life) instead of recognizing what's within (the right approach to life). It's often only at the self-revelation moment that a character realizes that they must shift their focus from without to within.

Of course, this is simply the most common pattern and doesn't reflect every type of character arc. Not all characters change and thus don't necessarily need to explore the internal battle between want and need (as is the case with Luke in *Star Wars* and Forrest in *Forrest Gump*). The character doesn't need to approach their journey in an incorrect or immoral way. Some characters are "traveling angels" who are morally pure and influence the morality of the surrounding community (it's worth noting that we might also see a "traveling devil" who's morally corrupt and negatively influences the morality of the surrounding community).

> *Takeaway*: It can sometimes be helpful to think of the character as starting the story with a false belief about what will bring them happiness. They may believe, "If I just do [x], or attain [y], or become [z], I'll be happy and fulfilled." Their central desire tends to be based around this false belief.

Desire From Thematic Opposition

Recall that we can often think of a thematic dilemma pair (such as individual versus community, love versus duty, and reason versus faith) as a form of want versus need. We may want to serve our own selfish interests, but we can sometimes live a fuller life by serving the community. We may want to value love over duty, but sometimes we need to fulfill our responsibilities. We may want to have a full understanding before we leap, but sometimes we just need to have faith.

With that said, some stories are best served by giving a character a desire for one side of the thematic dilemma (such as reason) and a need for the other side (such as faith). One side of the thematic opposition is then outwardly embodied in the character's want and later the other side of the opposition is embodied in the character's self-revelation and final thematic choice. In *Raiders of the Lost Ark*, for instance, Indiana Jones does eventually demonstrate his faith when he closes his eyes at the opening of the Ark.

Of course, the character's central desire doesn't necessarily need to be rooted in one side of the thematic opposition (especially if the character doesn't have a character arc). This is the case in *Star Wars* where Luke does not have strong feelings for the force one way or another. He later demonstrates his full commitment to it in the climactic scene where he turns off his guidance computer and trusts the force to help him destroy the Death Star.

> *Takeaway*: Some stories are best served by giving a character a desire for one side of the thematic dilemma (such as reason) and a need for the other side (such as faith).

Desire From Problem

Recall that a disruption is often either an opportunity or a problem. When the impetus (i.e. initial disruption) is a problem or a threat, the central desire is typically a desire to either avoid the problem or to return things to the way they used to be. We see this pattern when an obsession is threatened or lost, a ghost returns, a lie is challenged, or a façade is attacked. This is the case in *Shrek* where the initial disruption (i.e. the impetus) is the invasion of the fairy tale creatures, but there's not yet a clear plan for how to remove them. Shrek goes to Lord Farquaad to request that the fairy tale creatures be removed. The central desire and plan take shape when Shrek is offered a deal where he must save a princess from a dragon in order to get the fairy tale creatures removed from his swamp.

In these instances, the character typically responds to the impetus by trying to come up with a clear plan to conceal their ghost, maintain their façade, protect their threatened obsession, or defend their challenged lie. The dramatic question moment (also known as "plot point one" or the "lock-in" moment) may be the moment that the character devises the concrete plan to return things to the way they used to be (i.e. to solve the problem).

Where possible, we want to force the character to confront their void as part of the process of addressing their problem. They've got to do the thing they fear, hate, or dread in order to get things back to the way they used to be. In *Finding Nemo*, for instance, the only way Marlin can find his son is to confront the thing that epitomizes his fear of chaos and lack of control, the ocean.

> *Takeaway*: When the initial disruption is a threat or a problem, the central desire is typically a plan to avoid or reverse the consequences of the problem.

Desire From Opportunity

When the impetus is the appearance of an object of desire, an opportunity to solve one's ongoing problem, or an opportunity to chase one's dream, the dramatic question moment might be the formulation of a concrete plan to go after the opportunity or object of desire. The dramatic question moment may also be the moment that a clear plan or opportunity is either offered or assigned to the character (as in the case of *The Little Mermaid* when Ursula offers Ariel a way to become a human).

In this way, the story's central desire is typically a desire to pursue the opportunity or object of desire (perhaps after some hesitation). This is particularly the case when a character has some existing problem or some unfulfilled obsession (i.e. a dream or a longing). A character need not have previously done anything about addressing their problem or obsession up to this point in their life. They may also not have even realized that they had a problem or obsession until the moment of the impetus.

Recall that opportunities often come with a catch. When this is the case, a character may initially pursue the opportunity until they discover the catch. The catch may then become the overarching problem of the story that the character works to solve. In *Big*, Josh initially wants to be big. Once he gets that opportunity, however, he finds out that he doesn't want to be an adult and now desires to become a kid again. In *Onward*, Ian and Barley initially pursue an opportunity to see their father again. When the spell backfires and only their father's lower half comes back to life, the opportunity turns into a problem and the two set out to get the rest of their father back. In *The Little Mermaid*, an opportunity is presented to Ariel to become a human. The catch is that she has to kiss Prince Eric sometime within three days. Dealing with the catch becomes her new desire.

We ideally want to force the character to confront their void as part of pursuing the opportunity. This often means that we want to force the character to confront that which they fear or hate. In *Good Will Hunting*, Will is offered a way out of going to jail, but the catch is that he must undergo therapy and confront his ghost—the thing he most fears. In *Tootsie*, Michael Dorsey hears about an opportunity to act in a daytime soap opera. The catch is that the role is for a female. Michael must confront his misogyny and impersonate a woman in order to pursue the opportunity for acting work. In *The Silence of the Lambs*, Clarice is presented with an opportunity to work with Hannibal Lecter in order to get more information in her pursuit of Buffalo Bill. The catch is that she must answer questions about her past and consequently about her ghost—effectively undergoing therapy.

A character who's chasing an opportunity may also be chasing something concrete that's symbolic of a broader attempt to fill their void. A character might be relentlessly pursuing a particular plush toy from their youth, for instance, when that toy is merely symbolic of an attempt to repair their relationship with their mother. In the end, the character must typically realize what it is that will *actually* make them happy. Chasing *symbols* of happiness may only result in fleeting or superficial fulfilment.

> *Takeaway*: When the initial disruption is an opportunity, it often comes with a catch or requirement. Dealing with the catch or requirement is often the central desire of the story.

Justification and Rationalization

Some characters aren't willing to admit to themselves the real reason that they have a particular desire. For example, a character who's fiercely competing to win a local competition may not be willing to admit to themselves that they're only doing it because they think a win will make their father proud of them. The character will often come up with some sort of justification or rationalization for why they're pursuing their desire. They might say, for instance, that the competition money could really help or that it's always been a child-hood dream. When a character isn't willing to admit their true reasons for pursuing a desire, we may want to get a sense that there's more to their true motivation than the justification would have us believe. They may be inexplicably obsessed or inexplicably frustrated in the face of otherwise trivial setbacks.

This pattern tends to arise when a character is hiding their void, not just from others but also from themselves. They may not be willing to admit that they have an emptiness within them. With this in mind, this pattern is most applicable when a character has a façade (i.e. a false identity), including one that arises from a trauma, lie, or worldview. Characters who are aware that they have an empti-ness that's rooted in an obsession or longing tend to be more upfront with why they want what they want.

> *Takeaway*: A character may be unwilling to admit the true reason that they're pursuing their central desire. This tends to occur if the character can't admit to themselves that they have a void.

The Impetus and Dramatic Question Moment as One

As we've seen, it's possible that the impetus and the dramatic question moment actually occur at the same time in the same event. In other words, it's possible that the initial disruption is the thing that incites the central desire and thus the central dramatic question. This is especially the case when something of special value to a character is lost, threatened, or dangled via a clear opportunity. This might also be the case when an opportunity appears that promises to fix a character's ongoing problem. When there's an opportunity for or threat to something of intense value, the character will tend to jump into action with little hesitation. They craft and update their plan along the way.

We may also see the establishment of a strong and immediate desire if a character's façade is credibly threatened or endangered. We also tend to see an early dramatic question when there's a disruption to a well-defined or strict rule or moral code as defined by either the character or story world (as in the case of *Monsters, Inc.* when Boo arrives and puts Sully in danger of violating Monstropolis' rule of no human children).

Internal Versus External Impetus

We can think of the impetus as the initial trigger of the character's desire. Many times, this trigger occurs externally (such as a call to adventure, the arrival of a stranger, a mission, a problem that upends the character's life, or any other form of external problem or opportunity). It's important to realize, however, that this trigger doesn't need to be an external force that pushes or pulls the character. The impetus may simply be a moment that triggers within the character a calling of some sort. It may be a revelation. Perhaps the character discovers something or sees something from a new perspective that incites in them a feeling or obligation to embark on this journey. The calling might be based on their moral code or sense of honor or any other internal value system. It might be an otherwise ordinary object or line of dialogue that triggers the character's inner feelings. It's important to realize that not all impetuses need to be externally driven—some can be an awakened force from within.

Superseding Desires

The central desire raised at the dramatic question moment doesn't always last the full length of the story, of course. The two key points at which a desire is likely to dramatically change is the midpoint (i.e. the middle of act two) and/or the crisis point (i.e. the end of act two). Sometimes the central desire is attained or lost at the midpoint (as in the case of *Titanic* when Rose gets Jack). Sometimes the desire is abandoned and replaced at the midpoint (as in the case of *Avatar* when Jake Sully's desire to infiltrate the Na'vi is replaced by a desire to save them from the invading humans). Sometimes the desire is attained at the crisis point and it turns out to be a false victory (as in the case of *Up* when Carl realizes his trek to Paradise Falls is meaningless without Ellie). Sometimes the desire is lost at the crisis point, but the protagonist realizes there's something more important (as in the case of *Toy Story* when Woody realizes that being a good toy for Andy is more important than being the top toy).

As a general rule, whenever the central desire is replaced by another desire, the new desire must have higher stakes (i.e. the new desire is "higher" or nobler). In mystery stories, the truth behind the crime might be discovered at the end of act two, which then gives rise to a new desire: find and capture the criminal. Selfish desires might be replaced by altruistic desires. The desire for what one wants tends to eventually be replaced by the desire for what one needs.

> *Takeaway*: If the central desire is replaced by another desire, it typically occurs at either the midpoint or the crisis point. When a desire is replaced, it should almost always be replaced by a desire with even higher stakes (i.e. more valuable stakes).

Wrapping up Desire

Remember that these are simply common patterns and that our story need not necessarily follow them. Recall also that obsessions, lies, ghosts, and façades aren't mutually exclusive. While a character may have only one, they may also have multiple or all. And in this way, a character may fit multiple patterns when it comes to the impetus and the dramatic question moment.

As a general principle, we want the character to pursue whatever it is that they think will help fill, validate, or conceal their void. Sometimes this means pursuing an object of desire. Sometimes this means trying to change things back to the way they used to be. Sometimes this means desperately avoiding change. The character typically tries to move in the direction of retrieving or regaining what's most comfortable to them. In many cases, the character is pursuing what they *want* in life, but it stands in contrast with what they *need* in order to live a better life. In other words, the character's central desire is typically focused on pursuing a value system that's thematically opposed to whatever the character needs to learn in the end.

Need

When we think about the things we "need," we often think about the concepts that are low on Maslow's hierarchy of needs. We think "I need a glass of water" or "I need some food." But it may be more helpful for us to reframe our thinking and ask the question, "What do I need in order to live a happier, more fulfilled life?" Obviously physical needs such as air, food, water, and shelter tend to be among the most obvious needs. But once those needs are fulfilled, we get into self-actualization and other more ethereal needs having to do with morality, society, and relationships. These needs are just as valid as their physical counterparts and are the needs with which we'll be primarily focused when it comes to our stories.

A character with a weakness (or flaw) typically has a need to heal that weakness in order to live a happier, more fulfilled life. "Weakness" is subjective, of course, especially when it comes to the physical. We can break weaknesses into three primary categories: physical, psychological, and moral. Because there are three categories of weaknesses, there are also three corresponding categories of needs.

The first category of needs is the physical. Physical needs relate to living a physically healthy and fulfilling life. A character who's dissatisfied with what they perceive to be a physical weakness may seek some cure, treatment, or supplement. Physical needs are made most powerful when they're combined with moral needs. We can, of course, also make a physical need symbolic of a deeper moral need. Perhaps when the moral weakness is cured, the physical will be as well.

The second category of needs is the psychological. Psychological needs relate to living a psychologically healthy and fulfilling life. A character might have a psychological need to respect themselves, to be mentally stable, to enjoy their own company, or to be happy with their life. These needs are about the health of one's own psyche. Psychological needs by themselves are purely personal. Like physical needs, psychological needs are often most powerful when combined with moral needs so that the story can explore how the character's psychological weakness also affects their relationships.

The third and final category of needs is the moral. This is the most emotionally powerful of the three. Moral needs relate to living a morally healthy and fulfilling life. Recall that morality is about relationships. To be morally healthy, then, is to relate to others in a positive and healthy way for both oneself and for others. Because stories are often about relationships and how to live an emotionally healthy life, giving a character a moral weakness (and thus a moral need) can be a powerful way of exploring both the wrong approach to life and eventually the right approach to life and morality.

We generally want to give our character a moral weakness. As we've discussed, this weakness can arise from a character's coping mechanisms. These coping mechanisms can stem from an attempt to protect the character's façade (i.e. the false identity constructed to deal with the character's void). Coping mechanisms include projection, disassociation, detachment, lashing out, aggression, compensation (including, perhaps, trying to fill one's void with hollow pursuits), denial, repression, avoidance, people pleasing, humor, intellectualization, isolation, passive aggression, regression, and narcissism, among others. Consider how a coping mechanism may result in unsavory behavior in relationships. How might a character's desire to emotionally shield themselves result in harm to their relationships?

Once we've identified a character's moral weakness, we can then identify their moral need by asking, "What does this character need in order to live a truly great life?" What does this character need in order to reach their potential? What does this character need in order to be truly happy? What does this character need to learn in order to treat others with respect?

In order to overcome a weakness, a character often needs to do the thing that scares them most. A character might need to learn that they don't need to define themselves by their obsession in order to be valuable. A character might need to learn that their identity is separate from their past trauma or ghost. A character might need to learn that they can live a healthy and fulfilled life without their lie. A character might need to learn that they can only live a fulfilled life if they drop their façade and live in their essence. In short, a character needs to learn to become a healthy individual. They need to become individuated.

In *Finding Nemo*, Marlin needs to learn that he can trust others to protect themselves and that he doesn't need to define himself by Nemo. In *The Incredibles*, Mr. Incredible must learn that his value isn't derived from his role as a superhero but rather from his role as a family man. In *Toy Story*, Woody must learn that his value is derived not from being the top toy but merely from being a toy that takes care of his child. In *Legally Blonde*, Elle must learn that she's valuable as herself and not as what others want her to be.

Just like desires, needs are also hierarchical. A character might have a moral need to become selfless, but that moral need can spawn a more specific sub-need to be selfless when it comes to a specific thing. This is the case in *Toy Story* where Woody has a need to be self-less but more specifically he has a need to share Andy with Buzz. This hierarchical relationship between needs is often one reason why we might note different needs for the same character. We can think about how a general moral need can be made more concrete by specifying it within the context of the current story world.

Remember that not all characters have a need. Some characters are already psychologically and morally healthy. These characters tend to be innocent characters who spread their morality and change the surrounding community. In these stories, it's the community that arcs rather than the character.

> *Takeaway*: There are three categories of needs: physical, psychological, and moral. Moral needs tend to result in the most emotional story journeys. In order to overcome a weakness and fulfill a need, a character often needs to do the thing that scares them most.

The Lesson

A character will often construct a façade or use coping mechanisms in an attempt to avoid having to acknowledge or deal with their void head on. This is typically done out of a conscious or subconscious fear of confronting their void (which might more specifically be a fear of confronting their ghost or past trauma or a fear of living life outside of the protection of their lie). In other words, characters often act immorally because they're afraid. There's some great fear that they've internalized and it's negatively affecting their behavior.

A character might be afraid that they're not valuable if they don't hold some role or status or if they don't hold on to some idea or object. These are often fears that are implicit in a character's action. Marlin's afraid he won't be able to protect his family. Woody's afraid of being abandoned. Carl is afraid of living life without Ellie.

For each fear, there's a list of possible revelations a character might have that can counteract the root of the fear. A character who's afraid of being forgotten might need to learn that one's life is valuable regardless of whether one is remembered, or that no one can be remembered forever, or that the value of a life comes not from how one is remembered but from how one positively affects others. A character who's afraid of letting a family member take care of themselves may need to learn that their family member is a separate person who can and *should* grow on their own and experience their own life.

We want to consider what a character needs to learn in order to live a better life. What lesson do they need to learn in order to overcome their deep fear? Once a character has learned this lesson, they can begin to overcome the fear and address their void in a healthy way.

In his book *Story Trumps Structure*, Steven James offers a valuable piece of advice, "To uncover the meaning of your story, don't ask what the theme is, but rather, what is discovered." Here we're asking what the character will discover about the proper approach to life.

> *Takeaway*: What lesson does the character need to learn in order to overcome a deep fear that they may have? What do they discover about themselves in order to live a better life?

Want Versus Need Pattern

We've now defined both a desire and a need for our story's character. Recall that there can be an inverse relationship between the importance of a character's desire and the importance of their need over the course of a story. That which initially seems like the least important thing becomes the most important (need) and that which initially seems the most important thing becomes the least important (desire). Let's look at a few patterns for how the desire and need may relate to each other.

There are a few fundamental questions that we must answer when it comes to our character: Will our character learn their lesson about the best way to live a fulfilling life? Will our character end up getting what they initially wanted? If they do get what they wanted, will it be satisfying to them? What's the cost and is it worth it? If they get what they want, will it be attained before or after they learn their lesson? If they fail to get what they want, will they just accept that? If they fail to get what they want, will they lash out and permanently fall to immorality? Will they come to a false belief about why they didn't get what they wanted?

First of all, we want to decide whether the character will actually get what they need. Do they end up having a self-revelation about the correct way to live life? Not all characters have a weakness and thus not all have a need. These characters don't ever end up having a self-revelation because they don't need one. It's worth noting that some characters that *do* have a need don't ever end up having a self-revelation, perhaps because they're incapable of that level of self-awareness. Some characters do have a self-revelation, but it ends up being incorrect. These false self-revelations typically give birth to false beliefs about oneself or about the world and can lead to further corruption or moral decay (which can sometimes result in the birth of a villain). In the majority of cases, however, a character with a moral need will eventually have a self-revelation and learn the correct way to live life.

We send different messages to the audience based on whether the character gets what they need (i.e. has a self-revelation). When a flawed character has a self-revelation, we're taking a stance on the questions of whether people can change, whether mistakes can be fixed, and whether we can recognize our own mistakes.

Next we must decide whether our character will end up getting what they initially wanted and when they'll get it. In those instances where a character does *not* get what they want, we may want to imply that they won't get what they want without some sort of self-revelation. In fact, it's often the loss of the thing desired that *causes* the character to realize that they need to look within and change. The character might have a realization about *why* they didn't get what they wanted. It's also possible that a character has a self-revelation about what's truly valuable and this causes them to intentionally abandon the pursuit of their desire and instead be content without attaining the thing they initially wanted. In these instances, the character chooses the need over the want.

In some cases, a character might fail to get what they want, which leads to the character having a false self-revelation. In other words, they might come to the "wrong" belief about *why* they didn't get what they wanted. While the false self-revelation may involve blaming others or the world more generally, it's sometimes simply a rationalization or justification. In *Four Weddings and a Funeral*, for instance, Charles doesn't win Carrie over. He talks to his best friend and comes to the belief that love isn't about a thunderbolt moment, making us believe that he and Carrie just weren't meant for each other. This is revealed to be false by the end of the story. Other times, the false self-revelation can be more insidious. It can result in blaming others, society, and the world at large. These false self-revelations can give rise to villains. In these instances, the false revelation is left in place at the end of the story.

In those instances where a character *does* get what they want, it might happen *before* their self-revelation about the proper way to live life. In these instances, the attainment of the desire may be a hollow victory. The character has "won" but feels like something's missing and that they're not actually happy. They might wonder if the thing they wanted was worth the price that needed to be paid. This often causes the character to look within and realize that they need to change in order to be happy (thus triggering the self-revelation). In those instances where the character gets what they want *after* the self-revelation, it's often *because* of the self-revelation. Usually following a crushing defeat (or hollow victory), the character learns their lesson and this insight allows them to approach their journey of desire from a new perspective, typically resulting in success.

When a character has a self-revelation, they sometimes abandon their current desire in pursuit of a desire that's more aligned with their new-found lesson about the best way to live life.

Often a character will need to fail to get what they want in some way (or find it to be hollow victory) in order to learn their lesson and get what they need. If a character gets what they want before their self-revelation and they're satisfied with the price paid, they're never pushed to look within or to learn any lesson.

It can often be helpful to craft the want and need so that they're directly opposed. In *Toy Story*, for instance, Woody's desire is "to be Andy's favorite toy" or "to have Andy all to himself." We might think of Woody's moral need as "to be able to share Andy's love with others." On this level, the need and desire are in direct conflict, creating a thematic opposition and dilemma. Woody *wants* to be selfish when it comes to Andy (which spawns the desire to want to get rid of Buzz). He *needs* to be selfless when it comes to Andy (which spawns the need to accept Buzz and share Andy with him). This opposition between want and need often arises naturally when a character either tries to solve their problem using a coping mechanism or when their desire is to directly avoid doing what will actually fulfill them.

> *Takeaway*: Does the character get what they want? When? Is it a hollow victory? Do they get what they need? When? Do they have a self-revelation before or after they get what they want?

Character Arc

Recall that a character arc is the transition of a character from embodying one value system to embodying an alternate value system. It's an internal transformation. We discussed how a story's thematic opposition can be thought of as a pair of value systems. The opposition might be between ambition and integrity, between love and duty, or between the individual and the community, among others. At its core, the opposition is often between what the character wants to do (i.e. continue living comfortably with an incorrect value system) and what the character needs to do (i.e. embrace uncomfortable change and adopt the new value system).

Remember that not all characters arc. Sometimes it's the community surrounding the character that arcs. In either instance, we want to take this time to detail the arc of either the character or the surrounding community. We'll explore the specific beats of a character arc in a later section.

Central Relationship (The Influence Character)

In many stories, it's the central relationship itself that forces a character to change over the course of the story. In stories that have a character who undergoes some sort of thematic change (i.e. the transformed character), there's typically a thematic opponent who can be thought of as the "influence" character.

This influence character offers an alternate worldview or approach to life. The influence character is a thematic opponent who helps the protagonist or main character change (wittingly or unwittingly). It's through proximity to the influence character that the protagonist is forced to confront the fact that they may be living life incorrectly. The protagonist and the influence character might go through a life experience together (even if they're dramatically opposed) where the protagonist learns about themselves by observing how the influence character approaches life.

The influence character might be what's called a clone character. In his book *Invisible Ink*, Brian McDonald says, "Clones are characters in your story that represent what could, should, or might happen to the protagonist if he or she takes a particular path." Through comparison to another character, a central character may eventually realize they need to change. They might either be inspired to change or they might be moved by fear. In *A Christmas Carol*, for example, Scrooge serves as his own clone and influence character. He's forced to face his doomed future self if he doesn't change his current path.

When crafting a central relationship for our story, we might consider who will be able to best force the central character to confront their void. Who would most challenge the character's approach to life? Who would be the most confrontational thematic opponent? In *Toy Story*, Woody is so caught up in his obsession with being the top toy that the most confrontational opponent would be not just a character who doesn't want to be the top toy but one who doesn't even believe that he *is* a toy—which gives us Buzz Lightyear. It's also interesting to note that Buzz and Woody are symbolically opposed—a space ranger who represents the future versus a cowboy sheriff who represents the past.

Which character is most opposed to our character's worldview? That's who we want as the influence character. That's who we want constantly pushing our character to question their approach to life. Marlin has Dory (*Finding Nemo*). Linguini has Remy (*Ratatouille*). Woody has Buzz (*Toy Story*). Joy has Sadness (*Inside Out*). Rick has Ilsa (*Casablanca*). Note that the dramatic opponent can also be the influence character (as in *Toy Story*).

We'll later explore the ways in which this influence character acts to change our story's transformed character. And interestingly enough, a story can have a central character who is in fact an influence character on others. In these cases, the central character acts as a "traveling angel" (or "traveling devil").

Takeaway: An influence character offers an alternate worldview or approach to life. The influence character is a thematic opponent who helps the central character change (wittingly or unwittingly) by demonstrating a different approach to life.

14

GENRE AND STORY FORM

Genre

It's at this point that we want to begin thinking about a genre for our story.

We can think of a genre as an expectation of what will *basically* happen in a story (but importantly not *how* it'll happen). A genre quickly tells the audience what kinds of things they can hope to find within the story.

If the story is a thriller, the audience can expect suspense and mystery. If it's in the crime genre, the audience can expect there to be some sort of crime and an ensuing battle between law enforcement and the criminals. If it's fantasy, the audience can expect magic in the everyday world (either literally or metaphorically). If it's science fiction, the audience can expect fascinating technology and its implications.

We can think of a genre as the basic form that our story will take. Just as characters have archetypes, stories have genres. The genre we choose for our story will affect what the audience expects to get out of the story. John Truby says, "The biggest reason that writers fail at the premise (and by the way 99% of scripts fail at the premise line) is not that it's not a good idea, it's that they use the wrong genre to develop the idea."

Each genre also has its own familiar beats and situations. This is one of the great benefits of genre: we can explore and ground our unfamiliar ideas in the genre's familiar beats. This allows the audience to more quickly understand a new concept in terms of what they already know. We can think of genres as templates through which to explore story ideas.

When selecting a genre for our story, we want to keep in mind that each genre emphasizes different story elements. When we select a genre, we're implicitly promising to the audience of that genre that we'll emphasize specific elements and give them what they want. If we select a genre and fail to emphasize the story elements for which the audience consumes the genre, we'll create in the audience a feeling of frustration, disengagement, and distrust—resulting in an ineffective story for the target audience. To select a genre, we want to consider which elements are emphasized in each genre and compare that to which elements of our story we want to emphasize.

Fantasy

The fantasy genre emphasizes a unique, often magical world. The magic may not be literal but rather figurative. A fantasy story may explore "the magic in the mundane." It's about seeing the world with new eyes. Audiences of this genre tend to come for beautiful and dangerous story worlds that have never before been seen. Fantasy emphasizes wonder and style. It often blends well with the myth genre and consequently the "Hero's Journey" paradigm. Myth might be used to explain the creation and meaning of fantasy's beautiful and dangerous world. The fantasy genre can help explore the thematic opposition of faith versus reason.

Science Fiction

The science fiction genre emphasizes technology, progress, growth, and evolution. Audiences of science fiction come for the technology, the science, and the worldbuilding. The audience often wants to see technology that seems contextually plausible (and perhaps even argue about whether it could be possible in today's world). Peter Russell argues that in science fiction, problems should be caused by and solved by some aspect of the story world's unique technology. Like fantasy, science fiction also tends to blend well with the myth genre.

Horror

The horror genre emphasizes the monster. It compares the human to the monster (who often takes the form of either a machine or an animal). Horror is typically about exploring the question, "What is human?" And in some of the most interesting horror stories, we're forced into the realization that sometimes humans act in a way that seems inhuman. Horror tends to emphasize the thematic opposition of life versus death. Audiences of horror want to feel fear and the opposition between life and death.

Myth

The myth genre emphasizes meaning, symbolism, and the Hero's Journey. Regarding the myth genre, Shawn Coyne notes, "A myth is a story that's of so high resolution and abstract that it's true for all time. That's what a myth is—meta-true." Pamela Jaye Smith says, "Myths are the stories we tell ourselves to *explain* the world around us and within us. — and as a side note to both of those: to *justify* the worlds that we have created [around us and within us]." Myths often explore life and death. They explore man versus animal, man versus machine, and man versus God. The myth genre often emphasizes the journey of a hero to find out who they are. It's an external journey for an internal discovery. The hero is then tested over and over again to make sure they are who they were told that they are. For the myth genre, we can almost always refer back to the Hero's Journey with all of its Jungian archetypes and mythical symbols. The myth genre tends to emphasize the thematic opposition between want versus need, ends versus means, the individual versus the community, power in the hands of the many versus the few, and morality versus immorality.

Action

The action genre emphasizes war, strategy, tactics, power, and the warrior. Audiences of this genre want to see a fierce and clever battle between the protagonist and antagonist. They want to see both sides exercising a battle plan and then being unexpectedly undercut by their opponent, forcing improvisation. Action is all about the life of the warrior. It's about honor. It's about standing and fighting, even when it might mean the cost of one's own life. Action emphasizes the thematic opposition between life versus death and what it is to live an honorable life.

Mystery

The mystery genre emphasizes logic, reasoning, and the analytical process. Audiences of this genre often want to see the brilliant leaps of a logical and creative mind. This genre emphasizes the reveal of new information that changes our understanding of the problem and/or world. It's about missing information and the search to uncover it. In the mystery genre, the opponent is often unknown or hidden. The protagonist's goal is typically to uncover the identity of the opponent and sometimes to capture them. Mystery is about piecing together the truth.

Thriller

The thriller genre emphasizes suspense, surprise, twists, and clever strategy. Audiences of this genre like the thrill of the chase and the thrill of the hunt. Like the mystery genre, the true opponent is typically hidden. In the thriller, however, the opponent is on the attack. There's danger and unseen threats around every corner. Suspense is the key dramatic tool. Nothing is as it seems.

Romance

The romance genre emphasizes emotion. It emphasizes the unique ability for two people to see the essence of each other, even when they're unable to see the essence of themselves. Audiences of this genre generally want to see wooing, swooning, witty banter, the physical connection, beauty and the physical form, seduction, romantic gestures, and the beauty of a world.

Comedy

The comedy genre emphasizes humor. The most impactful comedy comes not from gags or witty one-liners but from the characters and their situations. Audiences of this genre want to laugh deeply and meaningfully.

Many stories are a combination of genres. It's important to note, however, that choosing multiple genres doesn't mean we get to pick and choose which elements we want to emphasize. We must emphasize the elements of *all* of the genres of our story. A comedy thriller must emphasize the hunt and comedic situations.

> *Takeaway*: If we select a genre and fail to emphasize the story elements for which the audience consumes the genre, we'll create in the audience a feeling of frustration, disengagement, and distrust—

resulting in an ineffective story for the target audience. If our story is a mix of multiple genres, we must emphasize the elements of all of the genres in our story.

Story Form

Just like we can categorize stories into genres, we can also sometimes categorize them into story forms. There are basic stories which are retold over and over in different story worlds. Examples include *Cinderella, The Prince and the Pauper, Romeo and Juliet, Hamlet, The Sorcerer's Apprentice, A Christmas Carol*, etc. These basic story forms can typically be found in fairy tales and myths.

A story form can be especially helpful when writing a story from scratch. We can follow the basic beats of a story form, just like we follow the basic beats of a genre. Just like when writing in a particular genre, of course, the key is to remember that while we know what *must* happen (the story form beats), we must be inventive with *how* they happen. For example, *The Lion King* uses particular elements of the *Hamlet* story form, but the beats are expressed in a unique story world.

Although not all stories fit a story form, it can be helpful to consider if there's a story that may serve as a helpful template to explore a theme. Story forms are often timeless and particularly suited for expressing and exploring particular themes. *Sleeping Beauty*, for instance, helps us explore a theme about the limits of beauty and the dilemma between earned success versus given success. Using a story form allows us to consider the story beats and elements that will help us best explore a theme and deliver the most emotional impact.

Takeaway: Existing stories can serve as templates for new stories.

15

DRAMATIC AND THEMATIC ELEMENTS

Opposition

We must now decide who or what will provide the primary dramatic and thematic opposition in our story. Recall from our discussion about dramatic tools that dramatic opposition arises when a character's desire is opposed, thus giving rise to dramatic conflict. When a character's goal is opposed by another character, we get a situation where only one of the two characters can get what they want. Their goals are mutually exclusive. Thematic opposition, on the other hand, arises when a character's belief or value system is opposed, thus giving rise to thematic conflict. We can say that thematic opposition arises when two or more characters have fundamentally different approaches to life.

We may choose to have both dramatic and thematic opposition in a single opponent. In *The Incredibles*, Syndrome provides both thematic opposition (believing that one doesn't need powers to be a superhero) and also dramatic opposition (standing in the way of Mr. Incredible's desire to keep society and his family free and safe). In the *Harry Potter* series, Lord Voldemort exists as both a thematic and dramatic opponent to *Harry Potter*. In *Toy Story*, Buzz provides both thematic opposition (essentially believing that being a toy isn't important) and also a bit of dramatic opposition (standing in the way of Woody's desire to be the top toy even if not doing so intentionally). Note that while Buzz is both a thematic and dramatic opponent, he isn't a villain because he's not immoral.

On the other hand, it's also possible for dramatic and thematic opposition to exist across different characters. In other words, just because two characters have a different value system or approach to life doesn't mean they need to be dramatic opponents. In *Casablanca*, for instance, Ilsa provides dramatic opposition to Rick's desire to win her love. The thematic opposition, however, exists as Rick's internal battle between love and duty. In *Finding Nemo*, Dory provides thematic opposition in that her approach to life is one of letting go and living carefree where Marlin's approach to life is one of clinging and worrying. Marlin's dramatic opposition comes in the form of episodic antagonists, the environment, and his own self-sabotage.

Thematic opposition can exist either internally (within a single character) or externally (across multiple characters). In *Casablanca*, Rick must deal with the internal thematic battle between his pull toward love and his pull toward duty. While we do often see a single character dealing with an internal thematic conflict, we also often see that same character surrounded by other characters who argue for and against each side of the story's thematic dilemma. We see this in *Star Wars* where Luke must decide between faith and technology. Obi-Wan and Darth Vader explicitly and implicitly argue for faith while Han Solo and Grand Moff Tarkin argue for technology.

Dramatic opposition can also occur either internally or externally. Dramatic opposition is internal when a character stands in their own way. Recall that an internal conflict occurs when a character has two desires that can't both be attained. This is a state of internal dramatic opposition. We can think of this internal dramatic opposition as a sort of self-sabotage.

Dramatic opposition is external when two characters have desires that are opposed. External dramatic opposition results in the conventional opposition between protagonist and antagonist. This setup can result in a powerful back and forth of strategy, foiled plans, and improvisation. An example of this traditional back and forth battle is *Die Hard*.

To craft a dramatic opponent, we generally want to determine who or what might oppose the protagonist's central desire (which arises at the dramatic question moment).

When crafting our story's opposition, one helpful trick can be to first start with an opposition of value systems or beliefs (i.e. thematic opposition). After we've created a thematic opposition, we might find that a dramatic opposition more organically follows. The reason for this is that if we have characters who are opposed in their *beliefs*, there's a high chance that they won't agree with what the other one *wants* (or the means by which they go about getting it), thus giving rise to dramatic opposition.

Thematic opposition is a powerful tool to create underlying conflict and a battle of philosophies. It's as if each character is saying to the other, "I not only disagree with what you're doing, I disagree with how you live your life."

Takeaway: Opposition consists of both dramatic opposition (opposition to a goal) and thematic opposition (opposition to a way of life). Dramatic and thematic opposition can be embodied in the same character or different characters. To create dramatic opposition, it can be helpful to first craft a thematic opposition.

Multi-dimensional Opposition

Recall that opposition can expand beyond a simple fight between two diametrically opposed views into a multi-dimensional opposition with four or more opponents, each with a nuanced approach to the story's theme or dramatic question. This multi-dimensional opposition can be either dramatic or thematic.

Multi-dimensional Thematic Opposition

As we previously explored, real arguments about the right way to live life are often complex and nuanced. Rarely do worldviews or approaches to life boil down to only two perspectives. This makes a more complex thematic opposition almost inevitable if we truly want to explore a thematic dilemma in depth.

Let's consider a few examples. In *Finding Nemo,* the primary thematic dilemma pair is dependence versus independence. Should we do our best to prevent harm in others' lives through a dependent relationship or should we trust others to take care of themselves and live independently? In this story, Marlin, Nemo, Dory, and Gil all stand thematically opposed. They all approach life slightly differently when it comes to this thematic question. Marlin is heavily co-dependent and can't trust others to take care of themselves. Nemo is in a dependent relationship with his father but *wants* independence. Dory not only lives a life of independence and letting go, but she's *incapable* of living any other life. Gil's approach to life is one of rugged independence and pulling oneself up by one's own bootstraps. He represents an argument that one should take care of oneself. Even though interaction between some of these characters is limited, the existence of this multi-dimensional opposition allows us to explore varied approaches to life when it comes to the central thematic question.

Notice that in *Finding Nemo*, we have a multi-dimensional thematic opposition, but these same characters aren't dramatically opposed. Each of these characters wants to see Nemo get back to his dad. There's no traditional dramatic opponent or villain.

Takeaway: Multi-dimensional opposition provides a nuanced approach to thematic opposition by exploring four or more different approaches to life when it comes to the story's thematic dilemma.

Philosophical Mentors and Antagonists

We can often view thematic opposition as a battle between philosophical allies (or mentors) and philosophical antagonists. Whenever a character expresses their view on the thematic dilemma and the best way to approach life, they're giving what Michael Arndt calls a "philosophical aria." It's a speech where a character's approach to life is explicitly stated.

We've previously discussed how *Star Wars* creates a multi-dimensional thematic opposition by exploring two dilemma pairs (faith versus technology and means versus ends). The thematic opposition consists of Obi-Wan and Darth Vader in the corner of faith and Han Solo and Grand Moff Tarkin in the corner of technology. Since *Star Wars* ultimately argues that one should trust faith, we might consider Obi-Wan and Darth Vader (as strange as that may seem) to be philosophical mentors or allies (in this dilemma). It's worth noting that Darth Vader is a philosophical antagonist in the thematic dilemma between means versus ends but a philosophical ally in the dilemma between faith versus technology. This makes Han Solo and Grand Moff Tarkin both philosophical antagonists when it comes to the dilemma of faith versus technology.

There are two prominent philosophical arias (where a character's worldview or approach to life is explicitly expressed) in *Star Wars*. The first is given by Obi-Wan in support of faith as a value system: "The force is what gives the Jedi his power. It's an energy field created by all living things. It surrounds us and penetrates us. It binds the galaxy together." The second aria is given by Han Solo as a rejection of faith: "Hokey religions and ancient weapons are no match for a good blaster at your side, kid. ... I've flown from one side of this galaxy to the other. I've seen a lot of strange stuff but I've never seen anything to make me believe there's one all powerful force controlling everything. There's no mystical energy field that controls my destiny. It's a lot of simple tricks and nonsense." Notice how each character takes a firm stance on their worldview and the thematic opposition.

The primary thematic dilemma in *Ratatouille* is essentially whether power belongs in the hands of the many or the few. It's expressed in the terms of the story world of cuisine as, "Can anyone cook or can only a select few cook?" In *Ratatouille*, this thematic question is explicitly argued by the characters. The main philosophical mentor is Chef Gusteau who believes that "anyone can cook." The primary philosophical antagonist is Anton Ego who says, "I, on the other hand, take cooking seriously, and no, I don't think anyone can do it." We also have Remy who certainly believes that at least a rat can cook. And finally, we have Chef Skinner, a man who thinks so little of high cuisine that he wants Remy to create a line of frozen food products.

> *Takeaway*: Any character on the "right" side of the thematic dilemma can be considered a philosophical ally and any character on the "wrong" side of the thematic dilemma can be considered a philosophical antagonist. When a character explicitly expresses their worldview in regards to the thematic dilemma, they're giving a "philosophical aria."

Multi-dimensional Dramatic Opposition

A multi-dimensional dramatic opposition arises when we have more than two characters who oppose each other's desires or plans. This setup where a character's goal is opposed from different angles naturally gives rise to more complex conflict and a more intricate plot. Multi-dimensional dramatic opposition can be a helpful tool for adding interest to a plot. Consider the various ways in which plans and agendas might collide between multiple characters.

In *Breaking Bad*, Walter White, Jesse Pinkman, Gus Fring, and Hank Schrader all stand in opposition to each other in various dramatic ways.

Ticking Clock

We explored in our dramatic tools how effective ticking clocks and urgency can be for heightening a dramatic situation. This principle holds true for the story as a whole. We often want to craft a structural ticking clock which will force the protagonist to take action before they're ready in order to meet a deadline.

This central ticking clock is the thing that will force the central dramatic question to be answered sooner rather than later. It's what "forces the stakes" by putting something of value at stake, which then requires immediate intervention by the protagonist in order to prevent its loss. This ticking clock is typically something that threatens to take away the thing that the protagonist most values or loves if they don't act sooner rather than later.

In *Toy Story*, the ticking clock is Andy's move. If Woody and Buzz don't get back to Andy before the move, they'll face the ultimate spiritual death as they lose their identities and become "lost toys." In *Finding Nemo*, Marlin must find Nemo before Darla arrives. It's implied that Darla will kill Nemo if she gets ahold of him. In *Monsters, Inc.*, Sully must get Boo home before Randall gets ahold of her. It's implied that Randall will essentially torture her and forcibly extract screams. In *Beauty and The Beast*, Beast must get Belle to fall in love with him before the last petal on the rose falls or else the curse will be permanent and he'll remain a beast forever. In *American Beauty*, the story opens with the character explicitly setting the deadline by saying, "In less than a year, I will be dead." In *Star Wars*, if the Rebellion doesn't stop the Death Star before it becomes operational, the Empire will attack the Rebel base.

Notice that many ticking clocks are driven by the dramatic opponent's plan (i.e. the antagonist's plan). As the antagonist gets closer to completing their plan, the thing that the protagonist values most is put increasingly in danger. This urgency heightens the global dramatic tension of the story.

This ticking clock is typically about pushing up the timeline of the philosophical battle and thus of The Great Decision Moment. It's all about pushing up that moment where a thematic (and dramatic) decision must be made. In short, what's the bad thing that will happen if the character's goal isn't met in time?

To craft a structural ticking clock, we first concretely define the central dramatic question. We then think about what would force the dramatic question to be resolved early (before the stakes are lost forever). What would threaten something of great value to the character? We might consider putting the character's comfort object at stake (i.e. the thing by which the character defines themselves) based on a particular deadline. The ticking clock might threaten to destroy it forever. The ticking clock is often most powerful when a relationship is put in danger. This is the case in *The Incredibles* where Mr. Incredible's family is put in danger.

While crafting this ticking clock, we also want to be sure to ask ourselves whether the resource that's running out is *actually* finite. In most cases, it doesn't make sense for the resource to be daylight, for instance, since there's always another day. The character could just wait for tomorrow's daylight. There should generally be a feeling that there's no more of the resource available after it runs out. It might simply be the arrival of a particular event.

This central ticking clock may be introduced at the midpoint of the story.

> *Takeaway*: The central ticking clock is the thing that will force the central dramatic question to be answered sooner rather than later by threatening the imminent loss of the stakes.

Directionality

Giving a story a clear direction is an important part of keeping the audience anticipating. Thus far, we've primarily focused on providing directionality via a character goal that provides a clear dramatic question that generates dramatic tension. The audience anticipates the obligatory scene where we answer the dramatic question and find out whether the protagonist gets the thing they want.

A story's directionality can be driven by other dramatic tools, of course. We can use dramatic irony to give the audience a piece of information that one or more other characters doesn't have. This typically takes the form of a protagonist with a secret they're trying desperately to keep or a deep fear they're trying desperately to avoid. The driving question becomes, "Will their secret be revealed this time?" or "Will they have to face that deep fear this time?" The story's direction is provided by the audience's anticipation of the moment that the information is revealed to other characters. This technique is one of the primary drivers of the show *Dexter*.

Directionality can also be provided using convergence. Recall that convergence is essentially a promise that something significant will happen at a moment in the future. It might be the collision of two characters, the arrival of a character at a destination, the arrival of a trigger event or deadline, etc. Directionality is provided as the audience anticipates the moment of convergence where the promise is paid off. In this scenario, we can continually tease the audience with threats of the collision or the arrival of a significant moment. This is one of the drivers of *How I Met Your Mother*.

And finally, directionality can be provided by a mystery. The audience anticipates the moment that the mystery is unraveled and any questions are answered. While a mystery may exist only in the minds of the audience, it may also be something that one or more characters is actively trying to solve. When this is the case, the story's direction is provided by both mystery and dramatic tension. This is the pattern used in detective stories.

Directionality is important not just for the overall story but also for each individual scene. We must keep the audience anticipating a moment in the future so that we can play off of that anticipation with suspense and tension (i.e. stretching it out) or surprise (i.e. subverting it).

Takeaway: As a general rule, we want the audience anticipating where we're going in a story so that we have the option of upending their expectations. While dramatic tension (i.e. a clear character goal) is one of the primary methods of creating directionality in a story, it's not the only technique. We can also use dramatic irony, convergence (i.e. promises), and mysteries.

Stakes

Recall that stakes can be defined as the potential risks, impacts, and rewards involved in a dramatic journey. We now need to define what will ultimately be at stake if the protagonist fails to attain their central desire. What will they lose if they fail? What will they gain if they succeed? Why do we care?

Something must be at stake that prevents the protagonist from throwing their hands in the air and walking away. Marlin can't fail to find Nemo or he loses his son and his identity as a family man. Woody can't fail to get home or he loses his child and his identity as a toy. In *The Little Mermaid*, Ariel can't fail to get a kiss from Eric or Ursula will take her soul. Mr. Incredible can't fail to stop Syndrome or he'll lose his family. If our character fails, they will lose [x].

Our story's stakes often naturally fall into place when we simply ask, "What does the protagonist care about most and how can we put it in danger?" In general, we want to identify the protagonist's Achilles heel and then threaten it. Marlin cares most about Nemo. Woody cares most about his position as the top toy (and Andy). Mr. Incredible cares most about his identity as a superhero and his family. Recall that characters often care most about the thing from which they derive their value (i.e. their comfort concept). This might be their obsession, their worldview, or their façade. What would the protagonist be most devastated to lose or confront?

We can, of course, take the opposite approach and offer the protagonist the promise of something they've been desperately searching for. In this technique, we offer the protagonist an opportunity to get what they've always wanted. We offer the protagonist the thing they think will make them whole. And now that it's within the protagonist's grasp, they can't bear to let it slip away. We must also keep in mind that all opportunities come with a catch—and a price.

In our discussion of dramatic tools, we explored how new dramatic interest can be generated by raising the stakes of a dramatic situation. This, of course, applies to the global story. We might initially simply threaten the character's comfort concept or introduce an uncomfortable opposition to it. We might then promise the loss of it forever if something isn't done.

Stakes should arise organically from the character's goal. We might be tempted to inorganically raise the stakes by introducing some threat that doesn't have anything to do with the character's central desire. The writers of *Indiana Jones and the Raiders of the Lost Ark*, for instance, could have had Marcus Brody threaten Indie's job at the university, but threatening his job has nothing to do with his pursuit of the Ark. As much as possible, we want to ensure that stakes arise organically from the central dramatic question and the associated story disruptions.

Organic stakes often arise as a result of a dramatic opponent (i.e. antagonist) enacting their strategy to attain their desire. When an antagonist advances their position in a dramatic situation, it's typically at the expense of the protagonist (assuming the desires of the antagonist and protagonist are structurally opposed). The closer the Empire gets to bringing the Death Star online, the closer the Rebellion get to being destroyed.

After we've established the stakes of our story, we must remember that the audience will need to be fairly consistently reminded of their existence. The audience needs to get drips of information reminding them that the ticking clock is in play and that the threat to the stakes is getting closer and closer. We might do this by switching to the perspective of the thing threatened (such as Nemo in *Finding Nemo*). We might also do it by checking in on the progress of the ticking clock (such as Andy and the moving van in *Toy Story*). This method is also used in *Star Wars* where we follow Darth Vader's perspective in order to be continually reminded of the progress of the Death Star.

Takeaway: Our story's stakes fall into place when we simply ask, "What does the protagonist care about most and how can we put it in danger?" We may also consider what thing of great value we can offer to the protagonist. Stakes should arise organically from the protagonist's goal.

Plan and Strategy

If a character doesn't devise or enact a plan to get what they want, then their desire is merely a longing. It's a dream. It can never come up against any opposition because it's never meaningfully pursued. In other words, it doesn't create dramatic tension. If we want our character's desire to generate dramatic tension, then we must ensure that the character devises a plan to go after what they want.

The way in which a character goes about trying to attain their desire tells us a great deal about the character. A character's actions tell us what they're willing to do in order to get what they want and perhaps more importantly, what they're not willing to do. A character's plan to get what they want goes to the heart of the thematic dilemma between means and ends. Does the character believe that the ends justify any means or that there are some lines that aren't worth crossing?

Characters tend to initially treat their problems like they'll be easy to solve. And why shouldn't they? The protagonist doesn't know how long the story needs to be. That is to say, the protagonist generally doesn't know what they're up against or the depth of their problem. In fact, the protagonist typically thinks, "If I just do this, all my problems will be solved." Almost every plan is a plan to solve the problem *now*. The protagonist starts with the easy plan and only moves to the difficult plan when that doesn't work. "Easy" is relative here, of course.

Initial plans are typically simple and implicit. Want to get back home? Catch a ride. Want to learn to fly? Take a class. In danger? Escape. There's not much thinking needed for these types of plans. And most often, these are what initial plans look like. They're simple and the character thinks that once their plan is complete, all their problems will be solved. It's only when opposition throws a wrench into their plan that the character is required to improvise a new plan with clever thinking. Even with this new plan, though, the character typically still thinks it'll solve all their problems. That's rarely the case, of course.

It's worth noting that when a character devises a plan to get what they want, they're also inherently creating a new desire. For instance, if a character wants to learn to fly and their plan is to take a class, then their new sub-desire is to take that class. In this way, plans are desires. As storytellers, we can craft opposition not just to the original desire to fly but also to the new desire to take a class. We can create disruptions to the character's plan, making it difficult to complete and forcing the character to devise a new plan.

Plans are perhaps most interesting when they require getting another character to do something. Getting people to do the things we want them to do is hard. Sometimes we can't settle for a simple request of someone because we can't risk them saying no. And coercing someone to do something may go against our morality (and usually the law). This is where strategy comes in. We've got to figure out a way to get someone to do what we want within the bounds of the actions we're willing to take (based on our moral code, available resources, and appetite for risk).

It's been said that a scene is either a negotiation, a seduction, or a fight. For the tactics a character may use to get what they want, we'll take these categories and rephrase them as persuasion, deception, and coercion. In other words, we can say that when a character wants something from someone else, they'll generally either try to persuade, deceive, or coerce the other character.

Persuasion is the art of convincing and negotiating. It's a method of getting what one wants through voluntary means and is thus the most moral of the tactics. Any method of voluntarily convincing someone to do something falls under this category. This includes telling a story, charming, dramatizing, selling, logically or emotionally arguing, negotiating, offering incentives, appealing to guilt or a moral code, offering a deal or bet, and other methods. Anytime a tactic is voluntary and doesn't involve breaking or bending the truth, we can consider it persuasion.

Deception is the art of creating or presenting a false reality. It's the realm of lies, half-truths, and omissions. We can also include various forms of manipulation in this category. Tactics include lying, offering false pretenses, committing fraud, wearing a mask or presenting a false identity, scamming, gas-lighting, setting up a sting, infiltrating, spying, using a Trojan Horse, sabotaging, obfuscating, omitting, presenting a false equivalency, using sleight of hand, seducing under false pretenses, planting false beliefs, distracting, and diverting, among other methods. Deception is the favorite tactic of the trickster and the shape shifter. These tactics are generally considered to be immoral.

Coercion is the art of force. Its tactics include using violence, threatening, blackmailing, extorting, bribing, controlling, striking fear, terrorizing, exploiting, kidnapping, and imprisoning, among others. Coercion is the realm of the villain and the immoral.

While deception and coercion are in most circumstances always considered immoral, we can argue that they could be considered moral tactics if they're done for a moral and noble reason, such as to save someone's life, for instance. In this way, intention is a key factor in coloring the morality of a character's strategy or tactic. This recoloring technique (as we'll explore later) is used in the movie *The Lives of Others* to show us that seemingly immoral tactics might be done for a target's benefit.

Some characters may begin to morally decay as a story progresses. In other words, they'll become so desperate to accomplish their goals that they'll begin allowing themselves to use tactics that move closer and closer to immorality. At first, the decay is often subtle and filled with rationalization and justification. Later the decay speeds up and sometimes loses justification. The character's allies may protest and note the slide to immorality. The character might finally look at themselves and wonder what they've become. In a moment of self-revelation, they'll recognize their moral decay and realize that this isn't who they want to be.

When it comes to character strategies and tactics, it's worth mentioning Damon Suede's book *Verbalize*. In it, he recommends that we assign to each of our characters a single verb. This verb is the backbone of the character and helps us consider what a character would *do* in any given situation. Suede offers the example of Severus Snape from the *Harry Potter* series and claims that Snape's verb is "to vex." "What Snape does in every scene in every one of those 7 books is 'vex'. He vexes everyone. He vexes Harry, he vexes his family, he vexes Lily, he vexes Voldemort, he vexes Dumbledore, he vexes everyone. He's always vexing."

> *Takeaway*: A character will almost always pursue an easy or comfortable plan before they try a difficult plan. Strategies and tactics used to accomplish a goal fall under three broad categories: persuasion, deception, and coercion. While deception and coercion are almost always considered immoral, the motivation for the use of a strategy can affect whether the strategy might be morally permissible.

Wrapping up Story Elements

All of the previously discussed story elements (such as the impetus, the dramatic question moment, the self-revelation, The Great Decision, etc.) are all character-centric. Each character can have their own impetus, their own dramatic question moment, their own self-revelation, and their own Great Decision—all occurring at different moments in the story. We can think of a collection of these character-centric elements as a story spine. A story may have multiple spines, all arguing different approaches to the central thematic opposition. This is perhaps one of the most powerful ways of exploring a theme.

Stage III Wrap-up

We've now covered many of the foundational elements that a story will need in order to convey the theme in a dramatically interesting way. We've also explored some of the core features of a character's arc as they progress in their dramatic journey. Next we'll assess a few more story elements and common questions we'll need to answer before fleshing out the rest of the story.

PART IV

IS THE FOUNDATION STURDY?

VETTING A STORY IDEA

Now that we've got the framing of our story in place, it's time to take a step back. It's important to ensure that our foundation is solid. If we build on faulty bones, our story is doomed no matter what story choices we make from here on out. It's worth stepping back and fixing any problems that may exist.

16

VETTING THE STORY PREMISE

Once we've got a story premise, we need to ask ourselves whether this is actually a story we're passionate about exploring and crafting. We'll be spending a great deal of time on it. Are the characters interesting? Is it a theme that resonates with us? Is it a world that intrigues us? Is it a subject matter we'd like to explore? Is this the kind of story that we'd like to tell? If we could only write one more story before we died, is this the one we'd want to write?

Once we've got a story we're personally interested in telling, we next want to try to poke holes in the premise. We want to put ourselves in the protagonist's shoes and consider how we might try to simply avoid the story journey altogether. We might ask questions like, "Why doesn't the opponent just...?", "Why doesn't the protagonist just...?", "Why can't they just...?". We want to harness our inner 5-year-old for every element of the premise: "Why? Why? Why? Why? Why? Why?" Why does the protagonist want what they want? Why does the opponent's plan conflict with the protagonist? Why can't the protagonist just wait until later?

We must try to identify any complications or challenges that are inherent in our story's premise. If we're going to have a passive main character, for instance, we must realize that there will be challenges with narrative drive. If there's a large cast of characters, we must realize that the need to switch between story lines may reduce the ability to fully explore character development and thus may hinder the emotional impact of the story.

Write What You Know?

We often hear the writing advice to "write what you know." Should we really only write what we already know? Partially. In reality, this advice only applies to a particular piece of "what you know."

We should write the *emotions* we know. We should write the human *experiences* we know. We should write what sparks memories and *resonates* with us—love and loss. We should write about the relationships that have changed us.

But we shouldn't be afraid to wrap these familiar emotions in unfamiliar worlds and characters. We should feel free to write about any subject matter that we want to *explore*. If you haven't physically explored other parts of the world, that obviously doesn't mean that you can't travel to imaginary worlds in your stories. We're free to carry the emotions we know and take them to places we've never been.

Emotion and Experiences

Stories that resonate with us tend to do so because they explore familiar human emotions and experiences. Whether the story takes place in a dragon-ruled kingdom, an underwater science facility, turn-of-the-century London, or the world of monsters, the characters must still go through familiar human experiences: birth, life, love, loss, and death. Relationships form, fall apart, and sever. We feel love, hatred, jealousy, resentment, regret, nostalgia, and hope.

Our stories must explore human experiences in a believable way. No matter the story world, human emotions will ground the audience in the realm of the familiar. This is critically important.

Fleshing Out a Story Idea

Once we've found a world, theme, and character we'd like to explore in a story, there are a few questions that we want to ask ourselves.

Main Character, Protagonist, and Transformed

First we want to consider whether we've chosen the right main character. And while we're on that subject, it's important to note that a story's main character isn't necessarily the same as its protagonist. Recall that the protagonist is a character with a strong desire that moves the plot forward. This is a dramatic function. The main character, on the other hand, can be thought of as the point of view character. In most stories, these two functions occur in the same character, but they don't necessarily need to.

Consider the movie *Good Will Hunting*. Will is the main character (i.e. the point of view character), but he doesn't have a strong desire that moves the plot. On a scene by scene level, he has a desire to avoid facing his ghost, but he's not the protagonist of the overall story. The protagonist and the one who moves the plot forward is Professor Lambeau. His desire is to make use of Will's intelligence by getting him successfully through therapy.

The movie *Ex Machina* also has a main character who isn't the protagonist. Caleb is the main character through whom we explore the world of programming and artificial intelligence. He doesn't have a strong desire that moves the plot forward, however. That role belongs to Ava, the robot. Ava's desire is to escape.

It's also worth noting that neither the main character, nor the protagonist need to change. In *Ferris Bueller's Day Off*, Ferris is both the main character and the protagonist. He's not the one who undergoes character change, however. That role belongs to Cameron. We might give the title "the transformed" to the character (or community) that arcs (i.e. changes).

Takeaway: There are three distinct character roles: the point of view character (i.e. the main character), the protagonist, and the transformed. In most stories, these three roles are embodied in the same character—but they don't have to be. We should keep this in mind when crafting our own stories.

Who Should be the Main Character?

So who should be our story's main character? A general rule of thumb is that the main character (i.e. the point of view character) should be whoever goes from knowing the least about the story world to knowing the most. The reason for this is a practical one. The main character is often the audience's surrogate. By ensuring that the main character is exploring the story world for the first time alongside the audience, we get the added benefit of organic exposition and a natural discovery of the rules of the world.

Of course, this isn't a hard or fast rule. Breaking this pattern does come with additional story challenges, however. How will exposition be delivered to the audience in an organic way? Obviously a knowledgeable main character wouldn't be curious about the story world since they'd already know the answers. We'll explore this later in exposition techniques.

There are plenty of stories where a main character is fully versed in the story world but perhaps not as much with themselves. The character goes from knowing the least about themselves to knowing the most about themselves. This is the case in *Inception*, for instance. *Inception* is, however, a bit heavy-handed with characters whose main purpose seems to be asking questions about the story world so that the audience can get the answer. This is a byproduct of a main character who's already well-versed in the rules of the world.

The main exception to this pattern of having the main character know the least about the story world is when a story has an explicit narrator or storyteller. This storyteller character often has the most knowledge about the story world but also implicitly acknowledges that an audience exists. The character understands that the audience knows the least about the story world and therefore takes them on the journey from knowing the least to knowing the most. The storyteller character may know the least about themselves, of course, and may come to learn about themselves over the course of recounting the story. We see this in *The Shawshank Redemption* where Red is the main character and has extensive knowledge of Shawshank.

Will our main character also be the protagonist? We can choose a passive main character for our story, but it'll severely reduce the narrative drive benefits we get from also making the main character the protagonist. If we go this route with our story, we may want to ensure that the passive main character has a strong fear or desire to avoid. This is the case in the movie *Lars and the Real Girl* where the main character's primary desire is to keep things the way they are and it's society that has a strong desire to force change. We see this in *Good Will Hunting* as well where Will has a strong desire to avoid and wants to keep things the way they are. We can give the role of the protagonist to another character (such as Professor Lambeau in *Good Will Hunting*) or to the community (as in *Lars and the Real Girl*). We may additionally or alternatively allow the story to be driven forward almost entirely by the opponent or antagonist.

When determining the main character, ask from whose perspective the world might be most interestingly explored. With the fact that the main character is the audience surrogate, consider also whether the chosen perspective aligns with that of the target audience for the story. Notice that *Harry Potter* isn't told from the perspective of the professors of Hogwarts but rather from the perspective of the students. Since the target audience is children, they can more closely identify with the perspective characters.

There are often many perspectives from which it's possible to explore a story world. *Harry Potter* could be retold from the perspective of the professors, from the perspective of the Aurors, or from the perspective of the Death Eaters, among others. Consider making a list of all of the possibilities. From whose perspective do we want to tell our story?

In most cases, the main character will be the one whose void the story is exploring. It's the one who'll face The Great Decision.

> *Takeaway*: The main character (i.e. the point of view character) should typically be the character that goes from knowing the least about the story world to knowing the most. This helps us organically deliver exposition by letting the main character make discoveries alongside the audience.

The Storyteller Character

If our story is going to have an explicit storyteller or narrator, we might consider asking the following questions:

- To whom is the storyteller speaking? (Note that it might be to multiple people, as in the case of *Forrest Gump*).
- Why is the storyteller telling the story now?
- How will retelling the story affect the storyteller or the relationship that the storyteller has with their audience or with other characters?
- Will the storyteller have a revelation after telling their story?

Who Should be the Transformed Character?

The "transformed character" is the one that arcs. As we've explored previously, a story doesn't need a character that arcs (it might instead have a community that arcs, for example). If we do want our story to have a character who arcs, who should it be? Generally we want to choose the character that goes from knowing the least about themselves to knowing the most about themselves. It's through this journey of self-discovery that they change.

The reason this transformed character is often the same as either the main character or protagonist is because the process of exploring the story world or pursuing a desire is often the thing that *causes* them to learn about themselves.

Recall also that we generally want this transformed character to go from one side of the thematic opposition to the other side. It's the transformation of character that helps argue the theme.

Who Should be the Protagonist?

The protagonist is the character with the strongest desire. It's this desire that gives rise to both a plan and action. It's this action that moves the plot forward. The reason the protagonist character is often the same as both the main character and the transformed character is because it's through pursuing a desire that the character both explores the story world and is forced to change internally in order to attain their desire.

Character Questions

There are a few qualities we want to look for in story characters and particularly in the main character and protagonist. First of all, who's the most interesting character? This can often be measured by asking which character will be forced to make the most interesting decisions or which character will be faced with the most difficult dilemmas. Who will be forced to change the most? Alternatively who will change those around them the most? Who will have the most interesting time exploring the story world?

Stage IV Wrap-up

We've now started to identify any inherent problems that our story idea may have. We've also started to consider who our story's protagonist, main character, transformed character, and narrator may be. Next we'll take a deep dive into story structure and the common beats of a story's beginning, middle, and end.

PART V

ROOMS

HOW TO STRUCTURE A STORY: STRUCTURE, PLOTTING, BEATS, AND PACING

We've poured our foundation, put up the framing, and made sure that our base is strong. Now it's time to turn those studs into legitimate walls. We're going to make this thing look like a home. Let's learn how we can arrange our story's structural elements to create a structured story and plot.

17

THE DISRUPTION CHAIN

Cause and Effect

As we'll later learn in a discussion of the narrative fallacy, humans have a deep propensity for drawing connections between events, even when no connection exists. We want to believe that the world is orderly. We want to believe that things happen for a reason. We want to believe that everything is connected.

While it's arguable whether life is a connected chain of cause and effect, it's not arguable whether good story is. The most emotionally impactful and effective stories consist of a clear chain of cause and effect. Event A happens and *because of that* event B happens and *because of that* event C happens. This organic connection between story events allows the audience to draw meaning from the story. This is a key principle in the realm of both drama and theme. If story events are unconnected, the audience will either grow frustrated or hallucinate their own connections (or both).

When we say that events should be causally connected, we're really saying that events should be *consequential*. In other words, every story event should have implications. It should have *effects*. For a story event to be effective is for it to have an effect. Narrative is a pond, rippling with echoes from an initial splash.

So how do we ensure that we're connecting our story events during the writing process? We create events in relation to a character's desire and plan.

> *Takeaway:* Story events should be connected in a chain of cause and effect. Every story event should have consequences that lead to one or more other story events.

The Disruption Chain

At any given point, a character wants something and they've got a plan to get it. Then something happens. In other words, there's a disruption to the character's plan (for good or bad) in the form of an opportunity or a problem. In either instance, the most effective disruptions can't be ignored by the character. The character either can't help but pursue the opportunity or can't help but address the problem. And in this way, a disruption gives rise to a new desire (to either solve the problem, avoid the problem, or pursue the opportunity). The character will then devise a new plan to pursue this new desire. Along the way, they'll likely encounter a new disruption to their plan. This is the basis of the disruption chain.

The disruption chain is a plotting tool that allows us to create a chain of cause and effect that alternates between a character's plan and a disruption to that plan. In this way, the disruption chain is character-centric and every character has a different chain. The character has a plan, then something happens that forces them to come up with a new plan. They enact this new plan until they're interrupted by another disruption. The chain is, in essence, a sequence of turning points that are connected by cause and effect. A disruption is a turning point that "turns" a character's journey in a new direction.

Recall from our dramatic toolbox that we can often identify a disruption by noting when the polarity of a situation turns from either good to bad or from bad to good. A disruption might also result in a change of magnitude instead of polarity. In other words, a disruption can alternatively make things go from good to great or from bad to terrible.

Takeaway: The disruption chain consists of a cycle of a disruption to a character's plan followed by a new plan or desire.

The Disruption Chain and Causality

A character-centric approach to structuring a story gives us a couple advantages. First it helps us avoid the dreaded writer's block because anytime we feel stuck, we need only ask, "What does the character want right now and how do they plan to get it?"

Second the disruption chain helps us maintain what Matt Stone and Trey Parker call the "But & Therefore Rule." The idea is that we want to ensure that we can use the words "therefore..." and "but..." to connect our story events (rather than "and then..."). Notice the distinction here. If two events can be connected with "therefore..." or "but...", then the second *relies* on the first." A happened and therefore B happened" or "A happened but then B happened." The second event *requires* the first for context. In other words, the two events are *causally* related if they can be connected with "therefore..." or "but..." If two events can only be connected with "and then...", however, they don't rely on each other to exist and therefore aren't causally related.

With the disruption chain's character-centric approach, we don't just throw together a series of random disruptions. Instead each disruption is crafted as a reaction (whether from other characters or from the story world itself) to the character's current plan. Or more precisely, each disruption occurs *because* the character is enacting their plan. Each disruption requires the context of the character's plan in order to make sense. The disruption chain helps ensure causality because it's desire-centric and plan-centric.

Takeaway: Because the disruption chain is focused entirely on a character's desire and plan, its events are causally related.

Woody's Disruption Chain in *Toy Story*

Let's consider a portion of Woody's disruption chain in *Toy Story*. Woody's life has been disrupted and turned upside down by the appearance of Buzz. Woody has an obsession with being Andy's favorite toy and a belief (i.e. a lie) that if he's not the favorite toy, he has no value. When Woody's position is threatened, he has a desire to remove the threat, but initially he has no clear plan. Woody eventually sees an opportunity to get rid of Buzz and regain his position as top toy. He plans to use RC to push Buzz off the dresser and get him stuck between the dresser and the wall.

Disruption! What was once an opportunity turns into a problem. Woody's plan backfires and Buzz gets pushed out the window. The situation turns from hope (that Woody's problems will be solved) to concern and panic. All the other toys notice the commotion and RC tells them that Woody pushed Buzz out the window. The toys revolt against Woody, but before they can do anything, Andy comes rushing in to get a toy to bring to Pizza Planet. Because Woody pushed Buzz out the window, Andy can't find Buzz and so he unenthusiastically settles for taking Woody.

Andy and his mom stop at a gas station where we see Woody debating what to do now. We hear him say, "How am I going to convince those guys that it was an accident?" This disruption has incited in Woody a new desire to somehow convince the other toys that he didn't intend to push Buzz out the window. At this moment, he has no clear plan.

Disruption! Buzz appears! He had fallen out of the window and grabbed onto the car. To Woody, this disruption looks like an opportunity. Woody's situation turns from despair to hope. In fact, he yells out that he's saved. His new plan is to take Buzz back with him to explain that it was all one big accident.

Disruption! Buzz wants revenge. He knows that Woody tried to "terminate" him. From Woody's perspective, the arrival of Buzz turns from an opportunity into a problem. The two begin a scuffle and the fight knocks both of them out of the car.

Disruption! Andy and his mom leave the gas station while Buzz and Woody are fighting outside. The situation turns from a problem (having to fight Buzz) to Woody's worst nightmare—being a lost toy. Notice here how we get a magnitude shift from bad to worse (instead of from bad to good).

Disruption! Woody sees an opportunity in the form of a Pizza Planet car. He devises a plan: hitch a ride on the Pizza Planet car to get back to Andy. Woody realizes, of course, that he won't be able to show his face back in Andy's room without Buzz. He now has a desire to return to Andy but also to bring Buzz. This becomes the central desire throughout the rest of the story. Woody's plan works this time and the two make it safely to Pizza Planet.

Disruption! Woody spots Andy! It looks like the plan has worked and that he's about to get back home with Buzz. The situation goes from good to great.

Disruption! Buzz has something else in mind. While Woody's plan is to simply jump in Andy's sister's stroller, Buzz wants to find a spaceship to get back to his home planet. Woody must now try to wrangle Buzz while Buzz jumps into a claw machine in the shape of a rocket ship.

Disruption! Sid arrives and takes Woody and Buzz from the claw machine. They're now both headed for Sid's house. As Woody reminds Buzz, once a toy goes inside Sid's house, they never come out. The situation turns to hopeless.

The Stages of a Disruption Cycle

A disruption chain is made up of a series of disruption cycles. A disruption cycle consists of four distinct stages and can be best understood as an OODA loop. An OODA loop is a model developed by United States Air Force Colonel John Boyd for combat operations, but it can be more generally applied in situations where information is fast-changing. It's highly applicable in the ever-changing environment of a well-paced story. OODA stands for observe-orient-decide-act. We'll explore these four stages in the context of a disruption cycle.

Stage One: The Disruption

Unsurprisingly, the first stage in the disruption cycle is a disruption. Something happens. Sometimes it's good, sometimes it's bad. It's a turning point that "turns" the character's path (and thus often the story) in a new direction. It's also sometimes called a "plot point." This disruption can be thought of as an impetus or a catalyst because it's the ultimate force that pulls or pushes a character into action (to pursue an opportunity or address a problem).

We can think of a disruption as a unit of story energy. It's the fuel that pushes a story forward.

When Nemo is kidnapped in *Finding Nemo*, that's a disruption. When Buzz shows up in *Toy Story*, that's a disruption. When Carl's house is threatened in *Up*, that's a disruption. When superheroes are banned in *The Incredibles*, that's a disruption. When Mr. Incredible gets a secret mission, that's a disruption. When Will is arrested in *Good Will Hunting*, that's a disruption. When the crew receives a distress signal in *Alien*, that's a disruption. A disruption is a moment when things change. It's when something of significance happens.

> *Takeaway:* Stage one of the disruption cycle consists of the arrival of a disruption.

Effective Disruptions

We can think of a story disruption as being "effective" based on whether it, unsurprisingly, has an *effect* on the story. In other words, an effective disruption has consequences. It's *impactful*. Disruptions that can be ignored by characters are ineffective. We generally want our disruptions to get a rise out of the character. We want the disruption to force a response in some way. This is generally why we want our story's initial disruption to be the granting of a longing or the revocation (or threatening) of something of deep value—the character can't help but respond out of either hope or desperation.

Sometimes crafting a disruption can be as simple as asking what would cause a character great pain or great joy. Where is the character emotionally sensitive? What would cause a character to be the worst version of themselves? We want a disruption to change the emotion of at least one character (in polarity or magnitude).

Here are a few disruption effects that will tend to force a character to respond:

- Put at risk, threaten, or take away something of deep value to the character.
- Offer an opportunity to attain something of deep value to the character.
- Raise a moral dilemma (by introducing a new, conflicting desire) that will test a character's mettle and give rise to internal conflict.
- Show the character a violation of their moral code (by either themselves or by someone else).
- Unexpectedly move up a deadline or the timeline of a plan. In other words, increase urgency. Ensure the character's existing plan will no longer work within the new timeframe. This will then force improvisation to account for the new time limitations.
- Remove or block resources, routes, or options on which a character's plan depends.
- Reveal that a problem is actually more complicated or formidable than first thought, often requiring a more sophisticated or creative plan.
- Recolor previous information to show that what was previously thought to be bad is actually good or that what was previously thought to be good is actually bad. The character will often need to reassess their beliefs and potentially their plans.
- Force the character to confront a deep fear, regret,

insecurity, or trauma. This will typically prompt action to avoid pain.

- Force a character to confront new information about their identity or their place/role in the world.

Takeaway: An effective disruption is one that can't be ignored by a character. It must be addressed.

Stage Two: The Debate

The second stage of the disruption cycle is "the debate" or "the negotiation." This is the character's first opportunity to orient themselves and react to the disruption.

By definition, a disruption is an impetus to action. It disrupts a character's life in some way and forces a response. It's at this second stage that the character is confronted with the implicit question raised by the disruption, "What will you do now?" What will the character do now that either a problem has been raised or an opportunity has been presented? And does this new reality conflict with the character's existing plans or desires? Does it make them obsolete? Does it require any alterations? Does the character need to improvise? This moment is sometimes known as "the crisis point."

The character must wrestle with this question of what they should do now that the disruption has upended their life and/or plans. Do they sacrifice their existing desires to address the problem or opportunity raised by the disruption? Or do they find some way to pay the price of sidestepping the complications of the disruption?

Sometimes this debate is entirely internal, but other times it may involve consulting with allies. Perhaps the character decides to talk to a loved one in veiled terms (thus creating subtext) just to have someone with whom they can share their emotions.

While some disruptions make a character's existing plan obsolete, others give rise to a mutually exclusive choice between the existing plan and a new path. A disruption might leave intact the possibility of pursuing an existing plan at the same time as it gives rise to a new desire and a new option. In these instances, the debate is a moment of inner conflict between the old path and the new. Should the character pursue the path they were on or should they take the new path opened by the disruption?

Inner conflict arises when a new desire makes an existing desire hard to *want* to pursue. It's a dilemma. In many ways, it's a crisis. For example, an assassin may be carrying out her duty to terminate an undisclosed target when she discovers that the target is actually her brother (disruption!). The debate now becomes a pull between fulfilling her mission and forsaking her brother, or protecting her family and forsaking her duty.

Sometimes the debate is between two desirable outcomes. In the pursuit of buried treasure, for instance, a character may discover that there's a path to a treasure of even greater wealth—but it comes at a price.

Sometimes the debate is between two undesirable outcomes (and thus the character must choose the lesser of two evils). The classic example here, of course, is *Sophie's Choice*. Which child does the character sacrifice? The choice is an impossible one where there's no winning.

In these instances, the debate is a dilemma between two outcomes of similar value to the character. The outcomes may be equally desirable or equally undesirable. The key is that there should be no obvious or easy choice for the character to make. When we ensure that both options are of similar value (whether desirable or undesirable), we ensure that the character must struggle to make a decision. This stage is called a debate because it's an inner conflict about what to do next.

Recall that one of our primary thematic tools is a Great Decision that occurs in the climax of a story where a character must decide between two opposing value systems. That Great Decision is an example of the "debate" stage of the disruption cycle.

Takeaway: After a disruption, a character must decide whether to pursue their existing path or the new path that has been presented by the disruption. This debate can lead to an internal conflict within the character.

The Reaction Cycle

Characters come to terms with the consequences of a disruption through a clearly defined sequence of reactions. This sequence of reactions is called "the reaction cycle." We can combine the reaction sequences defined by K.M Weiland and Arlene Prunkl in order to arrive at a character's full reaction cycle. First a character reacts physiologically, then physically, then emotionally, then analytically. This is the process of metabolizing a disruption. Notice that the reaction cycle begins with the immediate, subconscious, and involuntary reactions and then graduates to the deliberate, conscious, and voluntary reactions.

Physiological Reaction

After a disruption, a character first reacts physiologically. On her blog PenUltimate Word, Arlene Prunkl[1] notes that a physiological reaction consists of the adrenal system of the character preparing for either fight, flight, or freeze. This includes sweating, changes in heart rate, rushes of adrenaline, dilating of pupils, etc. This reaction is optional, of course, depending on the type of disruption.

Physical Reaction

Next the character reacts physically. These are the instinctual reflexes. The character's hands might cover their face or head, their eyes might close, they might jump backward, etc. Typically these reactions are in self-defense. This reaction is largely involuntary and may be different for each character and each situation. Like the physiological reaction, this reaction is optional depending on the type of disruption.

Emotional Reaction

Next the character reacts emotionally. The character might swear, sigh, cry, scream, attack, etc. It's in this moment that the character considers how the disruption makes them feel based on their value system. Is it fundamentally good or bad based on their feelings? How does the disruption change the character's emotional state for good or bad? While an emotional reaction can occur in a moment, it can also stretch on for days, weeks, months, or longer.

Although not a fully accurate model of emotional reaction to loss, the Kübler-Ross model (denial, anger, bargaining, depression, and acceptance) can sometimes be helpful when considering how a character might emotionally react to a disruption.

When crafting a character's emotional reaction, we must also consider their coping mechanisms. How will they respond in order to try to shield themselves from additional pain? Will they mock, belittle, lash out, project, disassociate, hide, rationalize, repress, etc.?

Unlike the physiological and physical reaction, the emotional reaction isn't optional. Some characters will spend more time on an emotional reaction than others, however.

We want to consider whether the character will try to process their emotions on their own or by going to others. Do they seek emotional counsel? Do they share their emotions with others? Do they do this overtly or subtextually? Do they only share their emotions with certain characters? Do they need to be around someone while they're emotional, but do they refuse to discuss how they're feeling? These are all part of a character's unique emotional reaction.

Some characters may internalize their reaction instead of externalizing it. They may experience their feelings on the inside. This process of reacting internally is called internalization. Internalization allows a character to feel one way but act a different way. A character may, for instance, internally react selfishly but then externally respond selflessly. A character may internally react to a car crash with the feeling, "Damnit, he's fine" but externally respond, "Is everyone okay?!" Regardless of whether a character's internal and external reaction are dichotomous, a character will always go through some sort of emotional reaction—even if other characters don't notice.

Analytical Reaction

Finally the character reacts analytically. This is a conscious process where the character weighs their options using their own logic and reasoning (even if it's faulty). The character's reasoning can still be driven by a certain amount of emotion, of course. Like the emotional reaction, the analytical reaction isn't optional. All characters undergo some sort of analytical reaction even if it's quick and/or internalized. Some characters analyze alone and some need to bounce ideas off of others.

In this analytical stage, the character may consider whether their current plan is still viable. They may consider whether their current plan is still *worth* it. They may consider whether any new opportunities have arisen. They may consider whether a new or adjusted plan would require more risk and whether that additional risk would be worth it. They may consider whether any routes have been cut off, whether any options have opened up, whether there are enough resources remaining, and whether there's still time left.

The character may also offer justification or rationalization for their past actions or any actions that they're currently contemplating. This can particularly be the case when the negative consequences of their past actions come to light or when others attack the character's actions. Justification is the process of offering a valid excuse whereas rationalization is the process of offering a self-satisfying excuse. Both justification and rationalization imply that a character recognizes to some extent that they're responsible for their actions. Both may sometimes (but certainly not always) imply guilt for the actions or line of thinking.

Anticipation

For each option in the debate, the character will use counterfactual simulations to anticipate the consequences of their potential response. In other words, they'll use their imagination to play out what might happen based on their choice. This is the stage of anticipation and is also a critical piece of making a decision.

Anticipation may itself look like a reaction cycle. The character may sit with the emotional weight of any action that they're considering. They may analytically consider the potential results of their potential actions. Some actions are so potentially consequential that they warrant time for reflection. Character anticipation can also serve to induce anticipation in the audience.

When it comes to the reaction cycle, some characters spend more time on certain steps than others. Some spend so little time that it may appear as if they're skipping the reaction (although they never do). Regardless all characters go through the reaction cycle in this specific order: physiological, physical, emotional, and analytical. This is then followed by anticipation of potential responses. The way in which a character reacts to a disruption is a large part of what defines a character's nature.

The reaction cycle is a process of orientation and evaluation. The character discovers how they feel about the disruption and what they think about it. Then they evaluate their options. In his book *The Secrets of Story*, Matt Bird asks us to consider three simple categories for the primary method by which a character may evaluate a new disruption: heart, brain, and gut. Does the character primarily evaluate their options based on their feelings and emotions? Does the character primarily evaluate their options based on their rational thought and analysis? Or does the character primarily evaluate their options based on their intuition and instinct?

A character may react differently to a disruption and ultimately make a different decision depending on where they are in their character arc. Are they just starting their journey? Are they enveloped by their moral flaw? Have they already had their self-revelation? We must ask these questions when considering how a character would contextually react to a disruption.

> *Takeaway:* The reaction cycle consists of a specific sequence of reactions to a disruption. The cycle consists of the following reactions: physiological, physical, emotional, and analytical. The character then anticipates the consequences of their potential responses to the disruption.

Hesitation in the Face of Disruption (The "Refusal of the Call")

There's a key difference between how a character responds to a disruption that acts as a problem versus how a character responds to a disruption that acts as an opportunity. A problem *forces* change whereas an opportunity *offers* change. In other words, a problem disrupts a character's status quo whereas an opportunity invites a character to disrupt their own status quo. When we take into account the fact that most people have some level of emotional bias for maintaining their status quo or equilibrium (i.e. for staying in their comfort zone), it's not hard to see why an opportunity may be accompanied with some amount of hesitation. We can be tempted to stay in our comfort zone even after having seen its faults ("better the devil you know than the devil you don't."). We've got a natural bias against changing what we know.

This doesn't mean that all problems are met with action and all opportunities are met with hesitation, however. There's another distinction to be made based on the context of the opportunity. If an opportunity is presented as a solution to an existing and pressing problem, the character is likely to pursue the opportunity quickly. We might define a pressing problem as one that has some amount of urgency around its solution (which stands in contrast to a problem with little urgency, such as a longing or a dream). If an opportunity is presented when a character is in some form of equilibrium (even if that equilibrium has its faults), they're likely to meet the opportunity with some hesitation.

If the initial disruption of a story (i.e. the impetus) is an opportunity that presents itself as a solution to an existing and pressing problem, a character may pursue it with little or no hesitation. If the initial opportunity arises when a character is in a state of equilibrium, however, the character may approach it with some hesitation or uncertainty. It's worth noting that an opportunity may come in the form of a mission, an assignment, or an inner calling. These opportunities are invitations to break out of the character's comfort zone and consequently they activate the character's status quo bias.

Why might a character hesitate in the face of an opportunity? In most cases, they're afraid. They're being presented with a daunting journey outside of their comfort zone. It's not an easy decision to intentionally disrupt the equilibrium of one's own life. They may wonder if they're the right person to take this journey. They may be filled with self-doubt and wonder whether they have what it takes to pursue the opportunity. There might be a deep fear of failure. There may even be a deep fear of success.

It's in these moments of hesitation that a character may begin to make excuses about why now's not the time to deal with this. They may rationalize in any way they can in order to avoid making a decision. They may bring up their other responsibilities or obligations (we see this with Luke in *Star Wars* after Obi-Wan invites him on a journey). They'll lay the blame anywhere and make any excuse in order to avoid confronting the disruption. In the Hero's Journey paradigm, this is known as the "Refusal of the Call."

So how do we shake a character free from this state of hesitation? How do we force the character to accept the opportunity before them? This is perhaps best done by either removing the character's excuses or by raising the stakes to the point that the character is forced to respond (sometimes because there's a new problem). In *Star Wars*, Luke's initial excuse is that he can't just abandon his aunt and uncle. He's got responsibilities on the farm. This excuse is eventually undercut, of course, when Luke's aunt and uncle are killed. We might also imagine how we could "sweeten the deal" of an opportunity by increasing its benefits or lowering its costs.

If a character is faced with a disruption in the form of a problem that directly affects their life and they see a way of addressing the problem, there's little chance they'll hesitate. Why would they? The problem itself has already disrupted their life, throwing things into chaos and pushing them out of their comfort zone. They'll want to act to return things back to equilibrium (i.e. to solve the problem) as soon as possible. We see this in *Shrek* when the arrival of the fairy tale creatures quickly prompts Shrek to try to get rid of them. We also see this in *Finding Nemo* when Nemo is kidnapped.

There *is* an exception to this, however. If a character sees no clear path toward solving their problem, they'll have no choice but to either take time to devise a plan or to search for more information. In this case, we may not see a character immediately jump into action after a problem disrupts their equilibrium. We find this in *Breaking Bad* where the disruption is a terminal cancer diagnosis with no clear solution. Walt doesn't see a clear path toward fixing his problem.

Likewise a character may not take action toward an *opportunity* if there's no clear path toward pursuing it. In *The Nightmare Before Christmas*, Jack has a deep longing for something more in his life (which he views as a problem). He then discovers Christmas Town. This discovery appears as though it's an opportunity to fix his existing problem, but he doesn't yet see a clear path toward integrating the soul of Christmas Town into his life. In other words, he doesn't yet see how he can pursue this potential opportunity. This is also the case in *The Little Mermaid* where Ariel rescues Prince Eric from a storm and vows to find a way to be with him. It's an opportunity to fix her existing dissatisfaction with not being part of the human world. She doesn't initially see a plan to pursue Eric, however.

If the reason for the character's indecision or hesitation in the face of a disruption is that they don't see a clear path forward, we must present them with a clear path. In *The Nightmare Before Christmas*, Jack's path arises from a "eureka" moment where he realizes how Christmas can be integrated with Halloween Town. In *Breaking Bad*, Walt is presented with a clear path when he gets the idea to cook meth after seeing a drug bust carried out by his DEA agent brother-in-law. In *The Little Mermaid*, Ariel is presented with a clear path when Ursula offers her a deal to become human. In essence, we've got to help the character devise a plan.

A character may also freeze in the face of a disruption if they're unable to psychologically deal with the implications of the disruption. In these cases, a problem might strike the character in such a way that they don't know how to respond. They're in shock. And while the debate stage of the disruption cycle may last for quite a while, the character must eventually confront the disruption. If they choose to hesitate and hide out forever, we don't get much of a story.

A problem or opportunity may also give rise to internal conflict. But as we'll discuss in a moment, even internal conflict is best dramatized through character action rather than inaction.

The potential value in having our character hesitate in response to a problem or opportunity is that it emphasizes that the disruption is significant. It highlights the fact that the character believes this disruption is life-altering and that it shouldn't be pursued flippantly. Whether we choose to have our character hesitate in the face of a disruption or take immediate action, we must ensure that the reaction is believable. A character whose son was just kidnapped would not debate whether they should do anything about it. They'd immediately jump into action.

And just like not all characters speak indirectly (i.e. subtextually), not all characters will hesitate in the face of an opportunity. Some will jump at nearly any opportunity, even if it disrupts their equilibrium. A character's response to a disruption is part of what defines them. We must be aware, however, that if a disruption doesn't invite or force a character out of their comfort zone it's unlikely to have the same emotional impact as one that does.

Takeaway: A character may hesitate in the face of an opportunity that invites them to break their existing equilibrium. If the opportunity offers a fix to an existing and pressing problem, the character may jump into action without hesitation. Likewise a character may jump into action without hesitation in response to a problem. A character will only act, of course, if there's a clear path to respond to the disruption. If a character hesitates in the face of a disruption, we must remove excuses and raise the stakes to push them into action.

Dramatizing Inner Conflict

Recall that some disruptions give rise to an inner conflict by presenting a new path that conflicts with an existing one. In these instances, we want to show the character debating both possible paths. Dramatizing this debate is important because it shows us that this isn't an easy choice for the character to make. By highlighting that it's not an easy choice, we're emphasizing the fact that the character will ultimately be sacrificing something of value (by either giving up something good or paying the price associated with choosing the lesser of two evils). We need to see that this choice is a sacrifice in order to heighten the drama. We need to see that the character *could have made the other choice*. If we don't see the contemplation, the decision may seem trivial (which will kill the drama and consequently any interest).

Our initial instinct about how to dramatize inner conflict may be to show a character sitting and thinking intensely. After all, inner conflict is the state of having two desires that can't both be achieved. This makes sense since inaction is generally how we approach inner conflict in our own lives. In drama, however, inaction is boring. To maintain audience engagement and drama, we want to show a character struggling as they work toward both desires at the same time— whipping back and forth from one desire to the other. The whiplash itself provides interest and further proves to demonstrate the depth of the inner conflict.

Let's say a character is internally conflicted about whether she wants to go on a date with a man she met at a local café. To dramatize this internal conflict, we want to show her taking action toward the date and then taking action to cancel the date. First she begins to call his number but then immediately hangs up before he answers. After a couple of moments to calm her nerves, she calls again. She suggests a date for tomorrow night and he enthusiastically agrees. But then she decides against it and invites her brother. He's clearly disappointed but says it's a great idea. She decides she wants the date again so she asks him to bring someone else so that it's a double-date. She says, "See you later, buddy," and hangs up. Notice the unspoken battle within her. She jumps back and forth between her conflicting desires.

> *Takeaway:* To dramatize internal conflict, we want to show a character pursuing both conflicting desires at the same time, quickly alternating between paths. By dramatizing the internal conflict, we're highlighting that this isn't a trivial choice. We're emphasizing that the character will be making a sacrifice by making a decision.

The Short Debate

Not all disruptions give rise to an epic battle between two options of seemingly equal value. Not all disruptions result in a character tortured by inner conflict or paralyzed by fear. Sometimes a disruption just presents a clear opportunity that a character will want to pursue as soon as possible. Sometimes a disruption presents a clear problem that a character must address now.

In these instances, there's little debate about what should be done next. The path is obvious: pursue the opportunity or fix the problem. This tends to be the case when stakes are high. If a disruption presents an opportunity of intense value or threatens something of intense value, the character will simply jump into action. This is the case in *Finding Nemo* when Nemo is kidnapped and Marlin must go after him. There's little debate about what Marlin must do.

For these disruptions, the debate still occurs, but the decision comes quickly. As long as a disruption forces a character to respond and also has consequences, it's effective.

Takeaway: Sometimes there's no need for debate in response to a disruption. The path is clear.

Stage Three: The Decision

The third stage of the disruption cycle brings the character to a decision. They've observed the disruption, reacted to it, debated their options, potentially whipped back and forth between two conflicting desires, and now they're ready to make a decision.

In this step, the character makes a definitive decision and vows to pursue it. Note that this choice gives rise to a desire to either pursue an opportunity, fix a problem, or avoid a problem. In this way, this decision acts as an inciting incident (because it incites in the character a new desire).

Often as part of a decision, a character will also concoct a plan of action to pursue their desire. This is where that plan is formed.

Stage Four: Action

The fourth and final stage of the disruption cycle is the moment of action. The character has made a decision about what they're going to do and now it's time to make it real. Here the character enacts their plan. Where the disruption initially raised the question, "What will you do now?", the character answers, "This." It's the climax of the disruption cycle.

It's this stage in which the true nature of a character is defined. We only know a character by their choices and actions. Words are cheap but action speaks.

In the pursuit of the character's new plan, they may encounter a new disruption. This new disruption sends the character back to the beginning of the disruption cycle, resulting in a chain of disruptions as the character continues to work toward their ultimate goal.

18

DEFINING STORY STRUCTURE

Structure (and Narrative) as a Chain of Disruption Cycles

Traditional wisdom tells us that a story is a sequence of scenes. This can be a valuable perspective. After all, most stories *are* a sequence of scenes. But we can imagine a story taking place all at the same time and at the same location in one seamless take, resulting in one scene (close to but not exactly the movie *The Man From Earth*). And even though this story would undoubtedly consist of only one scene if we use the traditional definition of a scene as a continuous time and location, the story would still seem to have a more intricate structure than one might imagine for a one-scene story. Structure, then, isn't necessarily about a particular sequence of times and locations. Structure isn't necessarily about a sequence of scenes.

Instead structure is an ordered sequence of significant events. Sometimes these events occur in different times and locations, but they might also occur all at the same location and all within a continuous and seamless time. It's from the order in which these events are expressed that the audience makes connections and draws meaning (a la the narrative fallacy, as we'll later discuss).

On a rudimentary level, a story is simply a sequence of significant events where the order of those events is meaningful (i.e. where the order helps us draw some meaningful conclusion that doesn't exist in any one event—usually through a chain of cause and effect). By seeing a character's behavior and morality change over time, for instance, we may draw a conclusion about how the journey is affecting the character's mental and spiritual health. This meaning isn't contained in any one event but rather is drawn from witnessing the character's change as measured across multiple events (thus making the order of events meaningful). Ordering the events one way might show a character in decline while reversing the order might show the same character on the mend.

> *Takeaway:* Story structure is an ordered sequence of significant events where the order of those events is meaningful.

What's a Scene?

So what makes a single story event significant? To be significant is to have an effect. To have an effect, an event must incite a change in action or understanding. Or in other words, a significant event must disrupt the current path or understanding of the story. These are turning points. They're moments where the direction of a story "turns" in a new, often unexpected direction (to one degree or another). From this, we can say that story structure is an ordered sequence of turning points that alter action and/or understanding.

Viewed another way, we can say that story structure is an ordered sequence of significant disruptions (disruptions are, after all, turning points). These disruptions have effects. They turn the story in new directions, providing both dramatic interest through change and also thematic meaning through how characters respond to the disruptions.

With this in mind, let's revise our definition of a "scene" to be the dramatization of a disruption, along with any context necessary to understand or experience the significance of the disruption in the moment. By this definition, a scene always has a turning point—a disruption. In fact, a disruption is what a scene *is*. A scene then becomes a unit of story change. It's the dramatization of a significant event that turns the story in a new direction (to some extent). A meaningful sequence of significant scenes results in a story (note this definition expresses no judgment as to whether the story is "good" or not).

> *Takeaway:* A scene is the dramatization of a disruption along with any context necessary to understand or experience the significance of the disruption in the moment.

The Sequel / Interlude

With our new definition of a "scene" as the dramatization of a disruption, it's worth noting that a scene may consist solely of a character enacting their plan (i.e. taking action) followed by a disruption to that plan. So where does the rest of the disruption cycle go? Where does the character react, decide, and then form a new plan?

This is where the concept of a "sequel" or "interlude" comes in. A sequel is a span of time following a scene where a character goes through the rest of the disruption cycle. They react to the disruption emotionally and analytically. They deliberate and debate what should be done in response. They come to a decision and then craft a new or altered plan. Essentially a sequel is the aftermath of a scene.

Of course, not all disruptions call for a sequel. And some sequels are just tacked on at the end of a scene. The sequel might consist of only a few brief moments of deliberation and decision following a disruption. Sometimes the reaction cycle doesn't need to be dramatized and is merely implicit. Sometimes the plan is either implicit or will later be dramatized without explanation.

As a rule of thumb, the more impactful the disruption, the more time the character will need for processing and thus a sequel may be warranted. A sequel is differentiated from a scene in that there's no disruption in a sequel. It's all about dealing with what just happened and crafting a new way forward. It's all about sitting with the weight of the disruption.

> *Takeaway:* A sequel is a span of time used to dramatize the rest of the disruption cycle after the initial disruption of a scene. It's where we see reaction, deliberation, decision, and the crafting of a plan.

What's an Act? (What's a Narrative Unit?)

We previously explored the concept of the three-act structure. So what exactly is an "act" then? One of the most helpful definitions comes from Adam Skelter who says that an act is, "a story unit containing a strategy for the character to achieve an objective." We might say a new act is born, then, when a disruption fundamentally alters a character's strategy toward an objective or underlying desire. (We might also say that in most instances a scene consists of a disruption that alters or complicates a character's plan toward an objective but usually doesn't alter their fundamental strategy or underlying desire).

Even this definition of an act, though, doesn't hold up in all instances. Some stories are about characters without clear objectives and thus without clear strategies. Do those stories have acts? The proponents of three-act structure might certainly argue so.

An act can be thought of more broadly as a narrative unit, just like a scene, or a sequence, or the global story itself. A narrative unit is where something significant happens that's worthy of being told (and usually conveys meaning). The "significance" is provided by the narrative unit's disruption. In other words, a narrative unit is a span of significant change.

Every scene, sequence, and act ends with something of significance changing. The larger the narrative unit, the larger the disruption. This "something changing" is the *point* of the narrative unit. It's why it exists. It turns the story in a new direction and sets us up for the next narrative unit. In this way, disruptions act as structural glue that tie together narrative units.

What separates a scene from a sequence from an act? The relative degree of disruption. The difference between the narrative units is in the relative degree to which the story is turned in a new direction. Because of this, acts have more impactful disruptions than sequences, which have more impactful disruptions than scenes. There's a beautiful pulse of disruption that keeps the audience engaged. Structure consists of an ordered sequence of narrative units of varying degrees of disruption. In other words, structure is a sequence of disruption cycles.

Recall that we can often view story structure as a series of questions and answers. Large disruptions give rise to large questions (and sometimes answer large questions). Small disruptions give rise to small questions (and sometimes answer small questions).

Takeaway: A narrative unit ends with a significant disruption of some kind. Disruptions act as structural glue that tie together narrative units. The larger the disruption, the larger the narrative unit. Story structure is a sequence of disruption cycles.

Story Nomenclature

While there's little agreement on the strict definition of an act in the storytelling community, there's still value in understanding and using the terminology of the three-act structure. The writing community, unfortunately, is sorely lacking when it comes to an agreed-upon set of nomenclature. "Three-act structure" is a relatively common idea in the community that lets us communicate where we are in a story. When one writer says to another that they're having trouble with their second act, it tells us that they're having a problem with the section of the story after the dramatic question moment (i.e. after "plot point one" or the "lock-in" moment) but before the crisis or global turning point. There's value in being able to communicate that.

As we've seen, the terminology of storytelling is hardly set in stone. Is the initial disruption that kicks off a story called the impetus, the inciting incident, the point of first attack, or the catalyst? Is the end of act one called the lock-in moment, plot point one, the predicament, or the dramatic question moment? Is the end of act two called the crisis, the main turning point, or the "all is lost" moment? The unfortunate answer is that it depends on whom you're talking to.

One thing is true: These moments are all simply disruptions. They're all moments that turn the story in a new direction and give rise to a new desire. They're all moments that incite, complicate, simplify, elucidate, obstruct, or invalidate a plan. They're all moments that inject the story with additional fuel and push the audience forward to the next moment. Some of these disruptions are more impactful than others, but they're all disruptions.

But now may be a good time to take a step back and consider whether we're gaining anything by trying to rigorously define an act. We could concoct a new paradigm with some new number of story acts and tout it as the true secret of story structure, but would it help? Does this actually help us *write* a story? Does this even help us *structure* a story?

As we'll soon learn, the key to story structure is in story beats. The key to structure is the intricate interplay between the beats of character arc, genre, relationships, beginnings, endings, societal downfalls, and more. And nowhere in the unfolding of a story structure does the audience see a sign labeled "act," "sequence," or "scene." Structure is about the deep sequence of story beats. In other words, structure is about plot.

> *Takeaway:* All structural events, no matter what we call them, are disruptions. Structure is about the deep sequence of story beats. Structure is about plot.

19

PLOTTING AND REPETITION

Plotting

Plotting is fundamentally about how we sequence (or structure) the beats of our story. A beat is essentially a moment where something of significance happens. In other words, a beat is a moment where something *changes*. It's a disruption. It's a "plot point" that can often be summarized to fit on an index card. Examples include "the lovers meet," "the body is discovered," "the protagonist and the antagonist duel," "the protagonist loses their loved one." If we were summarizing our story, we would likely be recounting the story as a series of beats (or moments of change).

Because a beat is simply when something of significance happens, a beat can often consist of several smaller beats. The beat "the lovers meet" might consist of the smaller beats "the man drinks coffee alone," "the woman trips on his briefcase," "coffee spills on her dress," "the man frantically apologizes," and "the woman asks for the man's phone number." Each of these beats might further be broken down into smaller action/reaction beats with description and lines of dialogue.

When we plot, we'll often start with the high level beats and drill down into the lower level beats in order to "increase the resolution" of the story.

> *Takeaway:* A beat is a moment where something of significance happens. It's a disruption. Plotting is about how we sequence the beats of our story.

The Sin of Repetition

One of the greatest mistakes we can make when it comes to plotting is also perhaps the easiest one to make. It's a repetition of the same beat. If we go with our definition of a beat as a moment when something of significance happens, then a repeated beat provides nothing uniquely noteworthy (because its purpose has already been previously served) and consequently has the potential to result in boredom. It sounds easy enough to avoid in theory, but avoiding redundancy can be deceptively challenging when beats may appear unique on the surface.

The challenge here comes from the fact that two beats may appear to be unique based on their individual situations or characters, but they may contain the same *type* of action or revelation (i.e. the same *type* of disruption). Another way to think of this is that we want each beat to be a *unique type of change* to the story. We want each beat to be a unique turning point. If a character is simply stuck in a repeated loop of using their skills as a fighter to defeat enemies, we're not getting any new information. Even though the opponent may change, if a challenge isn't revealing new information about either a character, the theme, or the plot, then it's likely part of an episodic (i.e. boring) plot. New conflict must bring fundamentally new information.

As a general rule, the easiest way to identify whether a beat is unique is to identify whether the character must take a categorically new *type of action* or whether they're confronting a categorically new type of conflict. Let's say, for instance, that a character is trying to fix a car. She might find out that the transmission is broken. She fixes that but then finds out that the timing belt is broken. She fixes that but then finds out that the starter is dead. This is inherently boring. She's facing the same basic type of conflict over and over. But if she receives a call that she'll be fired if she doesn't get to work in the next twenty minutes, we've now got a new type of conflict. When our stories have beats with the same type of conflict, we get a monotonous and episodic plot.

Another way to help ensure that we aren't repeating the same beat over and over is to define the purpose of the beat within the larger story. We don't want to keep hitting the same purpose over and over. Once a beat has served its purpose in progressing the story, it's done.

Sometimes the repetition of a beat can be masked by extraneous details that appear to make two beats unique on the surface. We have to guard against this possibility by being clear-eyed about the fundamental purpose and effect of each story beat. We have to be honest about what information is being conveyed and whether that same basic fact has already been established. When our story repeats the same basic beat, we run the risk of the audience disengaging from boredom.

Takeaway: The cardinal sin of plotting is the repetition of the same beat. We must ensure that no two beats share the same fundamental purpose within the story.

20

THE BEATS OF CHARACTER ARC

The Beats of Story

For each story pattern, there are certain things that *must* happen in order to maximize that pattern. In other words, a story technique will typically imply a series of beats that will maximize the emotional impact of the technique or pattern. This principle is at the heart of our "tools, not rules" mindset. We first decide what basic effect we want in our story, then we decide what techniques can be used to create that effect, and finally we consider the story beats that heighten the technique. We might say that for every story pattern, there's a beat sheet.

Having a natural instinct for story is about having a natural instinct for story beats.

We've explored how a character arc is a strong method for exploring and expressing a story's theme. Let's now consider the specific beats of the most common arc, the positive character arc. This arc shifts a character from flawed to unflawed—from moral weakness to moral strength.

A character arc is about forcing a character to change their beliefs. To do that we've got to challenge the character's current beliefs, at first slowly, but then at a deeper level and at a more intense rate. To challenge a character's beliefs, we'll create disruptions and dilemmas that force the character to confront their lies, confront their insecurities, and witness the negative effects of their moral flaw.

Dramatize the Moral Weakness

First the character must have a moral weakness. We previously explored how this weakness is typically the result of a ghost, a lie, or an obsession. This weakness is a behavior that actively and negatively affects those around the character. In other words, a character's moral weakness must negatively impact the character's relationships. This moral weakness must play out through action. We must dramatize specifically *how* the flaw is hurting others.

A character's moral weakness is typically a part of a character's façade. It's a negative behavior that grows out of an attempt to maintain a false reality or identity. The character is driven by desperation to maintain this façade and avoid confronting their true self. In essence, the character begins the story with a flawed approach to life.

> *Takeaway:* The character must start with a moral weakness that's actively and negatively affecting their relationships.

The Influence Character

After we've dramatized the character's weakness and seen its negative effects in action, we introduce a disruption to the character's life. This disruption drags the character into the world of the thematic opposition where their beliefs will be challenged. The goal here is to disrupt the character's life in a way that allows us to put the character in situations where they'll be confronted with one or more opposing belief systems and approaches to life.

This initial disruption is typically followed by the introduction of the "influence character." The influence character is the one who can most effectively influence the flawed character (wittingly or unwittingly) to recognize that their approach to life is flawed. The influence character typically, but not always, does this through their actions, by living a life that's thematically opposed to the flawed character. In other words, the influence character helps the flawed character realize *what life might look like* if they were able to recognize their moral weakness and drop their façade. Sometimes the influence character is an antagonist and the only way to dramatically defeat them is to adopt the alternate approach to life (as with the hitman Vincent in the movie *Collateral*). Other times, the influence character is an ally who functions as a philosophical mentor (as with Dory in *Finding Nemo*).

It's worth noting that because the influence character's function is to introduce and argue an alternate approach to life (i.e. an alternate belief system), a character without a moral flaw *can* also be impacted by an influence character. This is the case in *Star Wars* where Obi-Wan acts as an influence character and philosophical mentor to Luke in the thematic dilemma of faith (i.e. the force) versus technology.

The flawed character is typically strangely attracted to the approach to life that the influence character embodies. It may be the first time that the flawed character has encountered this alternate way of life in the flesh. There may be curiosity and an unspoken desire to find out more.

> *Takeaway:* The influence character is the one who can most effectively influence the flawed character to recognize that their approach to life is flawed.

The Moment of Harmony

The character's moral weakness will continue to cause them trouble just as it did at the start of the story. At about the midpoint of a character's arc, however, the character will experience a moment of living in harmony with the approach to life embodied by the influence character. In other words, the character will briefly question whether their existing approach to life is incorrect and consider whether the alternate approach may be more valuable.

The character may drop their façade for a brief moment. It's a moment of doubt. It's fleeting. In *Finding Nemo*, Marlin begins to play a game with Dory in the jellyfish fields. Importantly this moment doesn't necessarily need to show the flawed character acting in harmony with the theme (although it can). The character might instead passively witness an event or witness another character who's living in harmony with the alternate approach to life. While there's a recognition of this alternate approach to life, there's often an unwillingness to fully embrace it. Perhaps it's not fully understood or not yet fully trusted.

After this midpoint moment of fleeting insight, there's a reversal and the character is viscerally reminded why their façade exists. Often something bad happens that causes them to recoil into their shell and fully embrace their moral weakness once again. The character might believe that this bad thing happened *because* they dropped their guard. They reaffirm to themselves that any dropping of the façade, even for a brief moment, results in pain. They won't let it happen again. In *Finding Nemo*, this reversal is when Dory is stung in the jellyfish fields.

> *Takeaway:* At the midpoint, the character experiences a moment of living in harmony with the theme. This moment may consist of the character acting in harmony with the theme or it may consist of the character witnessing another character living in harmony with the theme.

Moral Decay

The next beat is that the character's negative behavior must continue to make things worse in their life. The character will typically try to solve their problems by leaning heavily into their past behavior with the hope that if they just try harder things will get better. This, of course, doesn't work. Often as the character becomes more and more frustrated, they begin to forsake their morals in a further attempt to solve their problems (or attain their desires). This is the process of moral decay. The character may begin to feel that the ends justify the means. They'll offer excuses, justifications, and rationale about why their moral decay isn't merely justified but necessary. This is the paradox of animosity—we tend to become like that which we fight.

The character may be confronted with the question, "What are you willing to do to get what you want?" And they may answer, "Anything."

It's during this process of moral decay that we as the storyteller must continually attack the character's weakness. To "attack" the weakness is to attempt to *show* the character that it's their moral weakness that's the source of their problems and nothing else.

We can often do this most effectively through the use of clone characters. We might, for instance, show a clone character who's facing the thing the protagonist fears most. We might show the fate of other characters with the same moral weakness (which is the premise of *A Christmas Carol*). This can help us remind a character of their past mistakes and attempt to draw a connection to their weakness. Or we can play with philosophical arias where a character expresses their worldview related to the theme (which often relates to the moral weakness). We can have someone the character respects attack and criticize the character for their behavior. Or we can have someone that the character hates draw a parallel between the two. The reason for the effectiveness of clone characters is that while humans tend not to be able to see their weaknesses in themselves, they can easily spot weaknesses in others. This helps us keep the protagonist's fear ever-present.

Another powerful technique for attacking a character's weakness is to continually present the character with moral dilemmas where one choice is to use the moral weakness to solve the problem (which is typically rooted in fear, lies, and insecurity) and the other choice is to take the position of moral strength. When the character chooses moral weakness in response to the dilemma (which they almost inevitably will, due to it being the comfortable response), we punish them. We want to force the character into situations where their moral flaw gets them (or someone else) into trouble.

Often a character will continually attempt to blame others for their problems. This is part of the process of moral decay. They'll point the finger at anyone but themselves. It's only when a character has hit emotional and spiritual rock bottom that they tend to start looking inward. Things have to get bad enough or stressful enough in order for the character to consider that *they* might be the source of the problem and not others. It's our responsibility as writers to get them there.

Not all characters morally decay, of course. Some are bastions of morality that must resist corruption in the face of an overbearing community. Others persist in their moral weakness but never cross the line to immorality (such as Marlin in *Finding Nemo*). Whether a character morally decays or not, we must always push them to confront their moral weakness.

> *Takeaway:* As a character experiences failure in the pursuit of their goal, they may resort to immoral tactics. They'll offer excuses about why their immoral methods are justified. This is the process of moral decay. We want to continually show the character that their moral weakness alone is the source of their problems.

Introspection

The next beat is to get the character in a position to realize that they're the source of their problems. We need to get the character to drop their façade and fully embrace their true self (through the process of individuation). In order to get a character into the right headspace to look inward, we must force the character to pay the price for their weakness. This is the only way to show them that the weakness must be forsaken in order to live a better life. It's only when a character can't look outward that they begin to look inward and consider change. Often the loss is forced via some ticking clock (i.e. the trigger that will "force the stakes") that ostensibly prevents the character from attaining their desire.

As with almost every event in a story, this beat is most impactful when it's *caused*. It's often caused either directly by the antagonist (as they implement their plan) or indirectly by the protagonist (such as in the case of Walter White in *Breaking Bad* when his failure to save Jane indirectly causes a plane crash). This beat is perhaps most powerful when it's the protagonist's own moral weakness or inability to accept the correct value system that causes the loss.

The price paid during this beat doesn't necessarily need to be a loss (though it often is). It can also be a hollow victory (as in the case of *Up* when Carl arrives at Paradise Falls but realizes it's hollow without Ellie). It can be the realization that the attainment of what the character wanted can't help them live a fulfilled life (i.e. what they wanted was not what they needed). The character might wonder whether the thing they wanted was worth the price they had to pay to get it (which includes the character's moral decay). Sometimes this beat may come in the form of a Pyrrhic victory where the character suffers such a devastating toll that their "victory" is effectively a defeat.

Recall that a character's central desire may be based around a belief that "If I just do [x], or attain [y], or become [z], I'll be happy and fulfilled." We may want to let the character finally do, attain, or become whatever it is that they thought would bring them happiness. Now that they're confronted with "success," they can see that it's hollow.

Over the course of the character's arc, we're pressing the character to change their beliefs. In other words, we're trying to push them toward a self-revelation moment. Although this beat is often either a major loss or a hollow victory, it can be anything that gets the character in a contemplative or introspective mood. It's plausible that a character is moved to change by comparing themselves to a clone character. Recall that we define a clone as a character who represents "what could, should, or might happen to the protagonist if he or she takes a particular path." The key here is that the flawed character must be on the same path as this clone character. The flawed character must realize that, without any change, there's a major loss or a hollow victory on their current path. This is how we get them to reassess their trajectory.

In the story *A Christmas Carol*, for example, Scrooge doesn't actually lose anything or experience any hollow victory for himself. Instead he's confronted with his future self (i.e. a clone character) if he doesn't change his current path. In this way, he's moved to a self-revelation out of fear (combined with some nostalgia from his past). In essence, this beat could consist of a character witnessing a loss in someone else's life, which drives them to change their behavior before the loss occurs in their own life.

We might also have a character who's moved to a self-revelation through the inspiration of a clone's action or decision. This is the case in *Frasier* S08E05 when Frasier's butler, Ferguson, notes that "[Niles'] willingness to break social rank has inspired me." After witnessing Niles' act of love for Daphne, Ferguson has a revelation about his own need to break social rank by quitting and chasing his own love interest.

This beat (i.e. the crisis moment) may contain some sort of betrayal of the story's correct value system. Michael Arndt calls this the "Judas Moment of Betrayal." We may see one or more characters shun the correct side of the thematic opposition (at least temporarily). In *Star Wars*, for instance, Han Solo abandons the Rebellion and refuses to fight in the final battle against the Death Star. This can further heighten the feeling of loss and despair at this moment.

This beat is all about getting a character to look inward. We want the character to question what's truly valuable to them. Sometimes that's through a loss, through a hollow victory, or through comparison with a clone character. When this beat is a major loss, it's often known as the "all is lost" Moment (a la Save the Cat terminology) or the crisis point. This beat typically corresponds with the end of the main dramatic question of the story and thus the end of act two. Sometimes the main dramatic question is answered with success (i.e. a hollow victory) and sometimes it's answered with defeat (i.e. a major loss).

> *Takeaway:* After a character has experienced repeated failure in the pursuit of their goal, we must get them into a state of introspection so that they can realize that their moral weakness is the true source of their problems. This is typically done through a loss, a hollow victory, or a clone character.

The Self-Revelation

The next beat is the moment of self-revelation. It's the moment when the character realizes something about themselves (often that they need to drop their façade, heal their moral weakness, and become individuated). The self-revelation occurs once the character is in the right headspace to begin looking inward. There's often a specific trigger that causes the self-revelation. The trigger might be something familiar seen in a new light (i.e. in a new context). That which was overlooked gains new meaning after the character's passage through the "loss or hollow victory" beat. The self-revelation beat may give rise to a new dramatic question, which typically lasts until the climax.

The self-revelation trigger is perhaps most powerful when it occurs via an object that carries new meaning or significance to the character. In *Up*, the trigger is Carl and Ellie's adventure book. Carl sees a message from Ellie that says, "Thanks for the adventure — now go have a new one!" Carl also sees Russell's Boy Scout sash. Putting these two objects together helps Carl realize that in order to best memorialize Ellie, he needs to form new relationships and have new adventures.

A self-revelation trigger might also be a phrase, line of dialogue, a look, a smell, a discovery, a behavior, etc. In *Toy Story*, Buzz sees the word "Andy" written in Sharpie on his foot and he realizes the importance of being a toy and taking care of one's child. The trigger might also occur through the use of a clone character. For instance, a character might realize that they're a womanizer by seeing someone else they respected have an affair. It's only at this moment that they make the connection to their own immoral behavior.

It's in this moment of self-revelation that a "thematic desire" may be born within the character. This thematic desire is the character's desire to undo the negative consequences that they either caused through immoral action or allowed through inaction. The character must make things right, own their mistakes, prove their individuation, and more generally champion and defend the correct value system in the face of the opposing worldview. In *Up*, for instance, Carl sets out to have a new adventure by helping both Russell and Kevin.

Sometimes this thematic desire completely overrides the character's dramatic desire and thus the character's "need" overtakes their "want." Other times, the character may devise a way to attain their dramatic desire through the use of the thematic desire (such as Luke's use of the force and "faith" to destroy the Death Star). In other words, the character will use their new understanding or value system in order to accomplish their dramatic goal. This thematic approach to their goal will propel the character toward the climax.

It's worth noting that it's also possible for a character to come to a false self-realization in this moment. Instead of recognizing that their flaw is the source of all of their problems, they may instead decide to lay the blame on others and on the world at large. In these instances, the character has a change in their worldview but learns nothing about themselves. This moment of false self-revelation can result in the corruption or disillusionment of a hero and the birth of a villain. This false self-revelation may give rise to a negative thematic desire. The corrupted or disillusioned character may set out to prove their new immoral worldview correct or may seek justice against those who they blame for their loss.

While the character almost always realizes the error of their ways at the self-revelation moment, it's possible that the character won't reveal the specific details of their self-revelation (i.e. the lesson learned). The character may bolt into action as they pursue their new thematic desire, but they may also leave the audience in the dark as to what they're trying to accomplish. The details of the thematic desire will be dramatized through *action* at the story's Great Decision Moment (i.e. the climax). This pattern makes use of a dramatic technique called "unstated desire," which we'll later explore in detail.

> *Takeaway*: The self-revelation is the moment when the character realizes that their moral weakness has been the source of their troubles. This revelation results in a change of worldview and may result in a new thematic desire to undo the damage done during their moral decay.

Loss as the Trigger of Change (and the Ghost)

Now that we've seen the importance of the crisis moment in bringing about introspection and a self-revelation within the character, let's take a step back and consider loss more generally.

Thus far, we've explored two common moments of loss in a character's life: the ghost event and the crisis moment. In a positive character arc, the crisis moment is generally some loss in the character's life that invites them to look inward and consider whether they're the source of their problems. It typically leads to a revelation about oneself or about the world (whether correct or incorrect).

Recall that a character's ghost is some past loss or traumatic experience that haunts the character in their current life. We've explored how the ghost event is typically the trigger of a character's coping mechanisms and thus of their moral flaw. After the loss of his family, for instance, Marlin desperately holds on to Nemo and smothers him. Over the course of the story, Marlin must learn to let go of his ghost and trust Nemo to live his own life.

Like the crisis moment, the ghost event is a moment of loss that triggers change. In the prototypical pattern, the ghost event triggers a negative revelation. The character might believe that the trauma was their own fault. They might believe that they deserved it. Or they might place the blame on others and on the world at large. Regardless of where the character places the blame, they often create a façade that's meant to protect them and ensure that they never experience a similar pain again. This leads to a moral flaw.

In this way, the ghost event often leads to the adoption of a belief (i.e. a lie) that negatively affects the character's life. The character's journey over the course of the story is required for them to learn that in order to live a better life they need to drop the negative revelation (i.e. the lie) that arose from the ghost event.

Both the ghost event and the crisis point are milestones in the character's life. They're moments of loss that instigate change (for better or worse). They both trigger revelations and a new worldview. As a general pattern, loss is what catalyzes change. Success doesn't. After all, why would it? If a character succeeds in their goal or more generally experiences joy, why would they consider changing their strategies, beliefs, or value system? It's only when a character experiences loss that they begin to place blame and consider change.

We might consider the ghost event as the crisis moment of a past story. In this past story, however, the character's crisis moment led to a negative self-revelation that created their lie and moral flaw. In the current story, the character's crisis moment is typically the catalyst of a self-revelation that *heals* their lie and moral flaw.

This is perhaps most evident in the *Star Wars* trilogies. What was originally Darth Vader's unstated ghost event in the original *Star Wars* trilogy takes center stage as the crisis moment in the *Star Wars* prequels. The prequels are about exploring the ghost event that led Anakin to the dark side (i.e. the loss of Padmé). The original trilogy is about exploring Anakin's eventual self-revelation and the act of redemption that puts him back on a path to the light side.

Loss catalyzes change. It leads to introspection and the placement of blame. This tends to lead to new beliefs about the way the world works or about one's place in the world. It leads to new beliefs about how one should act. Sometimes this new worldview is correct and morally good, other times it's incorrect and morally bad. We must keep in mind the power that loss holds in sparking revelations and character change, whether on the path toward redemption or on the path toward corruption. This is an important pattern for both creating villains and for healing heroes.

> *Takeaway*: Whether it occurs in a ghost event or in a crisis moment, loss is an instigator of change. It invites a character to place blame and reconsider their approach to life, for better or worse.

Value System in Action

The final beat of the character arc is the dramatization of the character's self-revelation through *action*. Talk is cheap. In order to demonstrate to the world and to the audience that the character is truly changed, they've got to apply the lesson of the self-revelation through a difficult choice (i.e. The Great Decision). In *Legally Blonde*, Elle realizes that she must accept herself wholly as she is. She no longer defines herself by her relationship with her ex-boyfriend and no longer makes decisions in order to impress him. In the climax, Elle's ex-boyfriend finally tells her he loves her and asks for her back. She makes the *choice* to reject him (and importantly the viable *option* of taking him back must be present), demonstrating her individuation and growth. As we've discussed, The Great Decision must be an actual choice where the character could choose either side.

To complete a character's arc, we must see through action that the character can treat others (and themselves) in a healthy way and that they've cured their moral weakness.

It's worth noting that it's possible for a character to face The Great Decision before they have their self-revelation. It's only after they've already made their choice that they learn their lesson and face the consequences of whether their choice was correct or not. With this pattern, we run the risk of a character not being able to concretely demonstrate the stickiness of their self-revelation. This pattern may work particularly well when a character unknowingly makes the wrong choice and must deal with the consequences (as is the case in *Vertigo*).

> *Takeaway*: After the character has had a self-revelation, they must take action to demonstrate that they've learned their lesson. This action is typically the result of a difficult choice between value systems during the story's climax.

21

THE BEATS OF THE BEGINNING

"The opening is the single most important part of any script."

— JOHN TRUBY

Because story is a chain of cause and effect, the beginning is what makes the rest of the story not only possible, but inevitable. It's for this reason that the seeds of an ineffective story are buried in its beginning.

The beginning of a story must accomplish a number of jobs. It must prepare the story for the impetus (i.e. the story's initial disruption), introduce and establish interest in a character, establish the character's nature, foreshadow change, imply thematic patterns, deliver on the genre, and also capture the audience's attention. In short, the beginning provides what Corey Mandell calls the "essential context" we'll need in order to understand the rest of the story. We want to accomplish these jobs quickly and efficiently so that we can get to the impetus as soon as possible.

Prepare For the Impetus

The beginning of a story must contain anything that's required in order to either understand the impetus or to feel the emotional weight of the impetus. This is the story's "setup."

Establish Societal and Character Rules

First let's consider what must be included in order to understand the impetus. If the initial disruption will be based on breaking some societal rule, we must first establish both the existence of the rule and also its importance. This is the case in *Monsters, Inc.* where we have to know that children aren't allowed in Monstropolis in order for Boo's appearance to mean anything. If the prohibition of children had never been established, the "Fugitive" story form could never work.

If a character's journey takes place within the context of a larger story world conflict, ritual, or activity, we may need to first dramatize and explore the context of the story world before the character's journey can begin. This is the case in *Star Wars* where Luke's journey to help the Rebellion only makes sense if we first understand the larger context of the Rebellion versus the Empire.

It's important to note here, however, that we often want to resist the temptation to start the story from an "omniscient" perspective where the story world history is laid out for the audience as a series of long, detailed facts. We must remember that first and foremost, the audience is interested in characters. If our story requires that we first explore the larger context of a story world, we generally want to explore that context through the eyes (and ideally desire) of a character.

Note that the context of the *Star Wars* story world is defined and explored by starting the story with Darth Vader's pursuit of the stolen Death Star plans. The legendary title crawl of *Star Wars* provides a brief introduction to the story's context in a visually intriguing way and sets us up for a more in-depth exploration through the eyes of the Empire. As a general rule, the audience doesn't want a ten minute introduction to the seven clans and the thousand year war of the story world. They'll want that once they're invested in a character.

More generally, we must also establish any story world rules that will serve as character motivation (to either pursue or avoid). In *Monsters, Inc.*, Randall is trying to invent a more efficient method with which to extract the screams of children. This only makes sense if we first establish that the story world of Monstropolis requires children's screams to function. Contrast these requirements with a story like *Finding Nemo* where the plot (and consequently the setup) isn't driven by the story world but rather by the characters.

In *Toy Story*, we must first establish that each toy has their "spot" so that when Buzz knocks Woody off the bed, it means something. Likewise we must establish that toys can't move in the presence of humans so that we understand the magnitude of the situation when Woody violates the rule in the climax.

If a character starts a story with a clear objective or desire, we may want to provide their motivation. If a boy is preparing to burn down his house, we generally want to know why. The motivation doesn't need to be immediately clear in the beginning, of course. Obscuring a character's motivation can help create an initial mystery in the story (provided their desire or plan is made clear and intense).

We also want to establish any societal value systems that will be opposed. In *Coco*, we must first establish that Miguel's family doesn't allow music in order for Miguel's pursuit of music to be considered "wrong" or "dangerous." In *Ratatouille*, we must first establish that Remy lives in a world dominated by the value system that only the "chosen" can cook. By doing this, we emphasize that Remy's journey to become a chef goes against society's dominant value system and that it'll be an uphill battle. The movie *Up* opens with thematic antagonist Charles Muntz championing the value system of physical adventure, which will later stand in opposition to the value system of adventure as relationships.

The beginning of a story must also establish any character "rules" (whether implicit or explicit) that will be broken. Does a character have a particular moral code that they'll be forced to break? Does a character have a particular way of life that they swear they'll never break out of? Has the character set any limitations for themselves that they'll be forced to break? The opening is the time to establish these character patterns. Corey Mandell offers the example of *Breaking Bad* and notes that before Walter can begin cooking meth, we first need to establish that he's the last person in the world who would cook meth and that Jesse is the last person in the world he would do it with.

More generally, we need to see why a character is particularly ill-suited for, unprepared for, or unlikely to embark on the story's journey. This is the case in both *Breaking Bad* and *Finding Nemo*. Marlin is the last fish we'd expect to head out into the open ocean. On the flip side, a character may be unusually *suited* for a journey. If that's the case, we need to see how. This is the case in *The Da Vinci Code* where Robert Langdon is the world's preeminent professor on religious symbology—the perfect person to unravel a symbolic story world.

> *Takeaway:* We need to understand the status quo in order to appreciate the magnitude of both the disruption (i.e. the impetus) and the character's response to that disruption (such as upending one's boring, stable life in order to cook meth). Before we begin our story, we must take the time to consider which societal and character rules will be broken or used as motivation in our story so that we can first establish them.

Enhance Emotional Impact

We also need to use the beginning of a story to set the groundwork for the emotional impact of the impetus.

If the impetus will negatively impact something of value to the character (i.e. if a problem will be created), we first need to see how much the character values that thing. This typically means we need to see how much a character loves something or how much they fear losing something (or both). In *The Incredibles*, we need to first see how much Mr. Incredible loves being a superhero before the loss of that identity is impactful. In *Finding Nemo*, we need to first see how much Marlin loves Nemo before we can take him away. In *Toy Story*, we need to first see how much Woody loves both Andy and the position of top toy before we can threaten Woody's position. We additionally need to take the time to see how all of the toys fear being replaced. This heightens the emotion when Woody's great fear actually does come true.

If the impetus will force a character to do something they don't want to do, we need to first clearly see why they'd resist doing that thing. In *Hostiles*, for example, we need to see Joseph Blocker's hatred of an old enemy before he's tasked with escorting that enemy back home.

In short, if the impetus is a problem (rather than an opportunity) we've got to establish *why* it's the worst possible thing that could happen to the character. If we're going to take something away, we have to first see how much it matters.

If the impetus will offer the character something of great value or an opportunity to pursue something of great value, we first need to see how much the character longs for this thing. In other words, we need to see how much a character wants something before they're presented with an opportunity to get it. This is where a character's metaphorical "I Want" song can come in. In *The Little Mermaid*, Ariel has a specific desire—to be part of the human world. We need to establish this desire before Ariel sees Prince Eric, a symbol of the human world.

A character may not have a specific desire, however. Instead a character may simply be dissatisfied with their current situation. In this scenario, the character may have a metaphorical "Discontent with the Status Quo" song. This is the case with both Belle from *Beauty and the Beast* and Jack in *The Nightmare Before Christmas*. In this case, the character is unhappy with the current situation but doesn't know what to do about it. They might feel "stuck" or empty in some way. The impetus will present an opportunity that they'll often gladly pursue. Of course, opportunities always come with a catch.

The impetus might also offer a potential solution to a character's ongoing problem. If this is the case, we need to first establish the character's problem and see the depth to which it negatively affects the character. We may also see the character fall to a problem or create their own problem within the opening scenes of the story. Only once a problem has been established can we fully appreciate a character's willingness to jump at a potential solution.

> *Takeaway:* Before we either threaten, take away, or offer something of value to a character, we need to first take the time to establish the depth of the value. This heightens the impact of any problem or opportunity related to the thing of value. We need to define the stakes.

Establish Interest in a Character

It's not enough to simply introduce a main character and expect the audience to care about their journey. We must first give the audience a reason to *want* to follow the main character on their journey. Let's explore a few techniques to establish this connection between audience and character.

Some books recommend that we establish sympathy for the main character by having the character do something likable. To do this, we might have the character help someone, fight for a just cause, give a child their last piece of bread (as in *Aladdin*), or literally save a cat (as Mr. Incredible does in *The Incredibles*), among other techniques. While this is certainly a helpful method for establishing a connection between the audience and the main character, it's not the only option we have available to us (and sometimes we know our main character would never do something this likeable!).

Instead of getting the audience to *like* a character, our goal can be to get the audience to *feel for* a character. This is about establishing empathy rather than sympathy. In his book *Writing for Emotional Impact*, Karl Iglesias lists a number of techniques we can use toward this end. He notes that we're particularly drawn toward those that have humanistic virtues such as compassion, loyalty, responsibility, morality, etc. A character might simply take care of a plant, showing that they have a heart (as is the case in *Léon: the Professional*). We also feel that a character is human if someone else cares for them (which is the case in *As Good As It Gets* when the dog, Verdell, cares for Melvin).

Iglesias also notes that we're drawn to those who have desirable qualities such as charisma, passion, wit, wisdom, cleverness, intelligence, humor, courage, etc. This is one of the techniques used in *Good Will Hunting* when we're shown how witty and intelligent Will is.

And finally, we're drawn to those who have experienced undeserved misfortune. This can include betrayal, deception, abandonment, rejection, a disease, a handicap, or trauma more broadly. In *Finding Nemo*, for instance, we're drawn to Marlin after we see his ghost event where he loses his family during a barracuda attack. This technique is particularly applicable if a character's void grows out of a past trauma or ghost.

Another method to create empathy for a character is to show how their actions are misunderstood. We see the main character try to do something kind, but their gesture or action is misunderstood, and they're blamed or scolded. Because they feel ashamed, they seldom protest. We might imagine a child who tries to make a birthday card for his mom but unwittingly uses the papers for an important business presentation she's giving that afternoon. The mom scolds the boy for ruining her presentation, having no idea that he was making her a gift. This method plays off of our compassion for undeserved misfortune. But it goes a step further because we see that the victim received their misfortune *because* of their attempt to do good.

But even these techniques can be limiting in scope. In practice, all we've got to do in order to establish a connection between the audience and a character is make the character interesting. The audience doesn't need to like them or feel for them (although it often helps if they do)—they just need to find them interesting.

We're intrigued by characters who are unusually knowledgeable, unusually skilled, unusually wise, or unusually talented (as in the case of *The Age of Adaline*). The key word here, of course, is "unusually." The character must noticeably stand out from those around them when it comes to one of these qualities. What's the character's unique skill, talent, or strength that puts them above others when it comes to this thing?

We're intrigued by characters who have an air of mystery about them. This is the case in *Casablanca* when Rick is introduced and also in *Schindler's List* when Oscar Schindler is introduced. We're intrigued by characters who epitomize the dark side. This is the case with Darth Vader, Hannibal Lecter, and Tyler Durdin. There's a strange macabre attraction to the dark.

And finally, one of the fastest ways to get the audience to care about a character is to give that character an intense motivation. When a character wants something, we generally want to stick around to see if they'll get it. This is one of the techniques used in *Psycho* to get us attached to Norman Bates as he cleans up his mother's mess.

These techniques aren't mutually exclusive. We'd be wise to consider how we can use multiple techniques to quickly get the audience connected with our main character.

The most important thing is that the beginning of a story must give the audience a reason to want to follow the main character on their journey. We can make the character sympathetic, empathetic, or just downright interesting, but whatever we do, we must make the audience care.

> *Takeaway:* It's not enough to introduce a main character and expect the audience to care about them. We have to actively and intentionally get the audience to care about the main character. We may establish sympathy, empathy, or merely an interest in what the character will do.

Dramatize the Moral Weakness

As we explored in the beats of a character arc, if our character has a moral weakness, then we must use the beginning of the story to dramatize *how* that weakness is negatively affecting others. There's a careful balance between establishing empathy for a character and also showing how the character's moral flaw is negatively affecting their relationships. In general, we want to take advantage of the Primacy Effect (i.e. first impressions) and give the audience a reason to connect with the character before we dramatize their moral weakness. In other words, establish empathy first.

In *The Incredibles*, the moral weakness is dramatized in a few separate moments. First Mr. Incredible pushes away Buddy (and inadvertently creates the story's nemesis). Soon after, he declares to his future wife, "I work alone." He later reemphasizes this point to Buddy when he says, "Fly home, Buddy. I work alone." At the wedding ceremony later that night, the future Mrs. Incredible again emphasizes Mr. Incredible's moral weakness when she says, "If we're going to make this work, you've got to be *more* than Mr. Incredible."

Not all stories have a character with a moral weakness and thus this won't apply to all beginnings.

Establish the Character's Nature

When we first introduce a character, we want the audience to immediately get the gist of the character. What's this character all about? What's their essential nature? This moment is sometimes known as the "characteristic moment."

We can often establish a character's nature by dramatizing their void. If a character has an obsession, for instance, we can introduce the character in the depths of their obsession. In *Toy Story*, Woody is introduced playing with Andy in his position as the top toy, the thing he loves most. In *The Incredibles*, Mr. Incredible is introduced on the job as a superhero, the thing he loves most. In *Monsters, Inc.*, Sully is introduced preparing for a day at work, the thing he loves most. We might also think of this as dramatizing any skills, talents, or powers that will become particularly important or relevant. *Ratatouille* opens with us seeing Remy's skill with food, *Good Will Hunting* shows us how Will is able to solve math problems no one else can, *Arrival* establishes that Louise is a skilled linguist, and *Frozen* shows us that Elsa has magic powers.

If a character has a ghost, we may want to dramatize the character's ghost. Recall that a character's ghost is something from the past that continues to haunt them to this day. In this way, a character's ghost is a part of their current nature. In *Finding Nemo*, Marlin is introduced in the midst of his ghost event (i.e. the barracuda attack). This technique is also used in *Arrival* to show the death of Louise's daughter. We may alternatively want to show how a character is defined by their coping mechanisms (which arise from their trauma).

If a character has a lie or a strong worldview, we may want to show the character immersed in their lie or worldview. In *Little Miss Sunshine*, Richard is introduced giving a philosophical aria about life consisting of winners and losers. In *Jurassic Park*, Dr. Grant is introduced in the midst of his obsession (dinosaurs) at the same time as he's intimidating a kid (highlighting his lie that he doesn't think kids are worth taking care of). We want to show how the character lives life by their worldview (correctly or incorrectly).

Another pattern in the realm of character introductions is that of the comfort concept. If a character derives their value from some comfort concept (such as a relationship, an idea, an object, a role, etc.), then we may want to show the character desperately embracing their comfort concept.

Because a thing's nature is defined by what it *does*, we generally want to introduce our character *doing* something. Show the character expressing the core of who they are through action.

Takeaway: The introduction of a character should embody their essential nature. This is known as the characteristic moment. One method of quickly defining a character is to open with the character's void. We can show a character living in their obsession, experiencing their ghost, or expressing their worldview or lie. In general, we want to introduce a character in action.

Foreshadow Change

Some character arcs explore the shift from Y to Z rather than from A to Z. Some stories show a character already teetering on the edge. The impetus (i.e. initial disruption) will be the thing that breaks the camel's back and triggers what had been building up for a while.

In these stories in particular, we want to use the beginning to plant the seeds of our character's change. Just as the acorn portends the tree, the roots of our character's change may already exist within them.

Functionally this means we may want to dramatize doubt of some kind within the character about the way they're living their life. The character won't yet know what to do about it, but they may be unhappy or dissatisfied, which can lay the groundwork for change.

This can also mean that we may want to dramatize hesitation, reluctance, or doubt within the character about a value system that they have traditionally embraced wholeheartedly. This can be especially valuable in those stories where a character will descend into madness (like in *Black Swan*) or have a corruption arc. Show us hints that it's *possible* this character could fall victim to an alternate value system. The seeds of change are already there.

> *Takeaway:* If a character is going to undergo change from early on in a story, it can be valuable to use the beginning to show that the character is already on the precipice of change. The story may then explore the implications of that change.

Imply Thematic Patterns

Recall that in order to express a theme, we must *explore* the theme. In a powerful story, that exploration should start immediately by implying the thematic patterns we'll be exploring over the course of the story. In other words, we want to begin exploring the thematic opposition of the story. What value systems will be at play here and how will they conflict?

One concrete way to begin implying thematic patterns in the beginning of a story is to start with a character's worldview. This might be a thematic antagonist or it might be a thematic ally (or even the protagonist themselves). The point is that we want to begin defining a value system by having a character state or act on their worldview or beliefs.

Ratatouille opens with explicit worldviews being expressed by Chef Gusteau and Anton Ego. This sets up an early battle of beliefs and shows us what the thematic opposition will be. Likewise in *Little Miss Sunshine*, we begin with both the thematic protagonist and the thematic antagonist when Richard lays out his worldview about winners and losers while Olive is shown in the depth of her obsession.

In the opening of *Butch Cassidy and The Sundance Kid*, Butch asks a bank guard, "What was the matter with the old bank this town used to have? It was beautiful." The guard replies, "People kept robbing it." Butch says, "That's a small price to pay for beauty." This begins to imply one of the thematic patterns of the story: progress versus tradition.

In *The Incredibles*, Buddy sets up the thematic dilemma when he says, "This is because I don't have powers, isn't it? Well not every superhero has powers, you know. You *can* be super without them."

We can alternatively or additionally include a thematic choice right off the bat. We can force a character into a dilemma between the two value systems that will be at odds over the course of the story. If the protagonist will undergo a character arc (and thus a change in value systems), it may be valuable to show them initially making the "wrong" thematic choice in this dilemma.

Right from the beginning, we want to be mindful of the different ways of life that will eventually clash in the climax. We want to start laying the groundwork for these beliefs early on. We don't need to detail them or explore them in depth, but we do generally want to imply that they exist.

Takeaway: From the beginning of a story, we want to imply the thematic patterns that we'll later explore in depth. This effectively means that we want to provide the outline of the opposing approaches to life that will be present in the story.

Set the Tone and Deliver on the Genre

As we discussed in our exploration of genre, there are certain key elements of a genre that the audience not only expects but demands. By beginning our story with these elements, we're implicitly telling the audience what kind of story this will be. We're setting the tone and atmosphere that they can expect. We're also giving them some candy upfront and promising more in the future.

For example, the movie *Harry Potter* doesn't begin with ordinary *Harry Potter* in an ordinary house. Instead it begins with Dumbledore using magic to extinguish the street lamps. *Breaking Bad* doesn't begin with ordinary Walter White in his worn down life. Instead it begins with Walt driving wildly in a gas mask and his tighty-whities as a pool of chemicals and glass slides up and down an RV. The movie *Speed* takes this same approach by opening with a hostage situation and the opponent's initial attack. It's a perfect way to deliver on the promises of the action genre.

The romance genre should generally begin with romance. The action genre should generally begin with action (and perhaps the dramatic opponent's first attack). The science fiction genre should generally begin with science and technology. The fantasy genre should generally begin with fantasy and an unfamiliar world.

If we need to start the beginning of our story with action and adventure, we might consider opening with a ghost event, the antagonist executing on their plan, or a flash-forward to the story's eventual climax.

This isn't a requirement, of course, but this technique helps us promise the audience that if they just stick with us through the setup, they'll be rewarded with the treasures of the genre. The worst thing we can do is make an implicit promise about the tone of a story and then fail to keep that tone (such as a comedy that opens with a serious, dramatic, and tragic death).

> *Takeaway:* We can open a story by delivering on the key elements of the story's genre. This will set the tone and make promises about what the audience can expect in the rest of the story if they stick with us through the setup.

The Hook

The final and perhaps most important task of a story's beginning is to hook the audience. We've got to grab their attention and skillfully hold on to it. Essentially we need to use our dramatic tools to generate narrative drive.

The hook is necessarily the first scene of the story. Ideally we want to be economical with our first scene and attempt to accomplish multiple things. Not only do we want to capture the audience's attention, but we also want to introduce the nature of important characters, establish empathy, prepare for the impetus, imply the thematic patterns, etc. Our goal should be to quickly and efficiently lay the groundwork we'll need (i.e. the essential context) in order to start the story as soon as possible.

The basic idea of a hook is that we need to raise a question to which the audience will want to know the answer. This might be a dramatic question, a thematic question, or simply a mystery. A key point to remember here is that once we've used this hook to capture the audience's attention, we need to continue to use our dramatic tools to keep the audience engaged. Every scene of our story must be compelling—not just the first.

Dramatic Question Hook

Perhaps the fastest way to capture the audience's attention is to set up a few dramatic elements: a character who wants something, someone or something that opposes the character's desire, something at stake in the character's pursuit, and urgency for the character to accomplish their goal. We can open the scene with the character already pursuing their desire or we might consider opening with a disruption that incites the desire. This quickly sets up a dramatic question about whether the protagonist will get the thing they want. When this technique is combined with our techniques to establish empathy for a character, we've got a good chance at making the audience want to follow our character on a journey. This approach is a more prescriptive version of the general advice to "open with conflict."

We may also consider using a dramatic tool called "unstated desire" (which we'll explore in more detail later). We simply show a character in the process of enacting a plan and struggling to attain something. The exact thing for which the character is struggling isn't made clear. The added benefit of this approach is that in addition to the dramatic question of *whether* the character will get what they want, we additionally raise a question around *what* the character wants.

We'll later explore a technique called "the sequence approach" where we can view a story's structure as a series of dramatic questions. This dramatic question hook is essentially the establishment of the story's first sequence. The movies *Speed*, *The Incredibles*, and *Star Trek (2009)* all start with a dramatic question sequence. It's worth noting that the protagonist of the dramatic sequence doesn't necessarily need to be the protagonist of the global story (as in the case of *Star Trek*).

We might consider ending the initial dramatic sequence with a disruption, which will set us up for the next sequence and propel the audience forward. In *Speed*, the aftermath of the initial elevator hostage situation is followed by a bus explosion, which propels us into the main dramatic tension (and dramatic question) of the story.

If our story has a physical antagonist, we may consider opening the story in the middle of the antagonist carrying out their plan. This technique is used in *The Goonies* with a prison break and in *Star Wars* with Darth Vader searching for the stolen Death Star plans. If our antagonist is immoral, this can make for a particularly interesting opening scene because immoral strategies and techniques tend to be morbidly fascinating. This opening is particularly effective if our story's genre is action. We might consider this technique to be that of opening the story with the antagonist's void (which often grows out of an obsession and/or a strong worldview or lie).

> *Takeaway:* Dramatic interest in the beginning of a story can be established by raising a dramatic question. We can also use the technique of "unstated desire" to show a character enacting a plan. This dramatic question hook raises a question about whether the protagonist will get what they want.

Thematic Question Hook

Another option for a hook is to open with an opposition of value systems. In other words, we want to establish the opposition of two ways of life—two worldviews. There will be an implicit question about which is right and which will win in the end. This is one technique used in the opening of *Ratatouille* where we hear an argument from the thematic antagonist, Anton Ego, and an argument from a thematic ally, Chef Gusteau.

Sometimes the thematic opposition isn't as explicit, of course. *Little Miss Sunshine* opens with the thematic antagonist, Richard, giving his philosophical aria (i.e. thematic argument) about winners and losers as we also see his thematic opponent, Olive, embracing her obsession of beauty pageants.

We can also establish the thematic opposition by pushing a character into a dilemma. This is a combination of drama and theme where the character's choice in the dilemma will show us their position in the thematic opposition. We can set up a dilemma by giving a character two desires that are both opposed (i.e. internal conflict). The character must then make a decision.

Mystery Hook

Finally we can raise a question in the hook by establishing a mystery. We previously explored in our dramatic tools how we might create a mystery. Since this is the very beginning of the story and the audience doesn't yet have any context, we often want to start with a passive mystery (i.e. one driven by curiosity). The most common techniques to establish a passive mystery are to start in medias res ("in the middle of things") without context; show something unusual, unexpected, or contradictory; show something obscured, veiled, or clouded; or show explicitly that important information is missing (perhaps by showing someone seeking information to get what they want or by a character asking an explicit question).

The technique of opening in medias res is used often in openings. We usually want to start in the middle of a character either carrying out their plan or in the midst of a disruption to their life. We see this in the opening of Hitchcock's *Notorious* with a disruption where Alicia Huberman's father is being sentenced in court. We also see this in the first *Harry Potter* movie where Dumbledore is in the middle of carrying out his plan to hide *Harry Potter*.

We can also start with a promise. Recall that we can create a promise by having a character project into the future by attempting to predict or alter the future. This will create a "dangling cause" and the audience will generally want to wait around to see the eventual effect of the cause. For instance, a character might give a prediction, omen, or fortune. A character might also express a wish, hope, demand, request, or threat. We'll generally want to stick around to see how the wish, hope, demand, request, threat, prediction, omen, or fortune pans out.

Finally we may also start with the technique of convergence in the form of a promised collision or a ticking clock or deadline of some kind. We see this opening in *American Beauty* where the narrator tells us, "In less than a year, I will be dead." This technique raises a question of either when the convergence will occur or what will happen on the road to the moment of convergence.

Takeaway: We can hook the audience by establishing a mystery. We may start in medias res, with clouded information, with a promise, with the promise of convergence, or with a ticking clock.

Other Dramatic Tools

Since the hook is all about generating enough interest to make the audience want to know what happens next, we're free to use any of our dramatic tools. Some techniques will create a more engaging opening scene than others, but it can be helpful to consider our full toolbox when it comes to the hook. We may want to consider a hook that creates narrative drive via dramatic irony, for instance. Perhaps the audience knows about some trouble that a character is about to get into but the character doesn't. We can use suspense, surprise, misunderstandings, secrets, promises, or convergence. We'll later explore other dramatic tools that we might use, including irony, subtext, the Kuleshov Effect, subverting expectations, a stream of the unexpected, a false rehearsal, dramatic intrigue, physical gags, disruptions, etc.

We might also consider the technique of opening with (or hinting at) a sliver of a story's climax. This is done in the pilot episode of *Breaking Bad* where Walt is driving madly in his meth lab RV. We tantalize the audience with a stream of unexpected images combined with intense character desire (which often peaks around the climax). We might then cut to the chronological beginning of the story to begin the slow build to the climax. With this opening, we're promising the audience that the ride will be worth it if they stick with us.

22

THE BEATS OF THE FIRST DISRUPTION
THE IMPETUS

With the beginning of our story out of the way, we've established the essential context for the audience to understand what's to follow. Now we're ready to start the story. This is where we throw a rock into the pond of our story. This is the moment where we disrupt our character's life.

We previously crafted a disruption that will be tailor-made to attack our character's void. It should be the start of something truly life-altering (even if it's initially subtle, as in the case of *The Truman Show* where Truman slowly begins to question the authenticity of his reality). It thrusts the character into a new life experience, accompanied by a metaphorical (and sometimes literal) new world. So what happens after this initial disruption to the character's life?

Responding to the Initial Disruption

To know what happens next, we need only refer back to our disruption cycle. After a disruption, a character orients themselves to their new reality and then debates their options through emotion and analysis. In other words, the period following the initial disruption is a debate. What should they do now? The character then makes a decision about how to respond to their new reality. The response to the initial disruption is character-specific and disruption-specific. Let's consider a few possibilities.

If the initial disruption is a problem, the character will first grapple with their destabilized reality and then shortly thereafter likely jump into action to try to fix it and return their life to equilibrium. Through the process of trying to solve their problem, the character might learn what they truly need to do in order to get their life back to normal. The true solution is often more complicated than initially anticipated.

If the initial disruption is an opportunity that offers a solution to an existing problem, the character will likely jump at the opportunity as a means to solve their problem. This is assuming that the character believes they see a clear path to solve the problem or pursue the opportunity.

If the initial disruption is an opportunity that would require a character to upset their equilibrium, they may hesitate for a time. They're being called outside of their comfort zone and it's often a daunting prospect. When this is the case, we must shake the character out of their hesitation by removing their excuses (usually by raising the stakes). In other words, we raise the consequences of *not* accepting the opportunity, thereby compelling action. We might also force a character into action by increasing the benefit a character would get by accepting the opportunity.

There are times when the initial disruption doesn't present a clear path to the character as far as what to do next. A character might encounter an object of desire without a way to attain it or a problem may present itself with no solution. If a character sees no clear path toward solving their problem or pursuing their opportunity, they'll have no choice but to search for more information or take time to devise a plan.

We find this in *The Little Mermaid*, *The Nightmare Before Christmas*, and *Breaking Bad*. In these instances, we must eventually present the character with a clear path (often at the dramatic question moment). The character may see a potential solution to their problem (as in *Breaking Bad* when Walt sees the money confiscated from a drug bust). The character may have a "eureka" moment (as in *The Nightmare Before Christmas* when Jack realizes how the opportunity of Christmas Town can be seized). The character may be presented with a deal or an assignment (as in *The Little Mermaid* when Ursula presents Ariel with a deal). In any case, we must eventually present the character with a path to either solve their problem or pursue their opportunity.

If a disruption is an inner calling or a discovery that shakes a character's identity or reality, the character might embark on a mission to search and investigate. We see this in Disney's *Hercules* when he sets out to find out more about where he came from. We also see this in *Elf*.

> *Takeaway:* When all is said and done, a character will generally respond to the initial disruption by addressing or avoiding their problems, pursuing their opportunities, and investigating their discoveries.

The Dramatic Question Moment

A story's initial disruption is just the beginning. It'll inevitably lead to additional disruptions and a chain of cause and effect. And the first stop on that chain of cause and effect is the moment where the character's central desire is solidified. We call this moment the "dramatic question moment" because it gives rise to the dramatic question of whether the character will succeed or fail in the pursuit of their goal. It typically occurs around the 25% mark of a story and usually denotes the end of act one.

We previously discussed how to craft a dramatic question moment that organically arises from the story's initial disruption. Here are a few examples: The journey to investigate or solve the character's problem may lead to a deeper understanding of the problem and a more concrete plan to solve it. We find this in *Shrek* when he must rescue the princess and defeat the dragon in order to fulfill a deal offered by Lord Farquaad. An attempt to solve the problem may lead to a larger problem. We see this in *Toy Story* when Woody tries to get rid of Buzz but accidentally causes his own exile. The journey to pursue the opportunity may lead to a bigger problem which must be solved or to a mission that must be completed in order to reap the rewards of the opportunity. We see this in *The Little Mermaid* where Ariel must complete a mission in order to win the object of her desire, Prince Eric. The journey to investigate the discovery may lead to more opportunities and problems. We see this in Disney's *Hercules*.

We've also seen examples where the initial disruption *is* the dramatic question moment. This is the case in *Finding Nemo* where Nemo's kidnapping incites the dramatic question, "Will Marlin find and rescue Nemo?"

Exploring the New World

Recall that the initial disruption is the moment that introduces the character to a new metaphorical (and sometimes literal) new world. After the character enters this new world, they generally do what any newcomer would do: take a look around.

Upon entrance to the new world, the character will explore their unfamiliar surroundings. It's here that we introduce the character to the rules of the world and to some of its inhabitants. This is often where the protagonist meets the influence character. In *Harry Potter*, this piece of the story is where Harry is first introduced to the wizarding world via Diagon Alley. He meets a cast of characters, learns some of the rules of the wizarding world, hears the lore of the world, and learns his place in the new world.

We can optionally have a character who guides the character through their new world and introduces them to the "rules of the road." We find this in *Star Wars* with Obi-Wan and in *Harry Potter* with Hagrid. This is the "mentor" character. This mentor is often a thematic ally or someone who embodies the "correct" side of the thematic opposition. We might also have a thematic antagonist fill this role of introducing the character to their new world. The thematic antagonist could introduce the rules of the world from their thematically biased perspective and also deliver their antagonist aria about the best way to live life (saying, "This is the way the world works, kid."). This pattern of having a mentor or antagonist introduce the character to their new world is optional, however. It's perhaps most valuable when the story world has complexity that requires explaining before proceeding. Some characters will be forced to make sense of their new world on their own (such as in *Toy Story* and *Finding Nemo*).

Recall that the first half of a story is responsible for making promises and the second half of a story is responsible for paying them off. It's in this early stage of the story that we want to begin preparing for the self-revelation and climax by introducing any elements that will later play a significant role. This could be a character, a skill, a story world rule, a piece of technology, a phrase, a symbol, a strength, a weakness, a line of dialogue, etc. The key is that we set it up here (i.e. introduce it) so that we can pay it off in the self-revelation or climax (i.e. reveal its significance). By setting up important elements here (shortly after the 10% mark), we're "mirroring around the midpoint" so that the elements will reappear in their symmetrical position at around the 90% mark (i.e. the climax). In *Harry Potter*, it's around the 10% mark that we're introduced to Professor Quirrell who plays an important role in the story's climax.

Recall also the basic story structure of question and answer. The first half asks the questions and the second half answers them. This section of the story is where we ask our questions—explicitly or implicitly. This is where we raise mysteries. This is where the unknown, unusual, and contradictory shows its face to be explored and explained at a later time.

Takeaway: After the central character arrives in their new world, they'll need to learn the new rules of the world and meet its inhabitants. Sometimes the character must learn these rules on their own via discoveries and sometimes these rules are presented to the character via a mentor character. It's at this stage in the story when we want to introduce the elements that will become important in the self-revelation moment and the climax.

23

THE BEATS OF THE MIDDLE

There's a lot of story space in between the dramatic question moment and the crisis. So what happens in all that space? Now that we've established the story's main dramatic tension via the character's central desire, it's time for the character to go about trying to accomplish that desire.

Many stories are goal-based. They're problem-solving exercises. The problem a character faces typically requires decisions in the realm of value systems and morality, which is where theme comes in. *How* a character goes about solving their goal is a story's thematic argument. The strategies and tactics used in the pursuit of a goal show us the character's morality. The character simultaneously learns, decays, and grows in response to the new life experience that has been thrust upon them at the impetus. The middle of the story is where we explore a character's plan, their strategies, their decisions, their sacrifices, their morality, and most importantly their approach to a new life experience (whether correct or incorrect).

Perhaps the largest challenge of the middle of a story is giving it structure. We'll explore a couple of techniques to do this. In essence, we'll want to send a character on a journey of desire and then force them to improvise as they uncover the greater truth about their predicament. We do this by disrupting the character's plan and their understanding of their journey. As the story progresses, we'll create increasingly consequential disruptions.

While writing the middle of our story, we must have the courage to let the protagonist attain their goal if it's the most believable action. We shouldn't artificially stretch out the story with episodic complications that are merely meant to force the journey to last until the climax. If a character can solve their problem quickly, we must let them. We must have the confidence to believe that there will be another complication that arises from their victory. In *Avatar*, for instance, Jake Sully accomplishes his goal of infiltrating the Na'vi at the midpoint of the story. It's *because* of his victory that the humans are able to begin their main attack on the Na'vi, which gives rise to Jake Sully's next goal of protecting the Na'vi.

> *Takeaway:* Most stories are goal-based. The middle of a story is where we send the character on the journey to solve their problem. We introduce disruptions and force them to improvise as the true nature of the problem becomes clear.

From Naïveté to Understanding

When a character sets out on their journey, they don't know what they don't know. This makes the character's plan necessarily naïve. They don't know what sort of disruptions, revelations, and plot twists await them on their journey. They don't know what the opponent has planned. They don't know what strange story world rules await them. The journey is often a process of learning.

In almost every case, the character thinks their problem is relatively simple. Woody thinks that if he can just get rid of Buzz, everything will go back to normal. In *Monsters, Inc.*, Sully thinks that he'll just get Boo's door and send her back to the human world. In *Groundhog Day*, Bill Murray's character thinks he'll just commit suicide and break the time loop. In *Avatar*, Jake thinks he'll just infiltrate the Na'vi and then he'll get the use of his legs back. In *The*

Wizard of Oz, Dorothy thinks she'll be able to get back home if she just gets to the Wizard. "Easy," the character thinks. "I'll just do this and everything will be good." This is the character's naïve plan.

The naïve plan is important because we need to show the audience (and the character) that the "easy" way out won't work. If we don't show the character trying to take the easy route, the audience will likely grow frustrated and wonder, "Why didn't they just take the shortcut?"

> *Takeaway:* A character's initial plan is typically to take the "shortcut" to solving their problem. This easy route almost never works, of course.

The Midpoint

There's a particular moment in a story that often begins to illuminate the depth and scope of the character's problem. This moment is the midpoint. It's the moment where Woody's goal expands from not just finding Andy but escaping Sid. In *Avatar*, the goal shifts from infiltrating the Na'vi to wanting to save them. In *Titanic*, Jack and Rose go from wanting to win each other's love to wanting to survive. Of course, there doesn't necessarily need to be a categorical expansion or shift of the protagonist's goal at the midpoint, but there's almost always the start of a deeper understanding about what the character's up against.

The truth about the character's problem begins to show itself and the character begins the shift from naïveté to understanding. In *The Wizard of Oz*, Dorothy eventually learns she'll need to bring the Wizard the broomstick of the Wicked Witch of the West. The true depth of the problem likely won't all come out at once, but the midpoint is typically where the important revelations start.

We can also often think of the midpoint as the moment where the antagonist asserts their power and begins a barrage of attacks on the protagonist. This middle section of the story is where we build the opponent of the story. From the midpoint to the crisis moment, we often (though not always) find an escalating series of unfortunate events as the antagonist's full plan and power begins to come into perspective. We can also simply think of the midpoint as the start of a section of the story where the problems begin to stack at an increasing rate.

The midpoint may actually consist of two distinct pieces: the appearance of a major win and the actuality of a major loss. The midpoint moment often contains the mirror image of the crisis moment (i.e. the end of act two) in its polarity. In other words, if the end of act two will be a major loss for the protagonist, then the midpoint may initially appear to be a major win or completion of the protagonist's primary goal. The thing that the character has wanted since the dramatic question moment may be just within the character's grasp. Shortly after this, however, we rip it away and reveal that the character won't be able to get it that easily. The problem is much worse than they thought.

In *Toy Story*, for instance, Woody and Buzz have finally made it to Pizza Planet. Woody's on the verge of getting back to Andy. It looks like the end may be in sight and Woody may finally get back home. At the exact moment that Woody's about to reunite with Andy, Buzz goes wandering off to find a spaceship. Moments later, Sid captures both Woody and Buzz. They're now further from Andy than they have ever been. Woody's naïve plan looked like it was going to work. But it's quickly reversed and crushed.

The midpoint also typically consists of a moment where the protagonist takes some action that burns their bridges. The character fully commits to their journey in a way that prevents them from returning to the way things used to be (whether metaphorically or literally). In *The Godfather*, Michael Corleone shoots McCluskey and Sollozzo, solidifying his commitment to the family business. In *Avatar*, Jake Sully turns against the humans and begins attacking them, solidifying his commitment to the Na'vi.

Takeaway: The midpoint moment is a disruption that begins to illuminate the depth and scope of the character's true problem. The midpoint is also typically where the antagonist begins to implement their central plan in earnest. The central character may take some action that burns their bridges back to the old world.

The Advanced Plan

Newly committed (whether out of decision or necessity) and with a new understanding of the depth of their problem, the character must reassess their plan and determine whether it's still the best approach given the disruption of the midpoint. This is where the character begins to form their "advanced plan." The character is less likely to make the same mistake of underestimating the problem before them. Things are now serious and typically require a categorically new approach. This is where the pace of moral decay may increase.

Even though the character has now crafted a more informed plan, that won't prevent it from requiring change. The second half of the story will continue to throw disruptions at the character and require improvisation. And although the character may have a better under-standing of their problem, they typically don't yet have a better understanding of how to *solve* that problem in a thematically correct way. In other words, the character's new plan will still contain the faults inherent in the character's moral flaw. The character won't fully embrace the thematically correct way to approach their problem until they've had a self-revelation about how they're the root cause of their problems.

Plotting From Character and the Void

If we've defined our story elements correctly (especially the charac-ter's desire, plan, opposition, and urgency), plotting the middle of a story becomes an exercise in problem-solving in the face of disrup-tions. The character has a desire so they devise a plan. As they enact their plan, something unexpected happens that requires them to orient themselves, learn about their new situation, make a decision, and take action toward a new or revised plan. The story unfurls organically as a character enacts a plan and is forced to improvise. To "plot from character" is to follow a character's plan.

One of the central questions of plotting from character becomes: What disruptions do we throw at the character? The goal in creating disruptions isn't just to force a character to improvise (although it is that). It's also to force a character (or community) to *change*. How do we compel change? We force a character to confront that which is different than them (and specifically we force them to confront different approaches to life). We force them to confront the fears they have about dropping their façade, giving up their moral flaw, and living life differently. We try to show them over and over that when they make decisions that prioritize their moral flaw, bad things happen. We show them over and over that their moral flaw causes problems not just for others but for themselves.

This is where the importance of fully understanding a character's void comes in. If we can understand the character's fears, their insecurities, and what they value most, we can create disruptions that will force a character to change. By forcing a character to confront their void through their deepest fears and insecurities, we force them to consider the prospect that they're the source of their problems.

So where do these disruptions come from? Some disruptions are inherent in the character's problem. As the character embarks on their journey to rescue the princess, they discover a moat around the castle. Once inside the castle, the character discovers a dragon. These obstacles are inherent in the problem itself and are generally thematically weak because they tend not to be personalized to the character. They typically don't strike at a character's void.

A more potent source of disruptions comes from dramatic opposition. Recall that dramatic opposition arises when the protagonist and antagonist (i.e. dramatic opponent) are pursuing control of the same underlying thing (such as the soul of Gotham in *The Dark Knight* or the freedom of the criminal in any crime story). Control is typically exclusive. This means that often the opponent will realize (or understand intuitively) that in order to increase the chance of accomplishing their goal, they should act to disrupt the protagonist's plan. What this effectively means is that the criminal, for instance, will try to sabotage the police officer's plan and vice versa. Both protagonist and antagonist actively work against each other to foil each other's plan. The enterprising opponent will take advantage of that which the protagonist fears most (e.g. their ghost, their lie being revealed as false, their obsession being threatened, their façade being threatened, etc.). Of course, the antagonist may first need to discover what the protagonist fears most.

Not every story has an external antagonist who wants control of the same thing as the protagonist, of course. *Finding Nemo* has no traditional antagonist character. There are characters who serve as episodic antagonists but no single character who tries to work against Marlin for custody of Nemo. We might also see a story where the ostensible opponent doesn't ever actively work against the protagonist. In *Toy Story*, for instance, Woody sees Buzz as a dramatic opponent in the pursuit of Andy's love, but Buzz doesn't ever actively try to win Andy or try to prevent Woody from being the top toy.

So how do we create effective disruptions that strike at a character's void when there's no antagonist? We craft personalized situations for the protagonist that are designed to spark reactions of hope or fear. We might, for instance, craft a situation that reminds a character of the thing they fear most. We see this in *The Office* when Ed Truck dies and Michael must confront an imaginary reality where no one cares that the boss dies. He's concerned that one day his death may be brushed aside. This is an example of crafting a situation around a clone character where the protagonist must confront or consider a possible path that they fear. This is a large part of the premise of *A Christmas Carol*—crafting a series of situations that force Scrooge to confront his moral weakness and its negative consequences throughout his life. We might also craft a situation that makes a character insecure and thus forces them to confront their insecurity, for instance. We can also craft a situation designed to offer a character hope (which will almost inevitably be followed by the snatching of that hope).

We want to force the character to confront that which they hate or fear. If a character fundamentally hates or fears women (i.e. if the character is a misogynist), then we may force the character to become a woman in order to get what they want. This is the core premise of the movie *Tootsie*. The character must decide: *Are you willing to do the thing you hate or surround yourself with the thing you fear in order to get the thing you want?* In *Finding Nemo*, Marlin must continually confront his fear of the open ocean in order to get to his son.

Another potent situation is one in which a character must make a thematic choice. This situation should ideally be a thematic dilemma where the character must choose between the two value systems at the heart of the story's thematic opposition. In other words, the situation should be a small scale version of The Great Decision. Hitchcock's *Notorious*, for example, is a series of situations where Alicia Huberman and agent Devlin are forced to decide between their love for each other and their duty to fulfill their responsibilities.

We might also present a moral dilemma (i.e. a thematic choice) in which a character can choose to either use their flaw to address the situation or approach the situation from a place of moral strength. We find this type of situation in *Casablanca* where Rick is confronted by a woman who's considering sleeping with Captain Renault in exchange for tickets out of Casablanca for herself and her husband. This is a moral dilemma for the woman, but it's also a moral dilemma for Rick who must decide whether he's going to persist in refusing to stick his neck out (his moral flaw) or whether he'll help the couple in some way. He decides to help the woman's husband win some money at the gambling table.

One of the symptoms of a villain is that they tend to force others into moral dilemmas. Sometimes it's for fun and sometimes it's to prove or emphasize their worldview. This method of forcing a character to confront moral dilemmas is at the heart of The Joker's plan in *The Dark Knight*. The Joker crafts a series of escalating moral dilemmas for Batman in an attempt to prove that Gotham isn't a shining beacon of morality. The Joker forces Batman to decide whether the means are worth the ends.

Disruptions also arise from discoveries. As a character seeks to investigate and uncover the truth along their journey, they may not like what they find. If a character believes that reason always wins over faith, perhaps they make a series of discoveries that can't be explained by reason. If a character believes that duty is more important than love, perhaps they make a series of discoveries where those who chose duty over love live an ultimately empty life in the end.

We can also create disruptions that shake what a character believes to be true. Perhaps those they believed to be moral turn out to be immoral. Or those they believed to be immoral turn out to be ultimately moral. We can have a character discover that their worst fears are actually true. Revealing the secrets a character would be most afraid to hear can go a long way in prompting character change (provided the revealed information has some relation to the character's worldview, ghost, obsession, or façade).

We spent time crafting our character's engine. We know what drives them. We know the emptiness within them. We know what they fear. We know what they most hope for. We know what makes them insecure. We know their vulnerabilities. We know what they regret. Now we need to bring those fears, insecurities, and vulnerabilities to life. Make the character's worst nightmares come true.

> *Takeaway:* The middle of a story is all about testing the character's commitment to their moral flaw. To do this, we want to write toward the character's deepest fears. We want to force them into difficult moral dilemmas where they must decide between two approaches to life.

Plotting From Opponent

Perhaps the most straightforward method of plotting a story is to view the events of the story from the protagonist's perspective. We define what the protagonist wants, what they'll do to get it, and who might stand in their way. We then let them enact their plan to get what they want.

But we know we can't make the protagonist's journey too easy. We know that the middle of a story must throw new disruptions at the protagonist as they work toward their goal. We also know that we don't want to just create random disruptions that are rooted in coincidence. We need the disruptions to flow organically from the story's chain of cause and effect. The solution is to change our perspective from the protagonist to the antagonist.

The key to a more intricate plot that's rooted in cause and effect is to switch back and forth between protagonist and antagonist. Because we've crafted an antagonist whose goal is diametrically opposed to the protagonist's goal, we know that when the antagonist gets closer to what they want, the protagonist gets further from what they want—and vice versa. The benefit of now plotting from the antagonist's perspective is that any genius plan that the antagonist comes up with will necessarily create a problem for the protagonist— and vice versa. The middle of a story becomes a dueling battle between two characters who are both going after their respective goals.

The antagonist comes up with a plan and enacts it. This creates a disruption in the protagonist's plan. The protagonist must craft a new plan, which they then enact. The antagonist is foiled. The two thrust and parry, constantly improvising and crafting new plans.

In some stories, of course, the antagonist's plan anticipates the protagonist's plan from the beginning. The antagonist's plan is deep, organized, and doesn't require any improvisation. As the antagonist enacts their plan, the protagonist learns that they've been outwitted every step of the way—until they start to get creative and do something the antagonist didn't anticipate.

This back and forth between protagonist and antagonist will eventually lead to a final battle: the climax of the story.

Takeaway: Organically plotting the middle of a story is often about switching perspectives between the protagonist and antagonist as each duel for ultimate control.

Avoiding an Episodic Middle

One of the keys to writing the middle of a story is to avoid a plot that becomes episodic or repetitious. In general, an episodic plot arises when the protagonist is tasked with performing the same basic action over and over.

For example, if a character has to fight an ogre, then fight a swamp monster, then fight a dragon, etc., then we're hitting the same basic action and consequently the same beat. We tend to see this when a character is sent on a laundry list of tasks that they must complete before they can get to the thing that they actually need to accomplish. In order to defeat the villain, for example, they might need to first defeat his three henchmen or find three pieces of an item, etc.

An episodic plot commits John Truby's cardinal sin of plotting—the repetition of the same beat. How do we avoid this? One of the key techniques is to ensure that the journey is one of discovery, not only one of action. We also generally want to avoid a story where a character's plan is known from the beginning and is never forced to change (which is what we tend to see in laundry list plots). As a character sets out on their journey, the opponent's plan should be throwing new disruptions at the protagonist, forcing improvisation.

If we know the character's plan from the beginning and there's never a change in that plan, then the story is driven by the boring question of, "Will the protagonist be able to do the thing that we know they're going to be able to do because otherwise there'd be no story?" Instead the protagonist should be learning new things about the nature of the opponent's plan and potentially their identity. Lean into revelations.

As a general rule, we don't want the protagonist to understand the true nature of their problem from the beginning. If they do, let them confront it head on from the beginning (and be disappointed when they're faced with failure or the complications of success).

And finally, we must have the courage to let dramatic questions be answered. Instead of sending the protagonist on errands, we must let them directly confront the villain the moment it's possible. We must avoid delaying confrontation in order to extend the story's runtime.

> *Takeaway:* An episodic plot is one in which a character must repeatedly perform the same basic action. To avoid an episodic plot, our story should be driven by discoveries and disruptions. As a general principle, the character's plan should be forced to change.

The Sequence Approach

We've discussed how we can follow a character in the pursuit of their goal and then create disruptions that make their worst fears come true. Let's take that principle and implement it in a way that provides a bit more structure to the middle of the story.

In his book *The Sequence Approach*, Paul Gulino details a helpful technique for sectioning a story into a series of dramatic sequences. Each sequence consists of a protagonist with a desire, giving rise to a dramatic question. The sequence, just like any other dramatic unit, ends with an impactful disruption that turns the story in a new direction. Using this sequence structure can help ensure that we maintain dramatic interest via dramatic tension and disruptions.

We can think of a sequence as a section of the story in which a character is enacting their plan. The character almost invariably believes that the plan will work this time. Regardless of whether the plan does actually succeed or not, the end of the sequence typically ends with a disruption that requires the formulation of a new plan to address the disruption.

When it comes to whether the protagonist will succeed in their goal, the sequence might answer with "no, and...", "no, but..." or "yes, but..." We can think of a "no, and..." as saying, "No, you lose, and here's an additional problem." A "no, but..." says, "No, you lose, but here's a bit of hope." A "yes, but..." says, "Yes, you win, but there's a catch."

We can take the traditional three-act story structure and break it up into eight distinct sequences. Let's take a brief look at "the sequence approach" and how it can provide us a new, more structured perspective of the three-act structure. Because Gulino already wrote the book on this subject, we won't spend too much time detailing the sequences.

First of all, the traditional act one gets two sequences, the traditional act two gets four sequences, and the traditional act three gets two sequences. Notice how again we can split act two into two halves at the midpoint, each half getting two sequences.

The first sequence contains our story's hook. While this sequence may contain a character trying to solve or address an existing problem, the sequence itself isn't necessarily driven by a dramatic question. The reason for this is because it's responsible for conveying the story's essential context and it's the only sequence before the impetus. In other words, it's the only sequence that exists before the story's main chain of cause and effect. The first sequence ends, of course, with the impetus and sends the story on its central trajectory.

The second sequence finds the protagonist responding to the impetus in some way. We've previous discussed a number of possibilities for how a character may respond to the story's initial disruption. The dramatic question of this second sequence typically revolves around whether the character's initial attempts at coming to terms with their new reality will be successful. This sequence often ends with the dramatic question moment, which gives rise to the protagonist's primary goal and the global story's main tension about whether the protagonist will get what they want. This brings us to the end of act one in the traditional three-act structure.

The third sequence consists of the protagonist enacting their naïve plan in the pursuit of their central desire. They may have some success in solving an immediate problem, but any success will almost always lead to a bigger problem. This sequence ends with a disruption known as "pinch point one." This pinch point deepens the character's predicament.

The fourth sequence finds the protagonist beginning to fall into desperation as their naïve plan isn't panning out. They typically persist in this plan, however. This sequence ends in the midpoint of the story. Recall that the midpoint of the story may show a moment when the character's naïve plan appears to work but is then quickly met with a reversal of fortune that results in disaster. The true depth of the character's problem begins to come to light.

The fifth sequence finds the protagonist responding to the disruption of the midpoint. Sometimes this results in a categorically new goal (such as in *Avatar* or *Titanic*) and other times it simply results in the need for a new plan for the character's existing problem. Regardless the character often crafts a new plan to solve their problem and thus a dramatic question is born for the sequence. This sequence may also contain a subplot. This sequence ends in a disruption known as "pinch point two" where the protagonist's goal for the sequence either succeeds or fails (and it often fails).

The sixth sequence is the last in act two of the three-act structure. The protagonist spends this sequence working with all their might toward trying to resolve their main goal that was raised at the dramatic question moment. This sequence ends with the crisis moment and typically results in a major loss or a hollow victory, bringing the central dramatic question to an end.

The seventh sequence typically finds the character grappling with the crisis that occurred at the end of sequence six. As with any major disruption, the character may spend some time in the debate stage of the disruption cycle. This post-crisis debate is sometimes known as the "Dark Night of the Soul" moment. This sequence usually contains the character's self-revelation, which may result in a redoubling of efforts and an active pursuit of the character's need over their want. There may be an unveiling of the depth of the antagonist's plan or powers. This sequence ends with the story's external climax and The Great Decision Moment where the character must make a choice and pick a side in the story's thematic dilemma.

The eighth and final sequence contains the story's resolution. We typically see the character living in harmony with their final value system. We also often see the character sharing their success with their loved ones.

There's no rule that a story must consist of eight sequences, of course. Some writers write with twelve sequences, for instance. Generally the more sequences we have, the more significant disruptions we have and thus the faster the pace of the story.

As with all of our tools and patterns, not all stories follow this sequence structure. This can, however, provide a helpful guide in giving a more concrete structure to our stories.

> *Takeaway:* The sequence approach breaks a story into eight sequences. Each sequence raises a dramatic question that will be asked and answered over the course of the sequence. This method provides a more detailed structure to the middle of a story than the traditional three-act structure.

Sectioning

The sequence approach is primarily about grouping scenes based on a dramatic question. We give a character a strong desire over a series of scenes and it creates a sequence. We can, however, create sections in the middle of our story that aren't grouped by a dramatic question.

Scenes can be grouped to create a "section." We might consider grouping scenes around time, space, or ritual. To group scenes by time, we might show a series of scenes that take place over a single day, a single night, or across seasons, for instance. To group by space, we might show a series of scenes that all take place in the same location where the setting contains some thematic significance. To group by ritual, we might show a series of scenes that all take place at one or more rituals such as a wedding, a funeral, a family gathering, a holiday, etc.

This method can help us provide an additional bit of structure to our scenes.

24

THE BEATS OF THE CLIMAX AND RESOLUTION

The climax of a story is the pinnacle of both drama and theme. It's where drama and theme become one in the final battle. It's by making the correct thematic choice that a character either wins or loses their dramatic goal. Let's consider the beats of the climax.

The climax is about testing a character's commitment to a value system. Recall that the way for a character to demonstrate their commitment is to make a decision that chooses one value system over an opposing value system in a Great Decision Moment. Typically this decision is between what the character originally wanted and what the character needs in order to live a better life. We'll need to set up this moment.

The character (or community) has likely already had their self-revelation about the "right" way to live. This revelation typically causes the character to attempt to make amends for their moral decay by pursuing that which they need over that which they want. This pursuit then leads the character to a showdown with the central dramatic opposition (which may or may not be an external antago-nist). The character knows what they need to do to make things right —and it's not going to be comfortable.

The self-revelation moment is all about the character's realization of the proper way to live life and the proper way to fix their predicament. The pursuit of that correct way of living leads them to the climactic moment. They're standing on the precipice. Frodo is standing at the fires of Mount Doom. Luke Skywalker is poised and ready in the trench of the Death Star. Rick is standing next to the plane on the way out of Casablanca. They're ready to take action to solve their global story problem.

> *Takeaway:* The climax is the moment where the character must demonstrate through action that they've learned their lesson. They must make amends for their moral decay. They must choose what they need over what they want by making a commitment to the correct side of the thematic dilemma.

Temptation

The first beat in this climactic moment is to set up The Great Decision Moment. To create this dilemma, we introduce temptation.

We tempt the character by offering them the option of getting the thing they originally wanted at the beginning of the story or we give them the option of forgoing the risk and pain that seems inevitable in the pursuit of their desire. We give Marlin the option of protecting Nemo from harm. We give Woody the option of getting rid of Buzz by abandoning him. We give Olive the opportunity to drop out of the pageant. We give Frodo the option of taking the ring for himself. We give Rick the option of taking Ilsa on a plane and leaving Casablanca. We identify the thing the character wanted most at the beginning of the story and we dangle it in front of them. We give them an option to avoid doing the difficult thing that they know they must do. This beat might best be thought of as the arrival of an opportunity to go back to or fall victim to the character's old worldview or incorrect value system.

What do characters originally want? They want to live in their façade. They want to reassert and live their lie. They want their obsession. They want to bury their ghost. They want to hold on tight to their comfort concept. They want to embrace their moral weakness. They want to avoid the emotional pain associated with change. They want that which feels good and comfortable but is ultimately unfulfilling. This is where we let the character taste it. We let them momentarily imagine what it might be like to give in to temptation. We make them an offer that they would never have been able to refuse at the start of the story. And we want to make this temptation *incredibly* attractive. If the audience knows the choice the character will make, then we don't have a powerful climax. This temptation will make it hard to *want* to choose the right value system. This is the character's ultimate test.

If a character came to a false or incorrect self-revelation after the crisis, it's possible that the temptation serves as the trigger of a correct self-revelation. In this pattern, the false self-revelation causes the character to move closer to the incorrect value system in such a way that creates responsibilities and obligations to this incorrect value system. This typically further separates the character from their need. We finally see the character on the precipice of the ultimate commitment to the incorrect value system, which will burn their bridges and solidify their unhealthy position. In the middle of this ritual of commitment, the temptation arrives. In this case, the temptation comes in the form of the *correct* value system. The arrival of this temptation causes the character to have a true self-revelation about what they really need in life. They realize that they've only got one shot to get the thing they ultimately want and it'll require a change within them. This is the pattern we see in *Four Weddings and a Funeral* where Carrie shows up at Charles' wedding and says she's now divorced.

> *Takeaway:* The first step in setting up The Great Decision is to introduce temptation in the form of the thing that the character has most wanted. Pursuing this temptation will represent the incorrect side of the thematic dilemma and may require the character to fall back into their moral weakness.

Commitment

The next beat is what Michael Arndt calls "The Kamikaze Moment of Commitment." This is where the character shuns temptation and takes a decisive action that proves their commitment to the correct value system. This is where the character makes the final decision in The Great Decision. The key to this action is that it should completely cut off any possibility of choosing the incorrect value system. It's an action that burns all bridges and commits fully, completely, and irreversibly.

In *Finding Nemo*, Marlin finds himself in a dilemma. Dory has been trapped in a net and Nemo wants to help her. Marlin is faced with The Great Decision between letting Nemo risk his life to help Dory (need) and preventing Nemo from getting involved in anything that could hurt him (want). Marlin commits to the correct value system and puts his trust in Nemo to keep himself safe while rescuing Dory.

This moment can be heightened by making it feel like the character is taking a great risk with little chance of success. The audience should scream, "No! What are you doing?!" In *Star Wars*, Luke shuts off his guidance computer when ostensibly it's the only way to defeat the Death Star.

We can often heighten this moment by having other characters push the protagonist to uphold the old value system or to abandon their pursuit of the new value system, even while the protagonist is facing their Great Decision moment. This emphasizes the difficulty of the decision. In *Little Miss Sunshine*, both Olive's dad and brother try to get Olive to back down from competing in the final competition of the pageant. When a character who, up to this point, has been a thematic ally encourages a protagonist to abandon the pursuit of the correct value system, this is a "Judas Moment of Betrayal." Olive rejects the temptation to abandon her pursuit, however. She forgoes the traditional standards of a beauty pageant and begins to dance to Super Freak (thus exemplifying that she's a winner by her own standards and not by anyone else's).

In *The Graduate*, Ben crashes Elaine's wedding by screaming, "Elaine!", thus choosing feelings over societal rules and traditions. In each instance, the character takes a massive risk that appears doomed to fail.

In many cases, we can think of commitment to a value system as being demonstrated through the *means* that a character uses to pursue their ultimate objective. Luke must decide *how* he's going to destroy the Death Star—through technology or through faith. Olive must choose *how* she's going to compete in the pageant—by her own standards or by society's. Ben must decide *how* he's going to pursue Elaine—by following his feelings or by following societal rules.

The climactic moment often finds the character running up against a deadline. The character must commit before the deadline approaches or the stakes will be lost. To heighten the drama of this moment, we may want to show the character running up as close as possible to this deadline (sometimes by moving the deadline up). The moment after the commitment may be a moment of suspension where time seems to stop. Did the character meet the deadline? Did they win or lose? We may want to prolong the reveal of the outcome as long as is believable.

While many characters will take a definitive action in order to demonstrate their commitment to their new approach to life, sometimes a character need only be *willing* to take this action in order to demonstrate their commitment. This is the case in *The Hunger Games* when Katniss and Peeta must decide whether one will kill the other or whether they will both eat the poisonous nightlock and commit suicide. The *willingness* to make a sacrifice is sometimes just as potent as making the sacrifice. It's once the character has convincingly demonstrated their willingness to take an action that we can spare them the sacrifice and let them reap their reward.

We can also optionally heighten this moment by making it *appear* as if the character is going to choose the incorrect value system. Generally we want this to be a twist where the choice appeared one way on the surface but is actually a different way in reality. This is the case in *Casablanca* where it originally appears as if Rick is going to sabotage Laszlo and take Ilsa for himself. We also see this in *Four Weddings and a Funeral* where it appears that Charlie is going to marry Henrietta and not pursue Carrie.

Of course, not all characters resist the call of temptation. Some characters *do* choose the wrong value system at The Great Decision Moment. In *The Lord of the Rings*, Frodo fails to resist temptation and gives in to the power of the ring. Although Frodo chooses the incorrect value system, he later struggles with Golem for possession of the ring and ultimately sends it into the fires of Mount Doom where it's destroyed.

> *Takeaway:* When faced with The Great Decision Moment, the character must make the ultimate choice in the story's thematic dilemma. It's at this moment that the character must fully commit to one of the value systems, completely cutting off any possibility of reversing their decision.

A Moment of Surrender

The character's moment of commitment typically requires the character to make an uncomfortable decision to let go and completely surrender in some way. In fully committing to a value system, the character also often puts their fate in someone or something else's hands. This is a moment where the character surrenders to a value system and essentially puts their fate (and often their identity) in the "hands of the divine." The character submits themselves to a sort of judgment.

In *The Graduate*, Ben surrenders his fate to Elaine. In *Finding Nemo*, Marlin puts his identity as a family man in the hands of Nemo and his ability to keep himself safe while saving Dory. In *Toy Story*, Buzz jettisons his rocket, surrendering his fate and waiting to find out if he can fly. In *Ratatouille*, Remy surrenders his fate to the judgment and food criticism of Anton Ego. In *Star Wars*, Luke surrenders his fate to the force as he turns off his guidance computer. In *Indiana Jones and the Raiders of the Lost Ark*, Indiana surrenders his fate to God as he shuts his eyes at the opening of the Ark (thus demonstrating his choice of faith over reason). In *Little Miss Sunshine*, Olive surrenders her fate to the pageant audience (although the point is that she effectively doesn't care about their judgment).

Ideally we want this moment of surrender and judgment to feel like it could go either way. We don't know how things will turn out. We can heighten this moment of uncertainty by making the moment of surrender feel like it has failed in the past. In *Toy Story*, we're previously shown that Buzz can't fly. So why should it work this time? In *Star Wars*, we first see an X-wing fighter fail to destroy the Death Star. We can first dramatize a moment where the character (or a clone) fails to pass the test associated with the moment of surrender in order to heighten the uncertainty of the moment.

After the character makes a definitive act of commitment and surrenders to a value system, we wait with bated breath on a moment of determination—for "the divine" to judge the character and make a determination of their fate.

> *Takeaway:* To fully commit to a value system at The Great Decision Moment, the character must often surrender in some way and submit themselves to a sort of judgment. The audience waits as the character's fate is left undecided.

Loss

The next beat of the climax is optional. We may want to make it *appear* that even after choosing the correct value system, the character has lost. The deadline wasn't met. The wrong decision was made. It's over.

This might be the failure to attain their ultimate desire or it might be a loss or sacrifice of something of great value. We may want to make it appear as if the character's sacrifice in The Great Decision was all for nothing. This might be where we appear to let the character's ultimate nightmare come true.

In *Finding Nemo*, we make it appear as if Nemo has died. Marlin's ultimate nightmare comes true. In *Toy Story*, we make it appear as if Woody and Buzz have run out of options to get back to the moving van and consequently to get back to Andy. Their abandonment is permanent.

We may also leave the character dangling on the ledge, unsure of whether their commitment to the correct value system will pay off. This is the case in *The Graduate* where it appears as if Elaine won't reciprocate Ben's vulnerability. He's in a state of excruciating limbo.

This is the moment of despair. It's the moment where the character has gone as far as they can go and has still fallen short. Their best wasn't good enough. It's typically at this point that we want it to feel like the character's goal is literally impossible to achieve. It's over.

> *Takeaway:* We can optionally make it appear as though the character's commitment to the correct value system has led to their defeat.

The Judgment

The final beat of the climax is the moment of judgment. The character has made an act of commitment and has surrendered themselves to a value system. Will their surrender be rewarded or punished? Fate will render judgment on the character.

In most stories where the character chooses the "correct" value system, this judgment comes out in favor of the character. The final beat of the climax reverses everything and we end with the character's success. A feeling of hopelessness and loss is turned into a feeling of joy. Nemo is alive. Han Solo returns and Luke is able to destroy the Death Star after having surrendered to the force. Anton Ego loves Remy's food. Indiana Jones and Miriam survive the opening of the Ark. Buzz *can* fly and they make it back to the moving van. Olive's family accepts her as a winner and dances with her onstage. Elaine screams back, "Ben!" and reciprocates with feelings of love. Ilsa and Laszlo make it out of Casablanca. Fate smiles on the character and rewards them with something that reverses their fortune, demonstrating that their commitment to the value system was the right choice.

The Resolution

After the climax comes the story's resolution. The character takes the lesson they learned and settles into a new normal. We can think of the resolution as the beginning of something new. It can often be considered the beginning of a new era of some kind. In *Casablanca*, Rick says to Renault, "Louis, I think this is the beginning of a beautiful friendship." In essence, endings are about new beginnings.

The resolution should show the character living a new life in harmony with the theme. In other words, we need to see the character living their new equilibrium with their new value system. At the end of *Finding Nemo*, we see Marlin letting Nemo go off to school on his own. At the end of *Toy Story*, we see Woody and Buzz living in harmony at Christmas.

The resolution is, in essence, a reaction cycle in response to the story's climax. It's for this reason that the resolution should be full of emotional reaction. It often shows the main character sharing their accomplishments and their joy with their loved ones. In the ending of *Monsters, Inc.*, we see Sully achieving positive catharsis. We end on a reaction shot showing his happiness while reconnecting with Boo. Of course, if the climax ends with a defeat or a great challenge ahead, the characters may instead share emotions of melancholy, fear, and reflection. This is the moment where the character must confront the repercussions of their actions and decisions (for good or bad).

We can use the resolution to show how any story world communities may have been changed by the events of the story. In *Monsters, Inc.*, the community value system changes from one of fear and scaring to one of laughter and fun.

The resolution is our final opportunity to answer any outstanding questions. It's also where we see the consequences and implications of the final decision made during the climax. The correct decision is rewarded and the incorrect decision is punished. *Star Wars* ends with a medal ceremony where success is awarded, recognized, and shared.

> *Takeaway:* The resolution typically shows the main character living in harmony with the theme. Because it's a reaction cycle to the story's climax, it's often full of emotional reaction (whether positive or negative). It's the final moment where right action is rewarded and wrong action is punished.

25

PACING AND A STRUCTURE RETROSPECTIVE

Pacing

A story's pacing is roughly the rate at which consequential information is revealed to the audience. Pacing is, at its core, the rate at which "things happen." In other words, it's the tempo of the beats. We might also think of pacing as the rate at which things change.

The pacing of a scene and the pacing of a story both follow the same general principle. On the global story level, pacing comes from the rate at which we get new revelations or disruptions. On the scene level, the pacing is typically set by the rate at which characters change their strategy toward their scene goal. In practice, it's all simply about the rate at which the audience gets new information.

As a general rule, high stakes allow us to wait longer until the next disruption. The high stakes keep the audience's attention and a new disruption isn't necessary to maintain dramatic interest. On the other hand, low stakes often give us less time until we need to provide the audience with new, consequential information. In practice, this means that high stakes scenes can (but don't necessarily need to) be longer and low stakes scenes must be shorter.

Good pacing, of course, isn't simply about getting information to the audience as quickly as possible. Good pacing is a pulse. The rate at which the audience wants new information ebbs and flows. Sometimes we want to speed up and sometimes we want to slow down. We want to feed the audience when they're hungry and let them digest when they're full.

The audience will be particularly hungry for new information when their appetite isn't being satiated by our dramatic tools. We must be sure we're generating narrative drive and keeping the audience captivated. Disruptions (i.e. new information in the form of a problem or opportunity) are merely one of the tools in our dramatic toolbox. And even though we can likely get away with keeping the audience's attention with our dramatic tools for quite a while, we do eventually have to provide new, substantial information.

Good pacing is about providing a feeling of progress. We generally want to escalate the rate of beats as the story progresses. In other words, we typically want the speed of the story to accelerate and crescendo as we approach the climax.

A key question with pacing is when we want to slow down. In fact, why would we ever want to slow down? Why wouldn't we just want to keep providing new, consequential information?

An onslaught of information can lead to mental and emotional fatigue. The audience can literally get tired. In these cases, experiencing the story can be a physically exhausting experience. If the audience gets tired, they may want to take a step away from the story. That's bad.

A barrage of information can also have the side effect of making revelations feel inconsequential or meaningless because the audience is never given the chance to sit with and contemplate the impact of a piece of information.

When Luke finds out that Vader is his father, we want to take some time to sit with that. How will this affect Luke? What will he do now? How would I feel if I found out that the villain were my father? If this information is immediately followed by additional consequential information, the revelation starts to lose its emotional weight. This is where the value of the scene sequel or interlude comes in.

A sequel follows a scene and exists to explore the emotional implications of an action that was taken or a disruption that occurred during the scene. Sequels don't contain disruptions and thus don't serve to increase the pace of a story. We want to take a break and consider the emotional weight of what just happened. The audience needs time to digest.

So when do we let the story breathe? When do we leave room in between disruptions and beats?

We'll generally leave room for a character to actually enact the first version of their plan (before we ruin it with a new disruption). We'll leave room for characters (and the audience) to emotionally respond to consequential disruptions. We want to provide characters time to think about the implications and weight of a revelation or action. We'll also give characters time to consider the emotional weight of any actions that they plan to take. We want to leave time for characters to share their emotions with others. These are all moments in which we want to let the story breathe. It's in these moments that we'll generally hold back delivering new information. We want the audience and the characters to sit with what they've learned and feel the weight of it.

After the audience has had time to sit with the impact of new information, however, it's time to move forward. It's time to keep up the pace and deliver new information. Delivering new information, of course, is only made possible when we intentionally *withhold* information from the audience (and potentially from characters). Withholding information is what *allows* us to reveal information and thus what allows for good story pacing.

> *Takeaway*: We want to ensure that the audience constantly feels like the story is progressing by providing new consequential information. When appropriate, we want to take a moment to let the audience appreciate the weight of new information (often by watching characters ruminate on the new information). After that, it's on to the next plan and the next beat.

Structure: A Retrospective

Now that we've explored the disruption cycle and the beats of story, let's take one last look at structure.

As we've discussed, drama is about making the audience want to know what happens next. Theme is about changing the audience's perspective or worldview. We might say that structure is the marriage of drama and theme in that its purpose is to change the audience's perspective by delivering the emotional beats of a story in a way that maintains the audience's attention.

If our story's structure keeps the audience's attention with dramatic tools but doesn't deliver the thematic beats in an impactful way, the audience will likely feel emotionally empty or unchanged at the end. They might merely feel the sugar high of drama without any of the protein of theme. If, on the other hand, our story's structure doesn't consistently maintain the audience's interest, then they'll disengage before we ever get a chance to deliver the thematic beats.

We've seen that in the context of drama, stories are made up of a series of disruptions. Each disruption injects a new bit of dramatic interest that helps maintain the audience's attention. It turns the story in a new direction that makes us wonder, "What will happen next?" The larger the disruption, the larger the narrative unit (i.e. scene, sequence, act).

We've also seen that in the context of theme, stories are made up of a series of beats. Each beat is responsible for delivering a piece of information that furthers a thematic pattern and helps to explore and deliver the story's theme.

Even though we use different terms in different contexts, a disruption is a beat and a beat is a disruption. They're the same thing. Each is when something of significance happens in the story that creates dramatic interest and furthers a thematic pattern.

As we've explored over the last section, every thematic pattern has a series of beats that best conveys the pattern. A positive character arc has a sequence of beats that tends to organically and believably change a character. Each genre has an expected set of beats (such as "the discovery of the body" in mystery). Each story form (such as the *Moses* story, *Sleeping Beauty*, and *King Arthur's Court*) has a set of beats. These beats are structured in a way that most effectively conveys the story's theme in an emotionally impactful way.

Structure then is about delivering the thematic beats (i.e. disruptions) in a dramatically interesting way that maintains a feeling of progress (i.e. pacing). The traditional three-act structure is one natural way of structuring the beats of a myth story. That's only one type of story, of course, and viewing all stories this way potentially cuts off a number of possibilities. Once we fully understand the first principles of story when it comes to drama and theme, we can expand our understanding of the possibilities of story structure.

The key to understanding structure is to first understand the beats of whatever thematic pattern we want to convey (a character arc, a community arc, a story form, a genre, a life experience, a moral dilemma etc.). We then want to deliver those thematic beats in a way that maintains the audience's attention using our dramatic tools. Our ability to deliver emotion in a dramatically interesting way *is* structure.

> *Takeaway:* Story structure is a consequence of delivering thematic patterns in a dramatically interesting way.

Stage V Wrap-up

We've now explored the core mechanics that make story structure work. We've learned about the disruption chain, the reaction cycle, plotting, and the beats of story. Now that we know broadly what's going to happen in our story, it's time to learn some dramatic tools to make each moment interesting.

PART VI

WINDOWS AND DOORS

DRAMATIC TOOLS FOR THE TOOLBOX

We've poured the foundation, laid the pipe, and raised the walls. We've got a solid structure for our story. Now it's time to start making the structure functional. We'll put in the countertops, windows, moldings, and doors. It's time to explore some tools that can make this place look desirable.

26

NARRATIVE DRIVE AND HEIGHTENING DRAMA

"Hollywood has three things above all that they're looking for in a script: narrative drive, narrative drive, and narrative drive."

— JOHN TRUBY

Narrative Drive

In our discussion of plot, we explored the importance of generating narrative drive. We must continually keep the audience wanting to know what happens next. The moment we lose that narrative drive, we lose the audience and our story comes to a premature end.

We've already explored the most fundamental dramatic tools in our discussion of plot, including dramatic tension (and the dramatic question), suspense, tension, dramatic irony, misunderstandings, secrets, mystery, surprise, promises, convergence, and urgency.

In the following section, we'll explore a few additional tools and techniques for creating narrative drive. While some of these tools build off of each other, many of them are independent and thus are in no particular order.

Heightening Drama

Once we've established a dramatic situation (such as a scene, sequence, or plot) using one of our core dramatic tools (e.g. dramatic tension, dramatic irony, mystery, and convergence), how can we heighten the drama?

Compelling Conflict: Making Things Hard to Want to Do

Not all conflict is equal. As Matt Bird says, the most compelling conflict is created by a goal that's not just hard to do, but hard to *want* to do.

To make a desire hard to want to pursue, we must necessarily create an opposing desire within the same character. This means that compelling conflict is an internal conflict. It's a dilemma. A character has two opposing desires (which may, of course, include a desire to avoid) and must decide which to choose. The desires must be mutually exclusive so that if one is attained, the other can't be.

To create an internal conflict, first determine the character's dominant desire. Then either create a new problem by threatening something that's personally valuable to the character or create a new opportunity by offering something to the character that's personally valuable. Ensure that the new problem can't be resolved without giving up the existing desire or ensure that the new opportunity can't be sought without giving up the existing desire.

In a previously mentioned example with *Das Boot*, a German woman desires to perform her duty to interrogate a Resistance fighter. At the same time, she desires that the Resistance fighter keep the German woman's identity concealed. This makes the German woman's desire to perform her duty to interrogate the Resistance fighter hard to *want* to do.

We can also think of this as forcing a character into a dilemma where each choice has a heavy benefit and a heavy cost. Let's consider a dilemma where a character and their best friend are scrambling to escape a hungry velociraptor. They're headed toward a blast door that's quickly closing. The raptor's racing toward them. The character's best friend trips and gets their leg stuck in a piece of debris. The character has the option to either continue heading toward the blast door, saving their own life (benefit), and sacrificing their friend (cost). Or they can let the door close and attempt to fight the raptor, risking their own life (cost), and potentially saving their friend (benefit). What does the character do? To heighten this dilemma, we can continually add new complications in the form of heavier costs and heavier benefits.

To create an internal conflict, we can start with a character's desire and then consider whether we can introduce an additional cost to accomplishing that desire. We might also consider how we could introduce an additional benefit to *not* accomplishing that desire.

To heighten drama, figure out what would make a character's goal hard to *want* to accomplish.

> *Takeaway:* Internal conflict makes a goal hard to want to accomplish. If a character wants to save their own life but can't do so without sacrificing their friend's life, the desire to save their own life is hard to want to do. This heightens the drama of the desire.

Urgency and Ticking Clocks

We previously explored urgency in our conversation about plotting from dramatic tension. It's worth noting that introducing urgency in the form of a ticking clock or deadline is one of the quickest and most effective ways of heightening a dramatic situation. Not only should our story have urgency, but ideally each scene should have some sort of urgency, as we'll later discuss.

Unavoidable

The dramatic situation must be unavoidable. There's no drama if a character can simply walk away with no consequences.

What makes something unavoidable? Stakes. Consequences. If a character is in some way penalized for disengaging, they'll be incentivized to face the dramatic situation. Ensure that the character has something to lose if they try to avoid the situation. Desire helps create organic stakes. If a character walks away, they'll lose the object of their desire!

Of course, the consequences of walking away don't need to be physical. The character might be driven by a strong moral code. Perhaps they made a promise to someone. Perhaps their identity or role within a group is at stake. These are emotional, social, and spiritual stakes.

This point is simple but crucial. To heighten drama, heighten the stakes.

> *Takeaway:* Any situation from which a character can walk away necessarily lacks drama. As has been said, "A problem that a character can walk away from is a book that a reader can walk away from."

No Obvious or Easy Solutions

Human nature being what it is, we tend to go for the easiest solution to a problem first. We tend to seek that which is the least uncertain and that will conserve the most energy. To show a character doing anything else would be disingenuous.

It's for this reason that a character who seeks anything other than the obvious solution to a problem will frustrate the audience. They ask the dreaded question, "Why didn't the character just...?" Needless to say, this is something we want to avoid.

This doesn't mean that our dramatic situation can't have obvious or easy solutions, of course. What it does mean, however, is that we need to first anticipate these solutions and then show the audience that those obvious or easy solutions aren't viable. The quickest and most believable way to do this is usually to have a character recognize the potential solution and try to solve the problem the easy way.

Then we need to show the reason that the solution fails. The character must discover that the problem is more difficult than they had initially anticipated. This can occur on both the global story level and the scene level.

The classic example is in a horror movie where the audience may be tempted to ask, "Why didn't they just call the police?" It's a good question! And we generally want to write characters who would ask that very question. So let's say that a character trapped in a house with a killer thinks, "Hey, why don't I just call the police?" Seems like a viable solution. Our job as storytellers is to let the character try the easy solution and show them why it won't work.

The clichéd answer to why the character can't call the police is that the phones are dead. We generally want to avoid clichés, but at the end of the day it's better to have any answer to the question than to leave it open for the audience to ask.

Why else might the character not be able to get the police involved? Perhaps they *did* call the police, but the character's story sounded like a prank call. The police will come to investigate, but it's not on the top of their list. Perhaps the character alerts the police, but nothing happens and the audience finds out that the "police officer" was just someone impersonating an officer (which we see in the movie *Hocus Pocus*). Perhaps the police are corrupt or paid off by the killer? Perhaps the police are too far away to provide any meaningful response time? Perhaps the police show up, but the killer ambushes them? Perhaps the killer already created a diversion or has in some way detained the police? Perhaps the police show up, but the killer anticipates their arrival and disappears (creating a "boy who cried wolf" situation)? Perhaps the character calls the police, but the character is so disoriented or delusional that they can't give their exact address? Perhaps the character gives their address, but the killer actually has them in a replica house at a different location? Perhaps the killer rerouted all the phone signals to call the killer's phone?

We might also consider whether an easy solution could arrive on the character's doorstep. In almost every case, of course, the character can't accept the solution for some reason. We see this in *Breaking Bad*

S01E05. Walt has recently been diagnosed with terminal cancer and is financially struggling to pay for treatment and to support his family. Walt's old business partner, Elliott, presents Walt a solution by offering him a job at the Gray Matter Technologies corporation. Walt, of course, can't accept this position for a number of reasons, including his personal history with Elliot, his personal history with Gray Matter, and his pride. The easy solution comes knocking and the character turns it away.

> *Takeaway:* Anticipate the obvious or easy solution to a dramatic situation. Let a character try this solution and show the audience that it's not viable (or subvert the expectation and let the easy solution work out). We must anticipate these plot holes and plug them before the audience becomes frustrated.

Irreversible

To further heighten a dramatic situation, make the consequences irreversible.

What makes something irreversible? What can't be undone? Often something is made irreversible by the depth, scope, or quantity of its effect. The wider the effect, the deeper the effect, or the larger the number of effects, the less likely it is to be able to be reversed. This is particularly pronounced in viral, exponential, and chain-reaction effects.

There are certain actions and decisions that open "Pandora's Box." They do something that, once done, can't be taken back. The genie can't be put back in the bottle. Words spoken can't be taken back. Disease released into the wild can't be taken back. The flame unleashed on a field can't be taken back.

Any action that "forces the stakes" of a desire can often be considered irreversible. Recall that to "force the stakes" is to force a decision about whether a character has won or lost their goal. If a criminal makes a mistake, they get caught. Their mistake forces the stakes of their freedom (i.e. of their desire to avoid being captured). Contrast this with the detective. If the detective makes a mistake, the search for the criminal doesn't come to an end. If a rock climber slips and falls, the mistake forces the stakes of their life (i.e. of their desire to avoid falling). In general, desires to prevent or to avoid don't tolerate mistakes. A simpler way to look at this is that some failures are fatal. Those are our irreversible disruptions.

> *Takeaway:* As stories progress, disruptions and decisions should generally get more and more irreversible. They should fundamentally change the story reality (internally or externally). We must feel that we can never go back to the way things used to be.

Foiling Plans, Moving up Timelines, and Forcing Improvisation

One way to heighten drama is to introduce a disruption that makes the protagonist's plan obsolete. But this technique becomes even more powerful when we drastically increase urgency by moving up the protagonist's deadline. We either move up the deadline threshold, move the urgency resource closer to the threshold in a significant way, or reveal that we didn't have an understanding of the true urgency resource.

The key here is to reduce the time until the protagonist's desire is either attained or lost. Or in other words, we "force the stakes." We force the protagonist to take action toward their desire, whether they like it or not. If they do nothing, they sacrifice what's at stake. Time's up. Action must be taken.

If the urgency resource is time, we simply reduce the time remaining. If the urgency resource is something like carbon dioxide level, we can either introduce a disruption that drastically increases the amount of carbon dioxide in the air or we can lower the threshold of toxicity in order to make a lower dosage toxic. We might also think of this dramatic technique as a reduction of the protagonist's margin of safety. In other words, we're reducing the protagonist's margin for error. There will be no mistakes allowed.

Of course, something must *cause* the timeline to be moved up.

Something must *force* a determination of the stakes. While it could be a coincidence that moves the timeline up, it's more dramatically satisfying for the urgency to be caused by another character.

It often makes the most logical sense for the antagonist to be the one who implements the next phase of their plan earlier than anticipated. There might be some disruption that *allows* the antagonist to strike earlier than planned. It's even better when it's the protagonist themselves who *caused* the thing that allowed the antagonist to strike early. This is the case in *Star Wars* where the protagonist's presence in the Death Star allows Vader to plant a tracking device that leads the Empire back to the rebel base. We might consider how the antagonist could take advantage of the protagonist's mistakes or weaknesses in order to implement their plan sooner than anticipated.

The timeline might also be moved up because the protagonist inadvertently stumbles into the antagonist's hands. This is the case in *The Silence of the Lambs* when Clarice shows up at the house of Buffalo Bill with no backup. Essentially the antagonist doesn't need to attack because the protagonist has delivered themselves in the process of pursuing their goal.

Foiling a protagonist's plan forces the quick formulation and execution of a new plan, resulting in improvisation. Improvisation is powerful because it gives us an opportunity to show off just how clever, creative, and resourceful a protagonist can be under pressure and with limitations.

Consider how time can be unexpectedly, believably, and significantly reduced for the protagonist. Remember that these dramatic tools apply not just to the global story but also to individual scenes. A protagonist's scene plan may be foiled. Their timeline may be unexpectedly moved up by the scene antagonist's strategy.

Takeaway: To heighten drama, disrupt a character's plan or unexpectedly move up the timeline until the character must take action. This often occurs as a result of the antagonist taking action earlier than expected. We might also consider how we could reduce the protagonist's margin for error. Take away the margin of safety. There will be no mistakes allowed.

Raise the Stakes

Drama can always be heightened by raising the stakes of the dramatic situation. In other words, make the potential consequences of the dramatic situation deeper and more personal. Force the protagonist to put more at stake in order to attain their desire. The more a character is willing to put at stake, the stronger they demonstrate the depth of their desire.

It's important to ensure that this process of raising the stakes is organic and not contrived. We don't want some arbitrary consequence of failure. To prevent this, the raising of the stakes should be *caused*. The best way to do this is often to have the antagonist (or some other character in the dramatic situation) enact a plan, which will put something of value to the protagonist at stake. Make characters advance their own position in a dramatic situation at the expense of other characters. This should be a relatively seamless and organic process assuming that the dramatic situation has been crafted to create a true opposition of desires (i.e. when one character gets closer to attaining their desire, the other necessarily gets further away).

To further heighten the raising of stakes, consider a categorical escalation of stakes. In other words, instead of merely putting a character's career in danger, put their relationships in danger. Instead of merely putting their life in danger, put their identity in danger. Put their moral code in danger. Put their beliefs in danger.

Raising the stakes can allow us to slow the pace of a dramatic scene. As a general rule, the length of a scene should roughly correspond with the level of stakes in the scene. A scene with low stakes should be relatively short and a scene with high stakes gives us the option to stretch it out.

Takeaway: To further heighten drama, raise the stakes. Make the potential consequences of the situation deeper and more personal to the protagonist. The antagonist's plan should naturally put at stake something of value to the protagonist.

Agitation

Introducing agitation to a situation is a surefire way to heighten drama. The idea is to introduce some element to the situation that makes it more difficult for a character to complete their goal. It might also simply make it more difficult to have a conversation. As a general rule, when we agitate a character we typically agitate the audience (though not necessarily in a bad way).

Some examples of dramatic agitators include bugs, loud noises, irrational or chaotic people, violations of personal space, violations of hygiene, approaching danger, and explicit timers (such as someone screaming out a countdown), among others. In *Titanic*, Rose is having a conversation with her mom and the scene agitator is simply the tightening of Rose's corset.

In *Frasier* S03E19, Martin is trying to watch TV and keeps telling Niles and Frasier to be quiet. The two proceed to have their conversation in a hushed voice. In another portion of the scene, the two are having their conversation, but Daphne is trying to listen to the radio. She keeps turning up the radio, making it harder and harder to have the conversation.

In *The English Patient*, Kip is trying to defuse a bomb. The frost on the detonator is thawing and when it fully thaws the bomb will go off. This creates suspense. Agitation is provided by two elements. First there's an approaching caravan of tanks, rumbling the ground and making us feel like they'll inadvertently detonate the bomb. Second Kip's new love interest is riding her bicycle to the site of the bomb in order to retrieve him, thus putting her in danger and making us agitated (which also introduces another element of suspense). These elements are crescendoing in a cocktail of suspense, agitation, and tension.

The key to an agitator is that it must affect or bother the character in some noticeable way (even if it doesn't change their action). An agitator can also sometimes act as implicit urgency in a scene.

> *Takeaway:* Introduce an element of agitation to heighten drama. A scene agitator is something that distracts or agitates a character as they pursue their desire.

Dramatic Credibility

It can be tempting to set up dramatic situations that serve the story without ever asking whether the situation might arise organically. Each dramatic situation must be credible. It has to make sense. If the audience doesn't feel like the drama is credible within the context of the story world, we'll lose them to frustration. And once the audience is frustrated, there's very little we can do to win them back.

Here are a few principles to keep in mind while crafting dramatic situations:

Actions must be motivated. Characters don't take action unless that action is driven by a desire. They don't do anything unless they want something (even if that something is simply to help someone else). It's a simple concept, but it can help counteract the temptation to have a character inexplicably do something for the sake of the plot. If a character acts, it must be toward their desires.

If a character is apparently acting against their own interests or desires as we know them, we say that the character is acting "out of character." We generally want to avoid this (unless the reason for them acting out of character will later be revealed as actually being in line with their desire or motivation). We might also say that a character is acting "out of character" if they're reacting or trying to solve problems (i.e. if they're using strategies, tactics, or methods) in a way that defies their modus operandi or moral code. Again we generally want to avoid this unless we're trying to highlight the fact that their strategy or moral code has changed.

Effects must be caused. In stories, we can make anything happen

—as long as we can *cause* it to happen. This is easier to overlook than it might seem. It's tempting to introduce new events that suit the direction of the story, but if these events aren't organically caused, the audience can feel consciously confused or even subconsciously frustrated.

For each dramatic situation, we can ask a few questions:

- What does the character want?
- How does the character plan to get what they want?
- Who or what stands in opposition to the character's desire or plan?
- Why does the character want this thing?
- What happens if the character doesn't get what they want?
- Why is this dramatic situation occurring now? Why didn't it occur previously? Why can't it wait? Why can't it be avoided? Why is it urgent?
- What caused this situation?
- Why don't the easy solutions to this problem work?

If we do happen to find ourselves with a dramatic situation that's completely necessary and at the same time not believable, there's one last resort. We can lean into the incredulity by having a character express how unbelievable or implausible the situation is. This technique is sometimes called "lampshading." A character might exclaim in frustration, "Seriously? How is this even possible?!" A character might incredulously sigh, "Am I seriously the only one here who can do this?"

In S02E08 of the show *You*, Joe and Fourty get kidnapped ostensibly because of Fourty's gambling debt. Joe says, "How's this for an act one turning point? Syd Field would be proud. Though, if this were a movie, I wouldn't believe it." It does later turn out, however, that the kidnapping was a façade put on by Fourty. The situation felt unbelievable for a reason.

If we have an implausible situation or story idea, we can let the story call out its own implausibility. To do this, we use a character who's especially knowledgeable about the subject matter and have them call out the situation as unbelievable. If the story explores a particular technology that's physically impossible, for instance, we can include a baffled expert who calls out the impossibility of the technology. The audience is more likely to take the impossibility as one of the "givens" of the story and allow it as part of their suspension of disbelief.

> *Takeaway:* Dramatic situations should be contextually believable. They should be plausible. Character actions should be motivated. Where a situation is implausible, consider using "lampshading" by explicitly highlighting the implausibility of the situation.

Revitalizing a Dramatic Situation

Once we've got a dramatic situation that's played out and fully exploited, how do we inject new dramatic life? There are a few tricks.

New interest can be injected by revealing new information to a stakeholder. We might consider how information about motivation, intention, allegiance, role, occupation, identity, or relationship can be revealed to a stakeholder (including the audience). Once new information is revealed, the stakeholder often alters their desire, strategy, or plan, which injects new interest.

We can also consider how we can invert our understanding of an existing motivation, intention, allegiance, role, occupation, identity, or relationship, etc. We want to take that which seems one way and reveal that it's actually a different way. Often we can recolor existing information to reveal that something which originally seemed bad is actually good and that something which originally seemed good is actually bad.

If the dramatic situation contains a secret, we can bring another character in on the secret. We can also bring in a character whose presence threatens to reveal the secret. This is a favorite technique of sitcoms. We see this in *Frasier* S05E03 where a misunderstanding about Roz's pregnancy is escalated as the "secret" is revealed to new characters.

And finally, we can often inject dramatic interest into a situation by introducing a new problem or threat to the stakes. In other words, we can introduce a disruption that takes the dramatic situation in a new direction.

> *Takeaway:* A dramatic situation can be revitalized by revealing new information to a stakeholder or by introducing a new disruption.

Schemas and Expectations

For every new piece of information, our brain tries to tie it to one or more known patterns that have been learned throughout life. These patterns can be called "schemas." A schema is essentially a list of all of our natural expectations about any given item, person, concept, situation, behavior, setting, etc.

If we're walking through the park and we see two groups of chairs that make an aisle leading up to a gazebo, a trail of flower petals, and a woman in a white dress, our brain will probably conclude that this is the schema for a "wedding."

After our brain matches the sensory evidence to a known schema, we then try to predict what else we can expect based on that schema. In the example of the wedding, we might then expect to encounter a groom, a marriage officiant, and a pair of rings. Once our brain has identified a schema, it begins making connections to associated concepts.

This process is the basis by which we form expectations. Later we'll explore techniques for creating expectations as well as how to subvert expectations in a satisfying and meaningful way.

It's important that for any dramatic situation, we consider the expectations of each stakeholder (including, of course, the audience):

- What information is the stakeholder missing?
- What is the stakeholder hoping for (desire)?
- What is the stakeholder fearing (desire to avoid)?
- What is the stakeholder expecting? What's most likely?

- What is the stakeholder *not* expecting? What's least likely?
- What expectations has each stakeholder formed based on the information they've gathered up to this moment?

Takeaway: For any given concept, our brain has learned a list of patterns that are associated with the concept. A concept and its associated patterns is called a "schema." Playing with schemas allows us to play with the audience's expectations. It's crucial for us to understand expectations so that we can cleverly subvert them.

27

INFERENCE AND THE KULESHOV EFFECT

We can also generate dramatic interest from what Pixar's Andrew Stanton calls the unifying theory of 2+2. "Make the audience put things together. Don't give them four. Give them two plus two." The concept here is that we maintain the audience's interest when we make them "figure it out." Andrew Stanton also calls this the "well-organized absence of information." Indeed the absence of information must be clear and well-organized. After all, the audience must know there's a puzzle in order to want to try to solve it.

This dramatic technique is based on the human propensity to infer. This is especially powerful when we get the sense that things aren't as they appear. We might say that this type of dramatic interest arises when the audience infers that there's a difference between what appears to be and what actually is—a gap between façade and reality.

Our job, then, is to first create a gap between what *appears* to be and what actually *is* and then imply that that gap exists. That which appears to be one thing is actually another. Not everything is as it seems.

This gap between surface and reality shows itself in powerful storytelling over and over. A character says one thing, but their body language tells a different story. An opportunity turns out to be a problem. A problem turns out to be an opportunity. The antagonist's plan is deeper than what it seems. A character is unable to see the hypocrisy in their actions. What a character wants won't actually get them what they need. Our beliefs turn out to be the lies we tell ourselves.

Meaning and the Narrative Fallacy

If we want to control what the audience infers, we must first understand how to intentionally imply. We want to learn to *suggest* something that's not explicitly stated. For that, we'll need to learn how humans assign and often hallucinate meaning.

Humans have a tendency to look for (or create) explanations where none are warranted. We take disconnected events or actions and assume there's some logical relationship between them. In other words, we have a deep propensity to draw connections between juxtaposed elements, even when no connection exists. This natural tendency to hallucinate relationships is called the narrative fallacy and it's the wellspring of meaning.

For instance, we tend to make the mistake of believing that two events that occur sequentially are causally related (a logical fallacy called "post hoc ergo propter hoc"). Just because a politician's poll numbers drop after they had dinner at a pizza place doesn't mean the two events are related or caused.

We also tend to believe that two elements that occur at the same time (i.e. elements that are correlative) are causally related (a logical fallacy called "cum hoc ergo propter hoc"). We often make these mistakes in thinking when we look back on someone's life and infer that something they did in their youth serves as an explanation for their pursuits or accomplishments in adulthood.

Let's explore a few ways in which the narrative fallacy can be practically applied. First what are the different ways in which elements can be juxtaposed?

. . .

Elements can be juxtaposed:

1. Across time (sequential elements).
2. Across space (contiguous elements).
3. Across mediums (overlaid elements such as voice and image).
4. Across context (associative elements).

Elements are juxtaposed in time when they occur sequentially in the same medium. This is perhaps the most common form of implicit connection in story and particularly in screenwriting. We assume that there's a connection between sequential images. When we see a character walk toward a house and then we cut to the inside of a house, we assume that the character entered the house they were approaching (even though this was never explicitly stated). This falls under the Law of Continuity within Gestalt psychology.

We tend to think that character action that occurs after an event or disruption was done in *response* to that event or disruption. We tend to think that a character's emotional state after an event was *caused* by the event. We tend to think that a character's fear while near an object or person is *caused* by that object or person. Now in most stories, we may be right to assume these things—but that meaning often only exists implicitly and not explicitly. Assuming a connection is a tendency. Being confident in the connection is a misjudgment.

In the movie *Friends with Benefits*, we see Jamie impatiently talking to someone on the phone as she waits for this person to arrive at the movie theatre. We then cut to Dylan swiftly walking and talking to someone on the phone, apologizing for being late. Based on the juxtaposition of these two moments in time, we assume that Dylan is the one who's late to meet Jamie. The writers took advantage of our propensity to make connections between sequential events. It's later revealed that both Jamie and Dylan are meeting separate people in separate locations and don't yet know each other.

Elements are juxtaposed in space when they occur simultaneously in the same medium. We tend to draw a comparison between elements that appear visually in the same scene, for instance.

Elements are juxtaposed across mediums when they occur simultaneously across different mediums. The most common example of this in screenwriting is the voiceover. One of the most powerful uses of this technique is found at the end of *The Godfather* when we hear Michael Corleone denouncing Satan at his son's baptism while we see the systematic assassination of Michael's enemies. The juxtaposition of the dialogue and visuals invites us to attempt to resolve the contradiction. With actions speaking louder than words, we understand that Michael's words ring hollow and that his chosen path is one of sin. His corruption is complete.

This technique is a staple of the show *The Office*. The writers often use talking head interviews juxtaposed against visuals of characters in the office. In S2E20, Jim is discussing Dwight's sacrifice for Michael in a talking head interview. He concludes, "I just don't get it. What does he get out of that relationship?" This dialogue is juxtaposed against an image of both Jim and Pam, which emphasizes the parallel feelings we have about Jim's unrewarded sacrifice in his relationship with Pam.

Elements are juxtaposed associatively when they occur in the same context. Context can be provided by either foreground or background. We might see the same foreground element in two different backgrounds, which then invites us to juxtapose and compare the backgrounds. In this case, the foreground element acts as context by which we compare the two backgrounds. Alternatively we might see two different foreground elements within the same background, which then invites us to juxtapose and compare the two foreground elements. In this case, the background element acts as context for the two foreground elements.

One prominent example of this is in the movie *2001: A Space Odyssey*. The black monolith appears in several scenes. This fact has resulted in film analysts trying to draw a connection between the significance of the scenes. In essence, the foreground black monolith acts as context for the scenes. One theory is that the appearance of the monolith marks a stage of human evolution. We tend to assign symbolic meaning to an element that appears across multiple situations.

We also tend to compare and assign meaning to two elements that appear in the same situation. In this instance, the situation acts as context by which we compare the two elements. This tendency is the foundation of a writing technique that makes use of what Brian McDonald calls "clone characters."

A story that perfectly embodies the concept of clone characters is *The Three Little Pigs*. This story is primarily about the last pig—the smart one that builds his house out of bricks. But his choice to build his house out of bricks is nearly meaningless unless we first compare that choice to one or more other characters who take a different path. The first two pigs are responsible for creating contrast and demonstrating what an *incorrect* choice would look like. This highlights the significance of the third pig's path. The three pigs all appear in the same situation and it's the way in which they treat it differently that brings out the story's message.

> *Takeaway:* The narrative fallacy causes us to hallucinate connections between elements where no connection may exist. It's often not any single element itself that produces meaning—it's the relationship between the elements that causes us to hallucinate meaning. Our brain considers a sequence of elements (whether rendered or merely in the mind's eye) and tells a story about their relationship.

The Kuleshov Effect

We might also better understand the relationship between story elements by reframing the concept of the narrative fallacy. We can say that a story element's significance (and/or its prominent features) changes based on its context. We might also say that our interpretation of something is dependent on its context.

The Kuleshov Effect is "a mental phenomenon by which viewers derive more meaning from the interaction of two sequential shots than from a single shot in isolation." We might abstract this concept and think of the Kuleshov Effect more broadly as the phenomenon where we extract meaning from two juxtaposed elements that doesn't exist in either of the individual elements.

Director Alfred Hitchcock provided an example by first showing an image of himself squinting, followed by an image of a woman with a baby, followed by another image of Hitchcock smiling. In this example, Hitchcock is a loving man. Note that the idea that Hitchcock is a loving man doesn't exist in any single image. It's the sequence of images that gives rise to this conclusion. We tell ourselves the story of a man reacting with joy at the sight of a woman and her baby. Hitchcock then offered an alternative sequence of images where we simply switch out the image of the woman with a baby for a woman in a bikini. Now when we see the image of the smiling man, Hitchcock notes, "What is he now? He's a dirty old man." Note, again, that the idea that he's a dirty old man doesn't exist in any single image. It's the sequence of images taken as a whole that allows us to extract meaning.

Let's consider a sequence of three scenes where scene one shows a mentally positive and healthy man, scene two shows a wandering and confused man, and scene three shows an angry and mentally deranged man. Taken as a whole, the sequence tells the story of the mental decay of a character. If we were to take these three scenes and play them in reverse order, the sequence would tell the story of the mental growth of a character. Note that the meaning of the story doesn't come from any one scene; it comes from the totality of the scenes and their relationship to each other. The labels "growth" and "decay" are only meaningful when considering the *order* of the images.

This phenomenon of an image being colored by its context can be applied more broadly to any two elements that can be compared. For instance, we can show a man walking down the street with happy ragtime music playing or we can show the same man with the same walk while we play tense horror music. Our interpretation of the exact same walk changes as the auditory context changes.

Any juxtaposition of elements creates a de-facto context (i.e. point of reference) for each individual element in the juxtaposition. We can't help but interpret things based on their context.

We can think of each element (i.e. context) as a schema (a list of all of our natural expectations about any given item, person, concept, situation, behavior, etc.). A schema invites us to create expectations about what else we'll see, hear, or experience. When we hear happy music, we expect happy things. When we hear sad music, we expect sad things. Each thing is colored by the context in which it appears. If there's a contradiction between what we expect and what we get, we infer additional meaning. A smile in a sad context takes on the additional significance of being either disingenuous or sadistic (neither of which is inherent in a smile on its own).

We can use the Kuleshov Effect when we want to make it clear to the audience that there's a connection between two things. In the opening of *Little Miss Sunshine*, we see Richard giving a speech about winners and losers. While we're still hearing the voiceover of his speech, we then see a shot of Olive watching a beauty pageant on TV. Olive watching TV is seen in the *context* of Richard's speech on winners and losers. This juxtaposition draws a connection between Richard's worldview and Olive's obsession with winning a beauty pageant. From this juxtaposition, we begin to infer meaning about Olive's obsession and how it relates to Richard's worldview.

The Kuleshov Effect is perhaps most powerful when we create a contradiction between context and what is dramatized. This occurs when sound contradicts sight, when dialogue contradicts intention, when reaction contradicts emotion, or when assessment contradicts reality, among others.

The cold opening of *The Office* S05E26 begins with Kevin describing his famous chili. Through a voice over he explains how cooking this chili is probably the thing he does best. While he's saying this, we visually see him spill the chili and frantically work to scoop it back into the pot. There's a clear contradiction between what he says and what we see. It also implies that Kevin doesn't do many things well.

We'll soon explore how contradiction and context (i.e. the Kuleshov Effect) is the source of subtext and irony.

> *Takeaway:* The Kuleshov Effect is "a mental phenomenon by which viewers derive more meaning from the interaction of two sequential shots than from a single shot in isolation." We can think of this more broadly as the phenomenon where we extract meaning from two juxtaposed elements that doesn't exist in either of the individual elements.

The Kuleshov Effect as Omniscient Commentary

The Kuleshov Effect allows us to make use of a unique phenomenon where a story appears to respond to itself. The basic idea is that we start with a situation that raises a problem, asks a question, or makes a promise and then we immediately switch to a new situation (sometimes with different characters) that presents a solution, provides an answer, or fulfills the promise.

In Hitchcock's *Sabotage*, for example, the story opens with a group of men huddled around a broken machine. One says, "Sabotage." The other asks, "Who did it?" The story has raised a question. Immediately the camera cuts to a man walking in the dead of night. The story is answering itself and implicitly saying, "This man did it."

With this technique, we're making a connection for the audience but not the characters. This allows us to subtly create dramatic irony (if the audience is savvy enough to pick up on it).

Using this technique, we can end a scene with a question and then provide an answer to the audience at the start of the next scene. It's almost as though there's an omniscient narrator responding to the questions, problems, remarks, etc. of the story and its characters. In these instances, the Kuleshov Effect acts as a commentary. This is a powerful "show, don't tell" method that can allow us to provide an explicit description in an implicit way. For instance, we might have a character say, "We've got a secret weapon." Then the camera cuts to a new character who's implicitly understood to be that secret weapon.

This method can also be used to connect two elements. In S09E04 of *Frasier*, the Kuleshov Effect is used to imply the solution to a problem. Frasier says, "There's got to be somebody on God's green Earth who can walk this dog." Immediately after this statement, the doorbell rings. Frasier opens the door and everyone in the apartment exclaims, "Roz!" Roz is the apparent, implicit answer to Frasier's problem.

The Kuleshov Effect as commentary is used quite often in *Frasier*. In S07E24, Niles is confessing his love for Daphne and says, "And [I would] ask you the question I had never dared ask." Then Donny barges into the room and asks, "What's the difference between a blister and a boil?" In S08E02, Daphne says "It's gotten to the point where you wonder what God-awful calamity is going to befall us all next." Daphne's brother, Simon, then walks in and says, "Something smells in your elevator."

We can use this technique to imply what a character is thinking. For instance, we might see a character watching a nature documentary. We see a penguin and the narrator says, "He's about to become a father." The camera then pans to the main character as he smiles at his sleeping wife. This implies that the character himself is about to become a father. It's worth noting that the Kuleshov Effect can also be used without any dialogue at all. Consider this same example, but instead of the narrator mentioning that the penguin is about to become a father, we merely see two penguins doting over their newborn. The camera then cuts to the man looking over and smiling at his wife beside him. In this moment, there's subtext.

We can use this technique to create irony by following a character's speech with a contradictory action. In *Arrested Development*, Michael says, "You know, Gob, you might want to start acting like the President. You're beginning to alienate some of the employees." Gob responds, "Yeah, like the CEO has to worry about alienating the employees." We then see Gob in the break room saying, "The worst that could happen is that I could spill coffee all over this $3,000 suit. Come on." The break room situation is an implicit, ironic commentary on Gob's assertion that a CEO doesn't need to worry about alienating employees.

> *Takeaway:* We can use the Kuleshov Effect to create a phenomenon where the story appears to answer itself or comment on itself. We do this by following an image or line of dialogue with a second image or line of dialogue that *appears* to acknowledge the existence of the first (while not *actually* acknowledging the existence in the story world). For instance, one moment may have a character asking a question and the next moment may show an image that's the answer to the question.

28

SUBTEXT

Subtext is the unspoken meaning underlying words, actions, or a situation. It's the truth and meaning that lies beneath the surface. Subtext is what a conversation, interaction, or situation is *really* about when it appears to be about something else on its surface. Subtext is one of the primary methods by which we can create dramatic interest through inference.

Subtext arises when text is incongruent with context. In other words, subtext is created when what appears to be going on (text) doesn't align with what's on the top of the audience's mind (via context).

So what's on the top of the audience's mind? It's whatever's the salient feature of the situation based on association. Or in other words, the thing on the top of the audience's mind is whatever's most prominent through association with the scene's characters, objects, setting, and/or situation (often based on what's occurred most recently or most vividly). For example, if a character just went through a tough breakup and is now standing by himself in a crowded movie theatre lobby sighing at other couples, the audience will likely think of the breakup (because of its emotional impact and the fact that it happened recently).

We might also say that subtext is created when what's going on reminds the audience of something else (often a subject that's more emotionally relevant or impactful).

Conversational Subtext

Conversational subtext arises when a conversation brings to mind (but doesn't explicitly state) a more relevant topic than the surface topic of the conversation. Often the more relevant topic is deeper and more emotional than the surface topic.

Humans use speech as one strategy to accomplish their desires. In other words, we use speech when we want something. However often our words aren't directly congruent with our desires. We dance around what's actually on our mind. There tends to be a gap between what we'd like to say and what we actually say. In other words, we tend to speak about our feelings and desires indirectly. This incongruity of speech (text) and intention (context) creates subtext in conversation. Conversational subtext arises when the audience knows or can guess what's on a character's mind (often through the character's recent actions, obsession, plan, or desire), but the character isn't directly saying what's on their mind.

Why don't we just say what's on our mind? Often it's because we feel it's in our best interest to hide the truth. Why might we think we need to hide the truth? We tend to hide the truth when we feel that the consequences of revealing the truth may be undesired (i.e. when we feel that stakes are high). If we fear the consequences or response to our words (whether that be rejection, abandonment, outrage, fear, sadness, sabotage, etc.), we tend to speak indirectly in an attempt to make our words more palatable or well-received. We might also hide what's on our mind because we're ashamed, guilty, or embarrassed of admitting our true intentions to ourselves (or to others). We might also hide what's on our mind because we believe the truth would foil our plans. This can result in ulterior motives.

Words don't need to *directly* contradict intent in order to create subtext (although they can, such as in *When Harry Met Sally* where "I hate you, Harry" actually means "I love you, Harry"). Words only need to be indirect or incongruent with what's on a character's mind in order to create subtext. We can create indirect speech by using metaphors, similes, parables, hyperbole, meronymy, metonymy, synecdoche, symbolism, allegory, etc.

Characters who are hiding their true feelings or intentions often find some way to indirectly respond with what's on the top of their mind (their current troubles, relationships, etc.) but while wrapping that subject in the terms of the current context or topic of conversation (e.g. what was asked or prompted). In *Sideways*, Maya asks Miles why he likes Pinot Noir. He responds by describing himself in terms of the wine, effectively projecting himself on to the wine.

A character might speak indirectly when they want to deliver information but the words are hard to *want* to speak. This technique of speaking indirectly arises naturally when a character is internally conflicted about delivering information.

It's also worth noting that not all characters speak in subtext. Not all characters are afraid or concerned with how their words may be received. Not all characters are ashamed or embarrassed by their desires. Not all characters have something to hide. Some characters don't care what others think.

Some characters are what we might call "high-status" while others are "low-status." A high-status character is one who leads or dominates a particular social group. This character is often powerful and influential. They're generally a boss, leader, or "head of household" of some kind. Because there are few consequences of a misstep within the social group (i.e. low stakes), the high-status character often speaks directly, without fear, and without hesitation. We tend to admire these characters for their ability to speak their mind.

A low-status character, on the other hand, is in a place in the social group where they must be aware of the consequences their words may have on their place in the group. These characters typically speak carefully and indirectly. A low-status character may feel that each conversation has high emotional stakes.

A high-status character may hide information for a reason that doesn't have anything to do with a fear of embarrassment or loss of social standing. Information is hidden when it appears to be in one's best interest to hide it. A high-status character may have a reason for withholding information from others and so may dance around what's actually on their mind in order to conceal from others.

Of course, character status is contextual. A character may be high-status in one social group (such as at work) but low-status in another (such as in their family)—or vice versa. Or they might be high-status in their hobby group but low-status at work, for instance. For this reason, a character may speak directly (without subtext) in one social group but indirectly (with subtext) in another social group. Social power and influence is contextual. By making a character's status change based on their current social group, we see how the character acts when they *have* power and how they act when they *lack* power.

We can take advantage of the fact that character status is contextual by forcing a character into a situation where their conflicting social statuses are on display. For instance, if a character is the boss at work but subservient in their family, we might explore a company picnic where families are invited. Now the character must navigate their power in a work environment with their lack of power in their family environment. Do they allow their family to boss them around in front of their co-workers? Likewise if a character is a subordinate at work but a leader in their family, perhaps the character's boss comes over for family dinner. How does the character navigate their conflicting roles as the social circles intermingle?

Subtext is perhaps most obviously on display when a character is keeping a secret from another character. A character with a secret may try to attain their desire without revealing the secret or may dance around any attempt by others to uncover the secret. A character's fear of revealing the secret may make it hard for them to accomplish the underlying desire (such as a desire to be with someone they secretly love).

A character doesn't necessarily need to be hiding something in order to speak indirectly. They might simply be uninterested in the current conversation and might instead desire to talk about what's on the top of their mind (but will have the courtesy of keeping it in terms of the current conversation). There doesn't need to be any subterfuge or ulterior motive. A character might just be absentmindedly self-centered.

For instance in *Once Upon a Time* S01E11, Emma and Sidney are discussing how they might expose the mayor, Regina. Sidney says, "You want to go by the book? Let's get a warrant." Emma responds, "What judge are we gonna find that she doesn't own? We're screwed." Sidney says, "Or there's my way." Emma protests and says, "I want to do this right, Sidney." He responds, "And what's right is exposing her. Sometimes doing a bad thing for a good reason is okay, right?" Mary Margaret then inserts herself into the conversation by saying, "Yeah. I mean, maybe you're doing something wrong, but if it's meant to be— if it's what's right—does that really make you a bad person?" Mary Margaret has been having a secret relationship with David and it's the only thing on her mind.

To write subtext, whether a character is trying to hide information or not, we consider how a character might find a way to respond to a conversation with whatever's on the top of their mind but in terms of the current conversation. What is [thing on the top of the character's mind] in terms of [the current conversation]? Or in other words, how can we express the character's obsession or desire in terms of the current conversation?

For instance, in *The Office* S4E3, Michael is angry and irritated that Ryan didn't invite him to the website launch party in New York so Michael takes it out on the pizza man when he says, "This young man needs to learn that this is not how you treat people. I don't care if it's pizza. Good business is about respect and accountability and follow-through. You don't just make promises and pull the rug out from under somebody, do you?!"

In *The Office* S7E13, Michael is angry and frustrated that Holly hasn't called off her engagement to A.J. so he rants about people not following through on their New Year resolutions and gives everyone else in the office a hard time. We see, of course, that he's really subtextually addressing Holly (highlighted by the fact that the camera focuses on Holly's reaction to his rant). There's then a follow-up subtext scene where Michael apologizes to Holly under the guise of apologizing to Kevin and Creed (whom he berated).

Because the thing on the top of a character's mind is being wrapped in the current conversation, a character might construct some sort of a metaphor, which necessarily contains similar characteristics and properties to what's on the top of the character's mind. "If I don't get out of this cab, I'm never going to get out." This might be a metaphor for, "If I don't quit my job, I'm going to die here. I'll never change if I don't change now."

Another technique for writing subtext is to consider how a character might indirectly carry out their strategy. For instance, let's say we have a scene where Jack wants to express his love to Jill. They're in a pet store, looking at a pair of birds. One bird is building a nest and the other is watching. Jack says, "How would one bird know if the other liked him?" Jill looks at the nest and says, "I suppose acts of service go a long way." Jack responds, "And what would one bird have to do to prove himself?" Jill smiles. In this example, Jack is trying to test and explore a potential relationship with Jill. Because of the emotional stakes, he does this indirectly, using the birds as symbols (and leaving the option of plausible deniability). Notice that this dialogue creates subtext. We understand there's something else on his mind. To use this technique, we can first determine a character's strategy and then figure out how to enact it through indirect communication.

Speech isn't the only outlet through which a character can express or communicate what's on their mind, of course. A character might take action in such a way that shows what they're really thinking. The expression of what's on the top of a character's mind might be dramatized through body language or through a focus on an object that's symbolic (i.e. representative) of whatever's on the top of their mind.

To write "on the nose" is to write exactly what's on the character's mind. To write in subtext is to write what's on a character's mind but in the veiled terms of something else (often the current situation, a recent situation, or a similar situation).

> *Takeaway:* Conversational subtext arises when a conversation brings to mind (but doesn't explicitly state) a more relevant topic than the surface topic of the conversation. Characters who are hiding their true feelings or intentions often find some way to indirectly respond with what's on the top of their mind (their current troubles, relationships, etc.) but while wrapping that subject in the terms of the current context or topic of conversation (e.g. what was asked or prompted).

Situational Subtext

Situational subtext arises when a situation reminds the audience of a topic that the current situation doesn't appear to be addressing on the surface (often something more emotionally relevant or impactful than the surface situation).

One method by which we can create situational subtext is to have a situation remind a character of something else. The character might then begin to speak with that other thing in mind, while staying in the terms of the current conversation. In S3E21 of *The Office*, Michael is hosting a girl's day at the mall and starts talking about how he wants to break up with Jan. Karen says sometimes relationships have their rough patches and you have to work it out (through context we know that her relationship with Jim is rough and she's reassuring herself that it just needs to work itself out), but then Pam counters that maybe Michael and Jan just aren't right for each other (implying that Pam and Jim *are* just right for each other). Both Karen and Pam are speaking about their relationship with Jim but in terms of the current situation.

We might see a situation where a character's words were not originally intended to have any subtextual meaning, but their deeper meaning is revealed upon inspection. In *The Office* S05E08, David Wallace has recently transferred Holly, the love of Michael's life, to a different branch. Michael is on a business trip to Canada where he's obviously trying to compensate for the loss of Holly by trying to find quick love. He sleeps with the concierge and feels empty. He's later in the business meeting talking about the benefits of Dunder Mifflin. In a rather sad voice he says, "Look, people continue to come back to us time and time again because they feel cared for here, they feel respected, and they feel that their needs matter. They are treated like human beings." As he speaks, he gets slower, more introspective, and begins to sigh. Clearly something's on his mind. We can tell he's thinking more about how Dunder Mifflin has treated him personally rather than how Dunder Mifflin treats their clients. The client notices something's wrong and asks, "Everything okay?" He looks up and responds with a sad smile, "Yes."

Situational subtext might arise when the current situation is inherently symbolic or metaphorical. Symbolism is made particularly strong with a physical object. In *The Office*, one of Michael's great fears is loneliness. This fear subconsciously drives nearly all of his actions. In S3E4, Michael discovers a dead bird outside the office and has an emotional freak-out. The bird died alone. Michael wants to have a funeral for the bird. During the funeral, Pam is reading a eulogy for the bird and Michael is taking the situation particularly hard—he's the only one tearing up. Referring to the bird, Pam looks at Michael and says, "We can't help but notice that he was by himself when he died. But of course, we all know that doesn't mean he was alone. Because I'm sure that there were lots of other birds out there that cared for him very much. He will not be forgotten." In this scene, Michael projects his fears on to the bird and it becomes symbolic of Michael's fear of ending up alone.

Situations can be inherently allegorical and thus create subtext. In the short story *Along the Frontage Road*, published in The New Yorker, the events take place in a pumpkin patch, but we quickly start to make connections to a deeper meaning. The child says, "I don't want a big pumpkin. I don't want to put a candle in it. I don't want you to cut it open with a knife." He also wants to name his pumpkin Kate. We come to understand that he's speaking subtextually and carving the pumpkin is symbolic of his mother having an abortion.

Consider making a dramatic situation force a character to metaphorically face their fears, vulnerabilities, insecurities, traumas, obsessions, and desires. Once we've established these elements of a character, we can bring them out symbolically through drama and thus create subtext.

The Kuleshov Effect can be used to create situational subtext—particularly when dialogue and image contradict each other. Through these contradictions, we're invited to guess what the dialogue could actually be referring to. In S3E1 of *The Office*, Jim has recently moved to Stamford and it's been clear all episode that Pam misses him. Michael has outed Oscar and is recapping the episode, saying, "What is love anyway? Maybe it's supposed to break all the rules like me and Jan or Oscar and some guy. Life is short. When two people find each other, what should stand in their way?" While Michael's saying this, we see a shot of Pam looking longingly at Jim's old desk (where Ryan now is). We see Jim looking longingly at an empty chair next to him. We understand the thematic subtext that the writers are implying.

> *Takeaway:* Situational subtext arises when a situation reminds the audience of a topic that the current situation doesn't appear to be addressing on the surface (often something more emotionally relevant or impactful than the surface situation). These subtextual moments tend to be the exploration of a character's emotional reaction to a past event but in the terms of the current situation.

Dramatizing Subtext

So how do we dramatize subtext? How do we bring it to life on the page? There's truth in the saying "actions speak louder than words." Whenever we, as the audience, see an incongruity between what a character says and what we believe is actually on their mind, we trust the subtext. Body language and tone of voice trump words. We know when "I'm fine" is a lie.

To imply that a character's words may not be the full truth, consider making a character's body language or tone of voice contradict their words in some way. If they say they're sure, show their eyes dart around. If they say they're happy, show a frown. If they say they're sad, show them trying to fight back a smile.

To suggest that a character has something on their mind other than what they're saying, show the character "looking inside" or acting introspectively in a situation that seemingly should require no introspection or contemplation. Perhaps the character is heavily observing when no observation should be required. Show the character "in their head."

By showing that a character is giving more thought to a situation or question than is warranted, we invite the audience to ask what's actually on the character's mind (which then invites the audience to consider the context of the current moment).

As a general rule, if there's a gap between what the audience expects to hear or happen (often as a response to another person or to a situation) and what the character actually says or does, the audience looks for subtext.

Consider the following when it comes to dramatizing subtext:

- Reaction that doesn't seem normal or proportional can be one way to make us look for subtext.
- Consider a character's state of mind and what it would take for them to "go off the handle" or to emotionally react. Is there any chance that another character's actions or words could be interpreted as attacking a character's insecurities or triggering something that's been on the top of their mind?
- Subtext can be evoked from unusual or intense focus on something otherwise trivial.
- If there's something we know that the character *should* be talking about but they're avoiding it 100% (and instead

focusing on trivial things or minutia, for example), that establishes that there's an elephant in the room.

- The incongruity between the apparent (the readable) emotions and speech/actions can result in subtext.
- If a character says something that's at odds with their characterization (i.e. if they do something uncharacteristic), then that can create the feeling that something deeper is going on.

Takeaway: To suggest that a character has something on their mind other than what they're saying, show the character "looking inside" or acting introspectively in a situation that seemingly should require no introspection or contemplation.

Using Objects With Subtext

Subtext can be made particularly powerful through the use of a symbolic object. Our goal here is to get the audience to understand that an object is a symbol for a more salient idea, character, relationship, or situation. Once we've established an object as a symbol, we then need only have a character interact with it or think about it in order to create subtext.

To use an object as a symbol, we must either establish the symbolism before we reference it or we must ensure that the object already shares inherent traits with the thing symbolized, perhaps reinforced by the way in which the object is being treated.

First let's look at how we might establish an object as a symbol before we use it for subtext. Let's say we have two people meet for the first time by bumping heads while both trying to pick up a dropped bracelet. The key here is to create an emotional connection between the object and the thing it symbolizes (the relationship in this case). We've done that by tying the bracelet to an emotional moment in the relationship—the first time the two met. From here on out, we can have one of the characters look down at the bracelet and twirl it in their fingers while saying to someone, "No, I don't think I'm ready to date yet." We can have one of the characters accidentally snap the bracelet and begin to hyperventilate as they rush to collect the beads. The bracelet is now symbolic of the relationship and provides subtext to any scene in which it appears.

An object might already share similar traits with the thing it symbolizes (this is perhaps clearest with a photo of someone serving as a symbol of the person). The object might also take on traits based on others treating the object as if it were the thing it symbolizes. This is the case in S3E4 of *The Office* when the dead bird symbolizes Michael Scott. Michael fears for the bird as if it were himself and Pam eulogizes the bird as if it were Michael. When characters project themselves on to an object, it may become a symbol (such as when Miles projects himself on to a glass of wine in the movie *Sideways*).

When writing subtext, ask the following questions:

- What's on the top of each character's mind?
- What has the character been recently obsessed or preoccupied with?
- What's the character's underlying fear?
- What are the character's insecurities?
- How does the character want to be perceived and how might that be at odds with what they're actually feeling?
- Is there any object that can symbolize what's on the character's mind?

Takeaway: Once we've established an object as a symbol, we then need only have a character interact with it or think about it in order to create subtext. To use an object as a symbol, we must either establish the symbolism before we reference it or we must ensure that the object already shares inherent traits with the thing symbolized, perhaps reinforced by the way in which the object is being treated.

29

IRONY

Where subtext highlights the gap between surface and depth, irony highlights the gap between expectation and reality. Because we tend to be fascinated by the unexpected and the contradictory, irony is a powerful tool for generating dramatic interest and keeping the audience engaged.

What is irony exactly? One definition is "incongruity between what might be expected and what actually occurs."[1] This is a good start, but it's clearly not complete. Consider a student who's expected to do well on a test but fails. Is that ironic? Not meaningfully.

Let's start with a few examples of irony and then work backward to identify the situations in which irony arises.

Here are a few examples of irony:

- A Parkour master trips going up the stairs.
- A racecar driver gets pulled over for going too slowly.
- A bank is foreclosed on.
- A fire station burns down.
- A gun safety instructor shoots himself in the foot.
- A child tries to avoid the sprinklers only to fall in the pool.
- American flags manufactured in China.

- The village idiot criticizes others for being dense.
- A cowardly lion.
- Monsters who are afraid of children.
- A rat who wants to cook.
- An anti-tech group who uses a website to recruit new members.
- Michael Scott criticizes the other branch managers for being idiots, as he himself makes an idiotic mistake.
- King Midas' search for wealth is his downfall.

Notice a commonality in each of these examples: there's an implicit expectation for each element (such as safety being associated with a gun safety instructor) and that expectation appears to be almost *deliberately* upended or contradicted.

We can't have irony without expectation. Fortunately our schemas provide implicit expectations. Rats are expected to be dirty. Lions are expected to be brave. Fire stations are expected to fight fires. Racecar drivers are expected to go fast. Things are expected to be helped by their positive traits and hurt by their negative traits. Things are expected to be hurt by their enemies and helped by their allies. People are expected to have some level of self-awareness of their nature (i.e. to understand and recognize their own strengths and flaws). These expectations are implicit and part of the patterns or "rules" of any given schema.

To create irony, we need to contradict or undermine the expectation of a schema. Generally it's not just any expectation that we're upending. We're often specifically contradicting or undermining an expectation about the schema's nature or identity. A thing's identity is what it *is* and its nature is what it *does* (or intends to do).

Irony is traditionally broken up into three categories: dramatic irony, verbal irony, and situational irony. We're going to clarify and adjust these categories slightly in order to make them more valuable in the writing process.

Takeaway: Irony is created when there's a meaningful incongruity between what's expected and what actually occurs. Often something is ironic when its nature or identity appears to be almost deliberately undermined.

Static Irony

We can use the term "static irony" to describe anything that exists as a contradiction of its own nature or as a contradiction of reality or of our expectation of reality. For example: an arsonist firefighter, a cowardly lion, a monster who's afraid of children, or a rat who wants to cook.

While static irony applies to any given thing, person, or situation that contains an inherent contradiction of its own nature or identity, it can also be extended to any line of dialogue that exists as a contradiction of what we know to be true. In *Die Hard*, Hans Gruber says, "And have no illusions, we have left nothing to chance." Moments after he says this, the elevator opens to reveal that one of his henchmen has been killed. Clearly things are getting out of his control. Reality contradicts the core of the line of dialogue, making it ironic. Some might call this verbal irony, but we won't due to the fact that it's not an intentionally ironic statement by the speaker.

At the end of *Angels and Demons*, a reporter says that the day's events have come to a conclusion "in one of the swiftest and smoothest conclaves in modern church history." Although the reporter believes it, this stands in stark contrast to the reality of the disaster of the conclave behind the scenes—as played out by the events of the movie.

Situations or scenarios can be inherently contradictory. For instance: it's ironic to expect that the most unpatriotic American will save the Allied cause (*Casablanca*). The Disneyland Jungle Cruise queue offers this ironic situation: "Due to monsoon season, all seminars on how to water-proof your boat have been rained out."

The focus in static irony is on the *existence* of an irony, not the creation of an irony. Static irony might also be called "cosmic irony."

Cosmic irony often feels as though fate itself is deliberately playing games with us and upending our expectations in a contradictory way.

> *Takeaway:* Static irony arises when something exists as a contradiction of its own nature or as a contradiction of reality.

Dramatic Irony

In the context of irony as a gap between expectation and reality, dramatic irony arises when the audience recognizes an irony (i.e. a gap between expectation and reality) that a character doesn't. Dramatic irony, then, can be seen as a static irony that the audience notices but that a character doesn't notice. A character might tell their loved one that they'll be home in twenty minutes when the audience knows that the character is about to be assassinated.

Dynamic Irony

The term "situational irony" is often used as an umbrella term for irony. We might also call this "dynamic irony." We'll define it in its broadest sense as a situation in which a schema's nature, identity, purpose, or intention ends up being contradicted or undermined. Notice that the focus here is on the *creation* of an irony, rather than the pre-existence of an irony.

A cowardly dog finds out that he's the bravest of his pack. A marriage counselor wants to file for divorce after a year of marriage counseling. A Parkour master trips going up the stairs. A man cures cancer but later dies of it.

There's an irony in working and struggling toward a goal only to have that work undermined by the unexpected, instant achievement of the goal. Consider this: a man works for three years to escape an island, only to have a helicopter save him on the day he plans to escape. Consider also *The Wizard of Oz*. Dorothy goes on a list of errands from the Wizard, only to find out in the end that she could have gone home whenever she wanted.

We can also define a more specific form of situational irony as being created when a schema (defined by nature, identity, purpose, intention, etc.) is contradicted or undermined as a *result* of its own nature or actions. In other words, it's the schema's action itself that causes the undermining. We can also think of this as one's actions backfiring or as one being the source of one's undermining.

For instance, a man is hit by a bullet that ricochets off of bullet-proof glass. In this example, it's the glass' bulletproof-ness itself that *causes* the wound. Consider the example of a boy who runs away from the sprinklers, only to fall into the pool. It's the boy's desire to stay dry that *causes* him to get wet. King Midas' search for wealth is his downfall. It's his greed that *causes* him to lose everything.

A character might also undermine themselves by unwittingly criticizing their own nature. In *The Office* S3E23, Michael has driven down to corporate (in New York) a day before his actual interview by mistake. As he's dialing Pam, he tells the film crew, "I have got it made in the shade. I know this company. The other branch managers are total morons." He then tells Pam, "Hey, Pam, I forgot what day the interview was. I drove to New York accidentally. I'll be, like, three hours late." It's Michael's words that undermine him. When he expresses his belief that the other managers are morons and that he isn't, he's creating irony because it stands in contrast to the reality that he's done something moronic.

> *Takeaway:* Dynamic irony occurs when a schema's nature, identity, purpose, or intention is contradicted or undermined in a situation. Where static irony focuses on the existence of an ironic gap between what's expected and reality, dynamic irony focuses on the *creation* of an ironic gap.

Verbal Irony

Verbal irony is created when someone communicates something that's intentionally contradictory to reality, without the desire of masking their true meaning. This intentionally contradictory communication is often thought of as sarcasm. Notice that this stands in contrast to subtext where one's true meaning is intentionally masked or distorted.

If a lion is acting cowardly and a character says, "Well, this lion isn't cowardly at *all*," that's verbal irony.

The Shortcut to Irony

All this theory about irony can make it seem more complicated than it actually is.

The shortcut to irony is to reveal the good as the bad and the bad as the good. Make the saint act as the devil and the devil act as the saint. Turn problems into opportunities and opportunities into problems. Take an attribute that makes an element good or powerful and have that attribute be the source of the element's evil, weakness, or undoing. Take an attribute that makes an element bad or unhelpful and have that attribute be the element's source of ultimate goodness or helpfulness. Turn allies into unwitting enemies and enemies into unwitting allies. Make our vices the path to salvation and our good intentions the road to hell. Force us to unwittingly support our enemies and undermine our allies. Make the actions taken in the pursuit of our desires be the cause of our losses. Make us unwittingly champion that which we most detest or fear. Make us corrupt that which we most want to protect. Make us derive joy from the thing we hate. Reveal that the thing we ostensibly love is the thing we hate. Make the rescuer the victim and the victim the rescuer. Make the serial killer heal and the priest kill. Reveal how the bad can be good and the good can be bad.

Of course, this won't necessarily result in an ironic situation, but it'll provide a good start. To create static irony, choose a schema, identify the common expectations about its nature, and then introduce a contradiction to that expectation. To create dynamic or situational irony, choose a schema and introduce an action that contradicts or undermines the schema's nature.

Irony creates dramatic interest. We find it inherently interesting.

As writers, we must consider how we can introduce irony not just into a scene but also into a character arc, a story world community, and the premise of our story itself. In *Ratatouille*, a rat (dirty) wants to learn to cook (clean). In *Monsters, Inc.*, the society of monsters is afraid of children.

30

REVELATIONS AND TWISTS

Revelations

A revelation is the reveal of new information to a stakeholder (often to the audience). As we've seen throughout the exploration of these dramatic tools, we can generate narrative drive by ensuring that there's at least one open question to which the audience wants to know the answer. We can also often generate dramatic interest by answering one of those questions.

When information is revealed that answers an open question of importance, the audience will get a boost of dopamine. In essence, one of the audience's goals (i.e. that of answering an open question) has been answered and therefore the audience is rewarded with dopamine. Provided there are still open questions, this reward will likely encourage the audience to seek more answers.

In other words, we can often keep the audience seeking more answers by providing an answer to a mystery or dramatic question. The key, of course, is to ensure that there's always at least one more open question.

We can maximize the opportunity for revelations by maximizing questions.

Consider the movie *Passengers*. In the movie, we open with Chris Pratt's character awaking from hypersleep. He can't go back to sleep and the ship won't reach its destination until after he's dead. Essentially he'll be alone for the rest of his life. He spends a good chunk of the movie falling in love with the idea of Jennifer Lawrence's character and finally decides to wake *her* from hypersleep. This is essentially a death sentence for Lawrence's character. Throughout this whole process, the audience knows all of the information that Chris Pratt's character knows. In essence, there are few open questions about what's going on.

YouTuber Nerdwriter1 offers a suggested change to the movie. He believes the movie would have been stronger had we started the story with Jennifer Lawrence's character waking up. With this change, we wouldn't know how Lawrence's character woke up and we wouldn't know whether Chris Pratt's character is an ally or an opponent. We could then later reveal the shocking truth that Pratt's character was the one who effectively sentenced Lawrence's character to death. Notice how this change withholds information upfront and maximizes the number of questions from the audience's perspective. This also allows us to maximize the number of revelations and thus the dramatic interest. Of course, the current version of the story allows us to play with the dramatic irony created by the knowledge that Pratt's character has doomed Lawrence's character. There's suspense there.

If a story feels like it's dragging on, chances are that the audience isn't actually learning anything of consequence. Characters might be *doing* things, but they might not be *learning* anything. It's possible that nothing's *changing*.

So how do we avoid a story where things happen but nothing changes? We need to ensure that we've got a structural source of organic revelations. Or in other words, information needs to be hidden and characters need to make discoveries. These discoveries might stem from either the story's plot (typically driven by the antagonist) or from the characters learning about themselves.

Dramatic revelations occur when a character learns new information about the story's plot. These revelations often come in the form of new information about the desires, plans, motivations, or actions of the antagonist. Typically a protagonist will start the story with only a partial understanding of the problem in front of them. They may initially not even know who the antagonist is. When they do learn the identity of the antagonist, they may still not fully grasp the antagonist's plan or connection to the larger problem. This provides a deep source of revelations as the protagonist discovers the true nature of their problem and the antagonist's plan, motivation, and actions. These types of revelations are generally associated with what is known as a "plot-driven" story.

We can also get dramatic revelations when characters reveal their true allegiances, when relationships are defined (e.g. "Luke, I am your father."), and when motivations are exposed. And, of course, unexpected disruptions are a potent source of dramatic revelations.

Thematic revelations occur when a character learns new information about themselves. They might have a revelation about their past, the consequences of their actions, their relationships, etc. These revelations are natural byproducts of a character going through a moral arc from either morality to immorality or immorality to morality. These types of revelations are generally associated with a "character-driven" story.

It's important that characters make significant discoveries, whether about themselves, about others, or about the story world around them. Without these discoveries, a story can drag on and feel lifeless. To create a story that sparks with new energy, ensure that the story starts with enough hidden information to allow a steady stream of revelations.

Takeaway: The reveal of desired information makes the audience want to seek additional answers to their questions. In order to maximize the number of revelations we can provide, we must withhold information and maximize the number of questions we pose.

Recoloring

New dramatic interest can be injected through the use of recoloring (which we might also call recontextualization). Essentially we can recolor the significance of an existing story element based on new information. In most dramatic situations, this means we can introduce new information to reveal that what once seemed bad is actually good (or at least benign) or that what once seemed good is actually bad.

Recoloring can perhaps best be expressed through the story of a Taoist farmer. All of the farmer's neighbors told him how lucky he was to have a horse to pull his cart. The farmer replied, "We'll see." One day, he forgot to close his fence and his horse escaped. "That's terrible!" said his neighbors. The farmer replied, "We'll see." After a few days, the horse returned along with three wild stallions. The neighbors told him how fortunate he was. The farmer replied, "We'll see." The next day, the farmer's son was training one of the new stallions. The stallion kicked the farmer's son, breaking the boy's leg. The neighbors exclaimed, "That's terrible news!" The farmer replied, "We'll see." The following week a conscription officer came by to draft the farmer's son into the army. The officer couldn't draft the farmer's son, however, due to his broken leg. The neighbors said, "That's fantastic!" The farmer replied, "We'll see."

This story is meant to highlight the fact that everything is contextual. We might say that nothing on its own is inherently good or bad. It can only be understood to be good or bad based on its context and specifically what comes after it. Bad things are bad unless they turn out to actually help in the long run. Good things are good unless they turn out to actually hurt in the long run. And in most cases, the "long run" can always be extended.

In an interview with Film Courage, Paul Gulino offers this example, "Suppose I show a movie where a husband is buying his wife flowers and chocolate and an anniversary card on his way home from work. Then, meanwhile, you see the wife and she's got a gun and she's hiding it in the bedroom drawer. What are you going to think?

He wants to make love and she has other plans. That's where the audience is going to go. And you could pay it off—he comes home with the flowers and she pulls out the gun and shoots him. Or you could then disclose later that he's a gun collector and this is a present for him—this is the gun he's been looking for. She saved up for it and she wants to give it to him for an anniversary present. And then you find out that he poisoned the chocolate." Notice how what seemed like a bad thing (i.e. the gun) turned out to be a good thing. Also note how what seemed to be a good thing (i.e. the chocolate) turned out to be a bad thing.

This recoloring technique is slightly different than starting with good news and then introducing separate bad news or vice versa. This method is instead about taking what's already believed to be good and making it seem bad in hindsight. It's about taking what's already believed to be bad and making it seem good or benign in hindsight. This technique is at the heart of the twist ending of the movie *The Lives of Others*.

To recolor a story element, we might simply consider the reasons that a bad thing might have been done for a good reason. Or we might ask how a bad thing could have a good effect. We might ask how a good thing could have been done for a bad reason. The question then becomes, "In what ways might the purchase of a gun be good or benign?" and "In what ways might chocolate be bad or dangerous?"

In *The Office* S5E19, Michael has a Golden Ticket idea. He places golden tickets in various shipments to give customers a 10% discount on their orders. Originally it appears to be a bad thing because the company's largest client finds five golden tickets, resulting in a cumulative 50% discount. However the idea later turns out to be a good thing because the client is so pleased with the promotion that they decide to make Dunder Mifflin their sole paper provider.

This technique is also used in *Frasier* S06E14 where Frasier spends the entire night trying to figure out if he's on a date on Valentine's Day. Every time it appears his date is flirting with him, we get an alternate explanation that makes us think that perhaps she isn't flirting with him. This back and forth persists all the way back to her place where he's still not sure.

We want to consistently be playing with the audience's conception of whether something is a disaster or an opportunity. We want to be consistently revealing to the audience that things aren't what they seem. This injects new dramatic interest and fascination into any situation.

> *Takeaway*: Everything is contextual. That which may have seemed bad may actually turn out to be good. That which may have seemed good may actually turn out to be bad. We can create dramatic interest by providing additional information that changes the audience's perception of something.

Cliffhangers

A cliffhanger occurs when a story intentionally cuts away from providing desperately desired information. We want to ensure that narrative drive is high before we cut away from a storyline (whether to go to a different storyline, to end a chapter, to end an episode, or to take a break from the story altogether such as in the case of an intermission or a commercial).

There are generally two types of cliffhangers. One type occurs when a moment of suspense is left unresolved. A character may be on the verge of success or failure in the pursuit of a desire when we cut away from the storyline. For instance, a character might literally be hanging from a cliff as the antagonist is stepping on their fingers. This cliffhanger is rooted in the dramatic question of, "Will the character get what they want?" In this case, the character presumably wants to survive.

The suspense of a cliffhanger can also derive from the audience's desire to learn a piece of information that other characters already know. A character might open a box and proclaim that the contents will change everything. If we cut away from the storyline while the contents of the box are hidden from the audience, we get a cliffhanger.

The other type of cliffhanger occurs immediately following a significant disruption. In this instance, there has been some significant revelation or action that makes us wonder, "What will the character do *now*?" In essence, the character enters a moment of crisis where some sort of decision or action is often required.

When we're working with cliffhangers, we must ensure that we're not making false promises. When we use a cliffhanger, we're making an implicit promise to the audience that the outcome of the current situation will actually matter. Let's say, for instance, that we've got a scene where the protagonist is tip-toeing down a dark, dangerous alley. A large shadow lunges at the protagonist and the scene ends. When we start the next scene, it's revealed that the shadow was just a piece of falling debris. This is an example of a cliffhanger with no payoff and it's a surefire way to cause audience frustration.

The better solution would be to fulfill the implicit promise by introducing a disruption of significance. We start the same way with the protagonist lurking down a dark alley when we see a shadow lunge at the protagonist. The protagonist feels a sharp sting in his shoulder from a knife. Holding the knife is the protagonist's wife, covered in blood. Now we cut away.

With this alternate cliffhanger, we're fulfilling the implicit promise that the looming shadow will be significant. Notice also that we're placing the disruption before the end of the scene. The question of this cliffhanger becomes, "What will the protagonist do now?" We've kept our promises and the audience wants to continue to the next scene.

We might alternatively keep the original use of suspense and mystery by ending the scene as the shadow lunges at the protagonist. As we cut away, the audience wonders who or what the shadow is and whether the protagonist will be okay. When the next scene starts, we keep our promise by revealing the identity of the shadow to be the protagonist's wife with a knife.

If a cliffhanger implies that something of significance will happen when we return to the storyline, that promise must be kept to the audience.

> *Takeaway:* A cliffhanger occurs when a story intentionally cuts away from providing desperately desired information. A cliffhanger is typically either a moment of suspense or alternatively a disruption (in the form of a revelation or action).

Contradiction

Recall Andrew Stanton's theory of 2+2 and our goal of maintaining the audience's interest by first creating a gap and then asking them to "figure it out." We've explored subtext as the gap between surface and depth. We've explored irony as the gap between expectation and reality. We've also seen how the gap between juxtaposed elements can create meaning through the Kuleshov Effect and the narrative fallacy.

Another powerful method for drawing the audience into the gap between façade and reality is to create a contradiction. We're inherently interested in resolving contradictions (and will want to gather more information in order to attempt to resolve the contradiction).

We've already seen how we might use the Kuleshov Effect to explore the contradiction between a message (in either text or audio) and the thing it apparently references (often an image). Let's consider a classic Volkswagen ad. We see a large image of a V.W. bug and right below it in large print is the word "Lemon." Through the Kuleshov Effect, the word "Lemon" implies that the Volkswagen is a defective car. But why would Volkswagen imply that their own car is a lemon? That doesn't make sense. It's a contradiction. This makes us want to read the small print of the ad to resolve the contradiction—a brilliant ploy to suck us in. We have a natural tendency to want to resolve contradictions (which means we have a natural tendency to want to get more involved in contradictions).

Other types of contradictory juxtapositions can work too, of course. We can break a schema. The opening of *The Umbrella Academy* begins with a woman seemingly becoming pregnant out of nowhere and giving birth minutes later in a pool. This contradicts our understanding of the schema of "pregnancy" where the gestation period is much longer than a few minutes.

We can also simply combine two things that don't belong together. A cat with a banana peel firmly situated on its head will raise some questions. A candle with a flame of water will also raise questions.

This technique of creating contradictions is particularly powerful when it comes to characterization. Characters are made especially interesting when they embody seemingly contradictory traits. Consider a woman who's publicly compassionate but privately cold-hearted or a man who's publicly cold-hearted but privately compassionate. A man might have a public objective but also a private objective that's completely contradictory. Characters who contain contradictions tend to be perceived as multi-dimensional.

> *Takeaway:* Contradictions are inherently interesting. They implicitly ask us to figure out how they're possible. Contradictions raise questions and are thus potent sources of dramatic interest.

The Twist: Creating and Subverting Expectations

Another method we can use to generate dramatic interest is that of subverting an expectation. To subvert an expectation is to make a story decision that's both unexpected and also satisfying. "Satisfying" is the key word here. It's easy enough to do something unexpected. Anyone can come up with a random and unexpected disruption. That doesn't make it a good story decision. This is, unfortunately, a mistake that can easily be made when a storyteller values shock over logic and surprise over cause and effect.

We can perhaps best think of the subversion of an expectation as a *twist*. A twist isn't about introducing a new element from out of left field. Instead a twist implies that we're taking an existing element and seeing it in a new light. A subversion often reveals a new understanding of existing elements—not the introduction of new ones.

Because we're discussing story twists, there will be spoilers ahead.

How to Create an Expectation

In order to subvert an expectation, of course, we've first got to have an expectation to subvert. Let's explore a few ways to create an expectation.

Schema Expectations

Recall that some expectations arise from schemas that exist outside of a story. For instance, cats meow, dogs bark, and birthday cakes have candles. These expectations are often implicit and we seldom consciously realize that we have them.

We also have implicit expectations when it comes to character archetypes. In fact, we might say that a character archetype is a character pattern that implies what a character will do, have, or be. In this way, a character archetype creates a collection of expectations about the character. We expect the detective to lead with their brain rather than their heart. We expect the warrior to jump into action and choose fight over flight. We expect the trickster to deceive and manipulate.

We can also look to clichés and tropes to identify our existing expectations. These are simply schemas in the realm of stories. Examples include the love triangle, good girl falls for bad guy, "the chosen one," etc. Genres themselves also create expectations about the story beats and what will happen.

To create an expectation from a schema, we often merely need to *imply* the pattern of the schema. We imply a schema by showing the schema in action (or by showing others reacting or interacting with the schema). For instance, people displaying birthday decorations and wrapping presents will imply the pattern of a birthday party. A character in a trench coat asking about a murder will imply the pattern of a detective. A man smiling and saying, "Who's a good boy?" with their arm moving in a petting motion will imply that there's a dog at the end of their hand (even if we can't yet see the dog). We can already see how humor can be derived from implying the pattern of a schema and then revealing that our expectation of the schema was mistaken. Perhaps it's revealed that the man is saying, "Who's a good boy?" to a newly purchased computer.

In Disney's *Atlantis*, Milo is giving a presentation. We see silhouettes of people and we assume it's a presentation to a live audience. Milo appears to be in front of an audience and we have no reason to believe otherwise. But it turns out it's a presentation to an audience of inanimate objects. This scene played off of our schema of a public presentation.

> *Takeaway:* Some expectations are implicit in our understanding of the rules of the world (i.e. schemas). Natural expectations can also arise from archetypes, clichés, tropes, and genres.

Creating New Expectations

While we all come to a story with certain expectations (i.e. those that we've built up through viewing other media and simply living life), there are expectations that are created within the story itself. These expectations often arise from the promises that the storyteller makes and from the beliefs that the characters have.

Recall that a promise can be created by having a character project into the future via a wish, a fortune, a hope, a demand, a request, a warning, a prediction, etc. If a character promises that there will be an arrest in a café later that night, we expect an arrest to occur (or at the very least it becomes a conscious possibility). If a character has a hope that something will happen, there's an implicit expectation that that thing might happen. If a character commands a subordinate to act a particular way, we expect the subordinate to act that way.

A promise can also be created through telegraphing. We can show people preparing for a birthday party, for instance. This creates an implicit promise that there will be a birthday party. We can also use explicit telegraphing by having a character say exactly what will happen. A character might say to another character, "Meet me behind the dumpster at noon." That creates an expectation that the two characters will meet behind the dumpster at noon.

Expectations are contagious. If a character expects something, the audience will tend to expect it as well. In other words, we can often create an expectation in the audience by first creating an expectation in a character. One of the best ways to create an expectation in a character is to give the character a strong belief.

Audiences will tend to adopt the beliefs of the characters they trust and tend to dismiss the beliefs of the characters they don't trust. We can take advantage of this by giving false beliefs to trustworthy characters and true beliefs to untrustworthy characters. If a trustworthy character believes that it's impossible to break out of a prison, the audience will tend to also adopt that belief. This is the case in *The Shawshank Redemption*. Red states his belief when he says, "Andy was right. I finally got the joke. It would take a man about six hundred years to tunnel under the wall with one of these." This then becomes an implicit belief of the audience.

To heighten the character's belief, we want to show the character *acting* on that belief.

We can give a character a belief by lying to them (i.e. by telling them false information and giving them no reason to distrust it). In *Star Wars*, Uncle Owen deliberately tells Luke that he's an orphan and says there's too much of his father in him—making us believe that his father is dead. Obi-Wan does nothing to counteract this when he says, "I knew your father." They all speak of Luke's father as if he's literally dead when in reality he's simply metaphorically dead through the death of his old self. Notice that when Uncle Owen and Obi-Wan lie to Luke, they're also implicitly lying to the audience. We also see a similar technique used in *Ocean's Eleven* when Danny and Rusty withhold the true heist plan from the rest of the crew (and thus from the audience)—effectively lying through omission. Consider why a character might be incentivized to lie to other characters or to the audience, such as in *The Usual Suspects*.

A character's belief might be born from an assumption. Once the character makes the assumption and adopts the belief, they might start telling others and may begin acting on the belief. This further solidifies the belief and any expectations that may arise from the belief. This is what happens in Pixar's *Coco* where Miguel believes that Ernesto de la Cruz is his great, great grandfather (even though the supposed head of Ernesto de la Cruz is cut off in the only family picture that serves as "evidence" for this belief).

Another important principle is that we form expectations about things based on how those things are treated. If characters are treating a situation like it's serious, we expect that it's serious. If a character is treated like they're a danger, we expect that they're dangerous. The opening of *Monsters, Inc.* takes advantage of this propensity for assumption. The beginning opens with a monster preparing to scare a child. The monster is treating the situation as if it's serious, but it's later revealed to be only a training exercise. This is an example of a technique we might call a "false rehearsal" (or "decoy") and can be a powerful tool for foreshadowing. A false rehearsal consists of a fake situation that's treated as real by its participants.

A key principle in setting expectations is that we believe people are acting on their intentions and desires. It follows, then, that the audience will make assumptions about a character's intention based on their actions. We see this quite clearly in the ending of *Casablanca*. Laszlo asks Rick to take Ilsa away using the letters of transit. Rick neither agrees to, nor refuses the request—but we know Rick's in love with Ilsa and he would *want* to run away with her. Later Rick tells Captain Renault that he's going to use the letters of transit to take Ilsa and escape from Casablanca. We have no reason to think this isn't true, especially since it was previously implied (though never explicitly confirmed). In this case, Rick is lying to Renault (and also to the audience) as part of a strategy to get what he wants (i.e. to free Laszlo and have him take Rick's place on the plane out of Casablanca). Rick tells Renault to free Laszlo so as to set up a sting where Renault (and Vichy France) can arrest Laszlo for a more serious criminal charge (as an accessory to murder). Rick's ostensible motivation for setting up the sting is to get Laszlo out of the picture for good so that Rick and Ilsa can safely escape. Notice how, on the surface, all of Rick's actions can be interpreted as selfishly motivated. Notice also how they can be interpreted at a deeper level as a selfless act in retrospect. As we'll see, the existence of two sets of facts is one key to a great twist.

We can also establish an expectation in a story through the use of repetition. The idea is that we create a baseline of expectation by establishing a pattern. If we see a character trip every time they get to the same location in a stairwell, we'll begin to expect that they'll trip the next time they head up the stairwell. As a rule of thumb, it takes two instances in order to establish a pattern and a third instance that begins like the previous two but ends differently. This is sometimes also called the "rule of threes" and is often used in joke telling in order to create and subvert expectations.

This concept of repetition extends to what we might call a "clone situation." A clone situation is a scene or situation that has a distinct similarity to a previous situation. When we show the audience an event that has clear similarities to a past event, we're creating a clear expectation about what should, could, or might happen (i.e. that it may be a repeat of the first event).

For instance, let's consider a clone situation in the movie *Forrest Gump*. It's Forrest's first day of school and he's about to get on the bus, but he hesitates. The bus driver asks him, "Are you coming along?" He says, "Mama said not to be taking rides from strangers." She says, "This is the bus to the school." He replies, "I'm Forrest, Forrest Gump." She introduces herself as Dorothy Harries and Forrest says, "Well now we ain't strangers anymore."

As Forrest looks for a seat on the bus, the school children all reject him. They say, "Seat's taken," "Taken," and "You can't sit here." Then Forrest hears "the sweetest voice in the wide world." Jenny says, "You can sit here if you want." This is the start of their deep friendship.

Later in the story, we get a clone situation. Forrest is an adult now. He's just enlisted in the army and he's about to get on the army bus. He treats the situation just like he did with his elementary school bus. He innocently says to the driver, "Hello, I'm Forrest, Forrest Gump." We immediately recognize the similarities to the past situation. We now have a strong expectation of what *should* or *might* happen. But the bus driver doesn't respond like the kind Dorothy Harris. This bus driver screams at Forrest, yelling profanities. The fact that we have Dorothy in our mind from the previous situation highlights the crassness of this bus driver.

Forrest again gets on the bus to try to find a spot. Again Forrest hears the voices he heard in elementary school: "Seat's taken" and "Taken." And once again, another character is there to accept Forrest when no one else will: Bubba. "You can sit down if you want to," he says. Because Bubba fills Jenny's role in this clone situation, we don't need any more information to know that Forrest and Bubba's relationship will be strong. An expectation has been set by showing the audience once already.

Finally we can create expectations using the Kuleshov Effect. In *No Country for Old Men*, there's a scene where we see the Sheriff outside of a hotel door. He's debating whether to enter the room. The camera then cuts to an interior scene where Anton Chigurh is waiting in the dark with a gun. Our minds tell us (via the Kuleshov Effect) that Chigurh is waiting inside the room that the Sheriff is considering entering. We find out this isn't the case, however, when the Sheriff enters and Chigurh is nowhere to be found.

Takeaway: We can create an expectation in the audience by creating an expectation in a character. This is typically done by giving the character a strong belief from false facts or from an assumption. We can establish an expectation based on how a subject is treated by others. We can also establish expectations from character action, repetition, clone situations, and the Kuleshov Effect.

How to Subvert an Expectation (and Create a Twist)

Now that we've learned how to establish an expectation, we can finally subvert it. In a way, a "twist" is the moment when the audience learns that they were part of a misunderstanding.

First we should note that some twists require more setup than others. Simple twists are often merely twists on a schema expectation (or a simple expectation setup through repetition or the Kuleshov Effect) and require little setup. These twists are usually relatively small and play off of the expectations we bring into a story before it begins. In Pixar's short *One Man Band*, there's a little girl named Tippy who's watching two street performers as they each impressively play a range of instruments. The two street performers inadvertently cause Tippy to drop her only coin. Tippy demands repayment, but neither of the performers has a coin. She finally exacts payment by seizing a violin. Given that Tippy is an exceptionally young child, our expectation is that she won't be able to play the violin well. After a few moments of awkwardly tuning, she begins playing like a virtuoso, subverting our expectation. This subversion of a schema generates a nice bit of satisfaction and dramatic interest.

We might also subvert a simple promise. We can use "false" telegraphing, for instance. Suppose we hear a man tell his boss that he'll be meeting an important client for lunch. We then watch him as he drives to a landfill for an undisclosed reason. This violates our expectation and surprises us. It's important to note that this only works if we first establish the expectation that the character will be meeting an important client. It's only then that we can subvert the expectation.

Intricate twists often require a decent amount of setup. For a climactic twist (particularly a battle or confrontation that the audience has been anticipating for a while), we need to create at least two realities (or two sets of facts). The first reality is the "surface" reality. It's what we assume to be the case (i.e. it's our expectation). The second reality is the "deep" reality and it's the truth. The twist is when the deep reality reveals itself and subverts the surface reality.

Let's consider a few twists and see what they have in common. As previously mentioned, spoilers ahead. In the original *Star Wars* trilogy, one of the big twists is that Darth Vader is Luke's father. In *The Usual Suspects*, the twist is that Verbal is actually Keyser Söze. In *The Sixth Sense*, the twist is that Bruce Willis' character has been dead the whole time. In *Fight Club*, the twist is that the narrator and Tyler Durden are one and the same. In *Psycho*, the twist is that Norman Bates and "Norma" are one and the same. In *The Planet of the Apes*, the twist is that the planet that's ruled by apes is actually Earth. In *The Shawshank Redemption*, the twist is that Andy is able to escape the prison by digging out through the sewer system.

So how might we create twists such as these? One method is to first decide on the truth. Who's the real villain? Who's the real mastermind? What's the true relationship between two characters? What's the true identity of the character? What's the true plan or strategy? Now we want to figure out a way to split this truth into two sets of facts—a surface reality and a deep reality.

We must first define the false reality. Who do we want the audience to think is the real villain? What do we want the audience to think is the true relationship between characters? What do we want the audience to think about the identity of the character? What do we want the audience to think is the plan or strategy? Once we've decided on the false reality, we've got to use our techniques to create that assumption in the audience. We've got to give enough evidence to plant the false belief.

One of the best ways to have the audience assume the false reality is to give a character a strongly held belief that the surface reality is the truth. In *The Sixth Sense*, Bruce Willis' character has a strongly held belief that he's alive. He acts on that belief. We can also have characters lie to other characters (and consequently to the audience). In *Star Wars*, Uncle Owen and Obi-Wan both lie to Luke about his father. In *Ocean's Eleven*, Danny and Rusty lie about the plan through omission. In *Psycho*, we never actually see Norman and his mother in the same scene. In *Fight Club*, we make use of the unreliable or faulty narrator technique where the narrator "hallucinates" a separate iden-

tity. From the narrator's perspective, Tyler Durden is indeed a separate entity. *The Usual Suspects* also uses this technique. The narrator
(Verbal) lies to the police officers and to the audience, leading us to
believe that Keyser Söze is a different person. To create the false reality, consider what evidence would need to be provided to the audience in order for them to make an assumption or adopt a belief.

It can be valuable to consider the rules that the surface reality
must follow. In *The Sixth Sense*, Bruce Willis' character can't ever
meaningfully interact with another human besides his patient who
sees dead people. In *Star Wars*, no one can explicitly say that Luke's
father is dead. In *Psycho*, we can never see Norman and his mother at
the same time.

To ensure that the audience doesn't suspect that the surface
reality is false, it can be helpful to provide clues that make the truth
seem impossible. In *Psycho*, for instance, we're shown a scene where
we see Norman's mother's shadow. We have no reason to question
that it's not the mother. In *The Usual Suspects*, Verbal seems too
incompetent to be a mastermind. In *Fight Club*, we see the narrator
and Tyler Durden interacting. In *The Sixth Sense*, we see Bruce Willis
interacting with another live human. In *Ocean's Eleven*, Danny explicitly lays out the heist plan to the crew (and consequently the audience). We have no reason to believe he'd lie to his own people.

Finally reveal that the deep reality is the truth. This may be done
by revealing to a character that their belief in the surface reality is a
lie or a faulty assumption. It may also be done by providing evidence
of the deep reality (such as the fact that Norman is "Norma" and that
Verbal is a highly intelligent con man).

The deep reality (i.e. truth) must be logical in retrospect. We must
be able to see how it could have logically occurred based on the
story's chain of cause and effect. If the twist isn't rooted in either
causality or logic, we're likely to upset the audience.

The basic concept of a twist is that we first want to make the audience believe that one sets of facts is absolutely true. We then later
reveal that it's not actually true. And most importantly, we provide a
plausible reason why that is.

Whether a simple or intricate subversion of an expectation, this method is a powerful way to generate dramatic interest.

Takeaway: To create an intricate twist, establish two sets of facts—a "surface" reality and a "deep" reality. Determine what evidence the audience will need in order to believe the surface reality. This is typically done by making a character believe the surface reality. Make the deep reality seem like it would be impossible or highly implausible. Then reveal the deep reality to create the twist. This may be done by revealing that a character's belief in the surface reality is false.

31

OTHER DRAMATIC TOOLS

Dramatic Intrigue

We can often generate dramatic interest through the simple method of introducing something unusual, unexpected, or intriguing. The idea is to pique the audience's interest through something that's just slightly "off." We want the audience to think, "Huh, that's odd." This technique is similar to that of presenting a contradiction.

We might see a character in a business suit but no pants. We might see a lawn chair being carried away by a pillar of balloons. We might see a dog in sunglasses with her elbow hanging out the car window. The idea is to pique our curiosity with a unique image.

One simple way to generate dramatic intrigue is to play around with blocking—the positioning and movement of characters within a scene. Perhaps two characters are having a conversation in the park except one of them is walking backward. Perhaps two characters are having a conversation at a table except one of them is standing on top of the table. Perhaps one is hopping up and down. We can consider how characters might be moving in an unusual way or might be unusually positioned.

To create dramatic intrigue, we might simply ask ourselves, "What would be an odd image?" We can later justify how it might be plausible within the story world. We want to brainstorm the visually and dramatically unusual, unexpected, obscure, unique, fascinating, awe-inspiring, and contradictory. Another example is the floating mountains in the movie *Avatar*.

> *Takeaway:* Use unusual, unexpected, or contradictory imagery to pique the interest of the audience.

The Familiar Wrapped in the Unfamiliar

There's a particular intrigue in seeing the familiar expressed in unfamiliar terms. This technique provides us a kernel of what we know but engages our mind to consider it in a new context. We're intrigued by the novelty of seeing the mundane in a new light. It piques our curiosity.

For instance, the *Harry Potter* series has a bank called Gringotts. We understand that it's a bank (familiar), but it's expressed in a wizarding world (unfamiliar). It has tellers, but they're goblins. It has security, but it's a dragon. It has clients, but they're wizards.

To use this technique, we can often simply consider a familiar occupation, location, setting, culture, task, or item and consider how it might function in an unfamiliar environment or story world. Sports and the Colosseum in the world of Pokémon looks like Pokémon stadiums. In *Monsters, Inc.*, energy production looks like monsters scaring children. In *Star Wars*, Samurai culture looks like the Jedi.

> *Takeaway:* Take the ordinary and express it in a new story world. We'll be intrigued by the novelty of seeing the mundane in a new light.

Immersion

We're trying to get the audience to mentally participate in decoding the story and the story world. If we spoon-feed them explanations, we remove a tool from our toolbox. Of course, we've got to balance Andrew Stanton's tool of "2+2" with the need to ensure that the audience knows what's going on (otherwise frustration and confusion arises). As a general principle, we want to make sure the story is clear but also let the story world feel strange, boundless, and unexplored.

Immersing an audience in a story world is all about throwing them into the deep end of the story world without a life vest. We must not be afraid to let the audience use their powers of deduction to figure out what's going on. Audiences *like* being immersed in unfamiliar jargon, rituals, rules, and culture. They *like* being trusted to figure things out on their own. We can't underestimate the audience's ability to understand what's going on through context and to enjoy the moment they figure it out on their own.

> *Takeaway:* Allow the audience to get lost in the story world and trust that the unfamiliar world will pique their interest. Inference is a strong dramatic tool.

Physical Comedy and Gags

Physical comedy transcends culture. When done well, it's a powerful source of laughter and amusement. People feel good when they laugh. They enjoy themselves. And so what does the audience want more of once they start laughing? More laughter. This is the simple yet powerful principle that makes the audience want to continue with a story that makes them laugh.

We generally enjoy watching characters physically struggle with incompetence as they try to accomplish their goals. In S6E14 of *Frasier*, Niles is preparing for a date on Valentine's Day when he discovers a crease in his pants. He pulls out the ironing board, but while he's ironing he notices a loose thread in his pants. He rushes to the kitchen to get some scissors but cuts his finger while yelling at Eddie, the dog, for eating his food off the table. Niles sees his blood from the cut and faints. All this time the iron has been fixed on one piece of his pants.

His pants light on fire. Everything spirals out of control through physical incompetence and he eventually lights the couch on fire.

Another great example is in *Friends* S5E11 when Ross is wearing leather pants on a date. He goes to the bathroom because his legs are sweating. He splashes water on his legs but can't pull his leather pants back up. He tries to use powder to dry up the sweat, but it combines with the water to form a paste. Hilarity ensues.

Pixar (and the genre of animation in general) makes heavy use of this technique. An example is when Woody first opens Buzz's space helmet, causing Buzz to begin gasping for air.

The caveat to this technique is that it must be suitable for the tone and atmosphere of the story. A dark, gritty drama should probably refrain from slapstick humor or risk alienating the audience. Likewise, gags should generally be avoided in moments of emotional weight.

> *Takeaway:* If it doesn't contradict the tone of the story, consider using physical comedy and gags where appropriate to capture the audience's interest.

Dramatization

We've heard the advice "show, don't tell." We can reword this as "dramatize, don't explain." In other words, don't tell us that something is happening—just show it happening.

Why is this advice helpful in generating dramatic interest? Dramatizing encourages the audience to decode the meaning of actions where telling just forces the meaning on to the audience with little to no inference. Dramatization requires active participation by the audience to figure out what's going on. As Andrew Stanton says, "The audience actually wants to work for their meal. They just don't want to know that they're doing that."

Don't tell us that two people are in love. Show us sideways glances and restrained laughter. Show us how he's uncharacteristically nervous around her. Show us how he stayed up all night carving a wooden locket for her.

Don't tell us that she's respected. Show the reactions when others speak her name. Show the hush when she enters a room. Show her ability to command attention and influence.

Don't tell us that he's dangerous. Show the lengths to which others have gone in order to restrain or ignore him. Show the faces turn pale when his name is whispered. Show the unending warnings others give.

YouTuber Thomas Flight succinctly sums up the benefits of dramatization in his analysis of *The Wire*: "*The Wire* doesn't try to grab and keep your attention—it requires it. And if you give it your attention, it will reward you." By requiring the audience to mentally participate in what's going on, we not only guarantee engagement, we reward it. Putting together the puzzle pieces laid out by dramatization makes the audience feel like they're active participants in the story.

> *Takeaway:* Dramatization forces the audience to actively participate in the story. They've got to take the pieces and infer a larger meaning from them. This helps guarantee the audience's attention.

Unstated Desire

We can use the principle of dramatization to generate dramatic interest by showing a character in the pursuit of something without telling the audience the character's desire. The idea is that if we show a character struggling and toiling at accomplishing something but don't tell the audience what the final goal is, we're inviting the audience to decode the character's actions and underlying desire. We're inviting them to infer and engage.

With this technique, we're simply showing a character enacting their plan. We offer no explanation to the audience about what the plan is meant to accomplish. We offer no explanation about where the plan will go. This creates a mystery. Audiences are smart. As long as the character is clear about what they're doing, the audience will begin to look for an explanation through context. We might also show a character saying something like, "I've got an idea." We then show them acting without explaining what the idea is.

This technique is used often in the shows *Breaking Bad* and *Better Call Saul*. In *Better Call Saul* S3E1, Mike appears to almost entirely disassemble his station wagon in the pursuit of something. We're not sure what it is, but we know no one would go to such great lengths unless they were trying to accomplish something specific. We see his frustration and persistence, further solidifying the fact that he wants something. We finally get our answer as to what Mike wants when he has a eureka moment and discovers a tracking device in his car's gas cap.

Once the character has completed or forsaken their pursuit, we might show the product of the character's success or failure. This will allow the audience to either confirm or deny their guess about what the character wanted. There's satisfaction in getting a definitive answer to one's guess. There's also satisfaction in piecing it all together on one's own.

One key to this technique is that it needs to be clear to the audience that the character is actually trying to accomplish something. The fact that the character has intention behind their actions needs to be especially pronounced perhaps through struggle, deep thought, or experimentation.

A slight variation of this technique is to tell the audience what the character wants to accomplish, but make it unclear *how* they'll accomplish it. We then show the character in the process of enacting a plan that hasn't been explained. We see this in the lead up to the climax of *Toy Story* where Woody recruits Sid's toys to help save Buzz. He says, "Okay, I think I know what to do. We're gonna have to break a few rules. But if it works, it'll help everybody."

As a general principle, we want to use this technique of unstated desire if the character's plan will succeed. This ensures that the dramatic situation is driven by mystery rather than a dramatic question (allowing us to avoid a dramatic question that's answered with success). If the character will fail in their plan, however, we may want to make the desire and plan clear upfront so that the audience can feel the tension as the plan spirals off course and out of control.

Recall that a character may also have a desire to prevent or avoid. When this is the case, the character has a fear that something may occur (such as the reveal of a secret). We can use the technique of "unstated desire" here to show a character in the act of trying to prevent or avoid something but without telling the audience exactly what it is the character is trying to avoid. We might think of this as the "unstated secret." This is one of the drivers of *Good Will Hunting* as Will tries to avoid confronting his past.

> *Takeaway:* Show a character struggling and enacting a plan without specifying their goal. This raises a mystery about what the character's pursuing and will typically capture the audience's attention as they try to solve the mystery. This technique is perhaps best applied when a character's plan will succeed.

Imagination

Imagination is activated by what Andrew Stanton calls "the well-organized absence of information." The central concept is that if we recognize that there's missing information, we'll go to work on trying to imagine what's missing.

We've got to know there's an open question in order to start imagining potential answers. For this reason, imagination is all about implication. It's activated by what is implied, not what is specified. It's the *absence* of what we suspect we should see, hear, or feel that activates imagination.

As mentioned, we start by first implying the *absence* of information. Generally we want to provide sensory "evidence" but not draw conclusions for the audience. This technique goes hand in hand with establishing a mystery but lets the audience fill in the missing information with their imagination (rather than wait for an explicit answer).

Consider showing only a piece of the whole. If we show one side of a conversation, for instance, we'll generate interest in the other missing half. We might also show a conversation but strategically cut out particular lines of interest through ambient noise or some other distraction. We can use this same technique to show only pieces of an image and leave the audience to guess as to what could be in the missing area. This also allows us to misdirect the audience by feeding them false information about what's missing (which is often done by giving a character a strong belief about what's missing).

Consider showing sound but not imagery. Imagination is our ability to create images in our mind based on what we suspect is missing. We can say that as a general rule, providing sight is less likely to activate the imagination than providing only sound (since the images are explicitly provided rather than being implied). To take advantage of this, let the audience hear something that they can't see. We might hear a murder, for instance, but not see it. This will activate the imagination. We can, of course, provide images that *imply* a thing but that aren't images of the thing itself. In the example of a murder, we might see bloody footprints or blood spatter.

Consider showing imagery but not sound. Our mind will want to "fill in the blanks" and imagine what the characters could be discussing, for instance, based on their body language. In *The Office* S5E28, Jim takes Pam to the hospital for an injury sustained during a volleyball game. In the final scene, we see Pam smiling and nodding as Jim is on the verge of tears. They embrace. This is shown to us, but there's no sound. We've got to use our imagination to deduce that Pam's pregnant. To create a scene such as this, we might first write out the scene with sight and sound, particularly emphasizing body language. Then we simply remove the sound. The visuals will likely need to be explicit or exaggerated.

Consider showing the effects but not the event. In other words, show us the consequences of the thing. Show the spider's webs but not the spider. Show the wake of the shark but not the shark. Show the mud tracks but not the trespasser. Show the ripples but not the splash. Show the ruins but not the bomb. Show the bullet holes in the returning vehicles. Allow us to imagine what the enemy might look like before we ever see them.

Consider showing the reaction but not the action. In other words, show us how others react to the event, but don't show the event itself. We see this in the beginning of *Arrival* when we first see the students' shocked reaction before we see that they're reacting to an alien landing. We also get some great use of sound but not sight. Before we see the alien crafts, the TV says, "Unfortunately, Montana right now is on complete lockdown. The object apparently touched down forty minutes ago just north of I-94. We're waiting to hear if this is perhaps an experimental vessel." We are left to fill in the images with our imagination.

Another example of showing reaction instead of the thing itself is in the shower scene of *Psycho*. We see the woman's reaction before we ever see the killer. We also see the shadow before we see the killer. These bits of sensory evidence ask us to fill in the missing information. Our imaginations can be far more haunting than reality ever could. This is good for all writers to keep in mind but particularly horror writers.

Imagination is about engaging with what is *not* seen. We create narratives and images in our head and we often become emotionally invested in those images. Imagination can create images far more powerful than we could ever hope to explicitly dramatize.

Takeaway: Imagination is activated by providing the outline of a puzzle but leaving out critical information. Show a piece of the whole. Show sound but not imagery. Show imagery but not sound. Show effects but not the cause. Show reaction but not the action.

Direction and Narrative Drive

"Drama is anticipation mingled with uncertainty."

— WILLIAM ARCHER

The majority of our dramatic tools are about giving direction to our story. They're about creating expectations and thus an anticipation of what will happen next. Once we've got the audience anticipating where we're going, we've got the upper hand. We can then play with their anticipation. We can subvert their expectations.

When we raise a dramatic question, we're also creating an obligation for ourselves. We're implicitly promising to the audience that the dramatic question will be answered. We're promising that they'll eventually find out whether the character gets what they want. And so we're additionally promising what might be called an "obligatory scene." That is, we're promising a scene in which that dramatic question is answered. In this way, we're giving the story direction by telling the audience what kind of scene they can eventually expect. This creates anticipation.

We can also set the direction of a story or dramatic situation using dramatic irony and promises. With each of these tools, we're implicitly promising to the audience that an informational disequilibrium will eventually be resolved and that a promise will eventually be fulfilled.

Convergence and ticking clocks also create an endpoint in the audience's mind. This creates a sense of direction as we careen toward the moment where the elements collide and the clock runs out.

We don't want the audience to wonder where we're going. We want them to think they *know* where we're going. That's the precise moment we've got them. We're then free to play.

At their core, these dramatic tools are all about getting the audience to ask the question, "What will happen next?" This forward momentum is called narrative drive and we must protect it at all costs. If a story ever loses its narrative drive, the audience stops wanting to know what's going to happen next. We lose them. If we lose the audience in the short-term, we lose our chance at conveying a meaningful theme.

We always want the audience anticipating. We always want them expecting. And we always want to have open questions. Story isn't a sequence of questions asked and answered. It's an overlapping mesh of unanswered questions sprinkled with consequential revelations as we crescendo toward a climactic moment. We don't answer a question until we've opened a new one.

Drama is about withholding information until revealing it is more interesting than hiding it.

> *Takeaway*: Use dramatic tools to give the audience a clear idea of where the story's going. We always want to provide directionality, anticipation, and expectation. Once we've got the audience anticipating, we're free to subvert their expectations and create additional interest.

Stage VI Wrap-up

We've now learned some of the core dramatic tools that we can use to make each individual moment in our story interesting. Next it's time to actually write those moments. We'll look at how scenes work and how they can be used to bring the beats of a story to life.

PART VII

BRING IN THE FURNITURE!

DRAMATIZATION AND SCENES

We've finally arrived at the stage where it's time to bring the house to life. It's time to put up the mirrors, lay down the carpet, move in the furniture, and make it feel like home. This is where the story takes its final form and turns from structure into words.

32

HOW TO WRITE A SCENE

The scene is where the story actually happens. We've defined the elements and beats of our story, but all of our work thus far has been effectively theoretical. The elements and beats only become real to the audience once we dramatize them. They only become real once we *show* them to the audience. The scene is the place where the rubber meets the road and the story takes shape through dramatization.

With that in mind, writing a scene is about first defining what we need to accomplish in the scene and then crafting an organic and contextually believable situation in which that purpose can be served. At the same time as we ensure that a scene serves its purpose within the global story, we must remember that we've got to maintain the audience's attention through the use of our dramatic tools.

Our first step in writing a scene is to ask, "What does this scene need to accomplish?" What's the scene's purpose in the global story? What story beat is it intended to serve? Does it need to define any foundational story elements? What information are we trying to convey to the audience? Are we revealing anything to a character? What effect will this scene have? Who or what will change by the end of this scene? Is the scene progressing the story? Has the information in this scene already been conveyed? In short, *why* does this scene exist?

Let's explore a few possible purposes that we might want a scene to serve. We might want a scene to introduce a character, establish empathy for a character, define a character's desire or plan, define the opposition in a dramatic situation, define or raise the stakes of a dramatic situation, define the urgency of a dramatic situation, establish a character's ghost, establish a character's worldview, summarize or reiterate the plot thus far, explore the dynamics of a relationship, foreshadow an important piece of technology or magic, reveal a secret, clear up a misunderstanding, show that a character is dangerous, etc.

It's important to note that a scene can (and ideally should) exist to serve multiple purposes. We might, for example, want a single scene to introduce a character, define their worldview, and define their desire. In these instances, we want to try to accomplish the scene's multiple purposes through the same situation, conversation, etc. rather than through trying to fit two situations or two conversations into the same scene. In these instances where we want to accomplish multiple purposes but can't figure out a way to serve them all through the same situation or conversation, we should split the purposes into their own individual scenes for clarity and dramatic poignancy.

Our next step is to determine how we intend to accomplish the scene's purpose. If we need to establish a character's worldview, we must ask ourselves how and in what circumstances a character might believably and organically express a worldview? *Little Miss Sunshine* does this for Richard by showing him expressing his worldview during a public speech. If we need to establish empathy for a character, how do we intend to do that? Are we going to show the character caring for someone or something? Are we going to show undeserved misfortune? And how can we do that naturally?

Scene work is about taking information we need the audience to know and figuring out how to express it organically through the story world. Instead of telling the audience that a character has a particular belief, we're going to show that character acting on their belief.

Instead of telling the audience that a character has an obsession, we're going to show the character obsessing. Instead of telling the audience that a relationship is deteriorating, we're going to show two characters as their behavior toward each other becomes colder and more hostile.

In defining the beats of our story, we've determined what information we need the audience to know and when we need them to know it. Now we've got to take that information and make it interesting through drama. Scene work is about *showing* the audience our story elements rather than telling them. In other words, scene work is about dramatizing information.

> *Takeaway:* To write a scene, we first determine the purpose we need the scene to serve in the story. What information does it need to convey to the audience? We then figure out a believable way to organically dramatize that information in the story world.

The Elements of a Scene

When writing a scene, we want to ask these questions:

- What do we want to accomplish in the scene? What information are we trying to get across to the audience? Is this scene progressing the story?
- Is the information conveyed to the audience fundamentally new? We should be honest with ourselves in asking whether the audience already knows the information in the scene (and cut it if they do).
- How will we dramatize that information? In other words, how are we going to express information to the audience through action? Are there any thematic strategies we could use?
- How are we going to convey information while maintaining narrative drive? In other words, how are we

going to convey information while maintaining the audience's interest?

- Will we use dramatic tension, dramatic irony, convergence, promises, or some other tool of narrative drive?

These are our primary questions as we craft a scene.

After we've established the essential context of our story, we may find that many scenes will depict a character as they enact a plan toward their desire. Let's look at how we might plan a scene that depicts a character working toward a goal.

The first step is to identify the basic elements of drama in the scene. We must define desire, motivation, plan, opposition, stakes, and urgency.

- Who is the protagonist of the scene? In other words, who is the character who'll drive the scene forward based on their desire? Remember that the protagonist of a scene isn't necessarily the protagonist of the global story.
- What does the scene protagonist want? Is the character trying to attain something (i.e. chase) or avoid something (i.e. escape)?
- Why does the character have this desire? What's their motivation?
- What's the character's plan to get what they want? What strategies and tactics are they willing to use?
- Who or what stands in the way of the character attaining their desire? What force opposes the character's desire?
- What does the character stand to lose if they don't attain their desire? In other words, what's at stake?
- What's the urgency behind the character attaining their scene desire?

Some of the most interesting story moments arise when a character wants something from someone else. In these instances, the scene's protagonist must devise a strategy to attempt to attain (or avoid) something from the scene's antagonist, typically via persuasion, manipulation, deception, or coercion. In this scenario, we need to ensure that the two (or more) characters in the scene are dramatically opposed in a structural way. In other words, the two must be vying for control of the same underlying thing and only one of them can get it.

We want to spend time considering the various strategies that the scene protagonist could enact toward their goal. What are the different methods they could use to get what they want from the opposing character? And how would the opposing character respond to each strategy? This is really where the back and forth of the scene plays out.

We'll also want to consider the following questions:

- What relevant information does each character know at the start of the scene?
- How will each character use their information against the other character?
- Does each character know what the other one wants?
- If a character knows what the other one wants, will they make it known that they know?
- Who's withholding information about what they know or don't know?
- How will each character's strategy undermine the other's?
- How would each character respond to a loss or victory in the scene?
- Will the scene resolve with a character victory or failure? Who will succeed or fail in attaining their desire? What technique will cause success or failure?
- Will the scene make any promises about what's to come?

Takeaway: We must define the dramatic elements of the scene, including desire, motivation, plan, opposition, stakes, and urgency. We must then consider the tactics and strategies that the scene's protagonist will use in the pursuit of their scene goal.

Scene Strategy and Subtext

It's been said that a scene is either a fight, a seduction, or a negotiation. In either case, a scene is often some type of exchange between two characters as one or both of them work toward a goal. In practice this means that at any given moment each character has a momentary strategy that they think will help them get what they want.

We can reduce a character's strategy down to a single verb. The strategy might be "to attack," "to defend," "to sabotage," "to entice," "to seduce," "to persuade," "to plead," "to proposition," "to vex," "to deflect," "to shut down," "to reject," or "to accuse," for instance. The character uses this strategy in an attempt to attain their scene desire.

Let's say that we have a protagonist who wants to extract a vault's access code from an opponent. The protagonist has two fundamental choices for how they can enact their strategy. They can do it either through physical action or through dialogue. If the protagonist were to attempt to extract the code via physical action, they might try to deceive or manipulate the opponent by impersonating someone or perhaps they may try to use physical seduction. They might alternatively coerce the opponent through force or torture (as they either try to gain access to a physical object or extract the information through pain). If, on the other hand, the protagonist were to decide to attempt to extract the code via dialogue, more nuanced approaches to deception and manipulation become available. Through dialogue the scene's protagonist might offer a persuasive argument as to why they have a legitimate right to access the vault's code.

When a character attempts to enact a strategy through dialogue, they can do it either directly or indirectly. Direct dialogue is when a character says exactly what's on their mind. Their surface goal and their actual goal are one and the same. The character might simply ask for what they want. They might use verbal coercion such as a threat, blackmail, extortion, etc. Enacting a strategy through direct dialogue is fairly rare for reasons we previously covered in our exploration of subtext. Sometimes the social stakes (i.e. the consequences of failure) are too high for the character to be direct. Other times, the character may not believe that the opponent would succumb to direct dialogue.

In the majority of instances, a character's strategy can be enacted through indirect dialogue. This allows for a subtler and often more effective tool for the protagonist to attempt to get something from the opponent. With indirect dialogue, a character can use deception and manipulation by masking their true intention. In this case, a character's surface goal is different than their actual goal. The character establishes pretext (i.e. a surface justification) for their words and thus creates a façade (i.e. a false goal) to present to others.

Let's say, for example, that a scene's protagonist is asking their spouse questions about where they've been. This might be distilled down to the strategy "testing." The spouse may give false information, which is a strategy of "lying." Instead of the scene protagonist directly saying, "Where were you last night?", they could instead say, "So I heard Rob won at your bowling league last night." Notice how the protagonist is still using the same strategy of "testing," but now they're doing it indirectly. Notice how there's subtext in this character's words now. The situation is being handled indirectly rather than directly. We can inject subtext into our scenes by having characters enact their strategies indirectly rather than directly. This creates a gap between what we're witnessing (the surface conversation) and what we know is actually on in the character's mind (the subtext).

When we look at dialogue this way, it's clear that dialogue is nothing more than a method by which a character can enact a strategy. Whether direct or indirect, dialogue is a strategy to attain a desire.

If a character is pursuing a goal through an indirect strategy, we have the option to either let the audience in on the goal (which makes use of dramatic irony) or to keep the goal hidden (which makes use of unstated desire). The first technique will create interest as we wonder whether the other characters will uncover the character's true goal. The second technique creates interest as we wonder what the character is doing (thus creating a mystery).

A scene unfolds as a back and forth between two characters as one acts and the other reacts. They each thrust and parry as the opponent's strategy forces improvisation and adaptation. As the scene progresses, characters may enact their strategy more directly, removing any subtext. Eventually one character may land a blow (intentionally or not) and bring about the turning point of the scene where a disruption occurs and a story value shifts.

> *Takeaway:* A character can attempt to attain their goal through persuasion, manipulation, deception, or coercion. These strategies can take the form of physical action or dialogue. When a character uses dialogue, their strategy can be indirect (thus creating a façade) or direct. As scenes progress, strategies tend to become more direct.

Philosophical Arias and Worldview in Dialogue

While some scenes are just about a character enacting a plan to get something from another character, the more emotionally impactful scenes go thematically deeper. These scenes are more than just the surface level of asking for a favor or extracting information. They're about two characters arguing over conflicting approaches to life. They're about characters promoting their worldviews in the face of thematic opposition. These characters are fighting about what's *right* and what's *wrong.*

Letting a character champion their worldview by arguing what is right and what is wrong allows us to explore theme through character. A character who's promoting a worldview typically wants others to adopt that view and they're ready to lay out their best argument for it. This is an argument of beliefs, morality, and the right way of living life.

This technique allows us to highlight a character's approach to life and to deliver a philosophical aria. In *Little Miss Sunshine*, for example, Richard makes his worldview clear when he says, "There are two kinds of people in this world: winners and losers. Inside each and every one of you—at the very core of your being—is a winner waiting to be awakened and unleashed upon the world."

We also see this in *It's a Wonderful Life* when George Bailey is conveying his worldview by challenging Mr. Potter. Bailey says, "Well, is it too much to have them work and pay and live and die in a couple of decent rooms and a bath? Anyway, my father didn't think so. People were human beings to him, but to you, a warped frustrated old man, they're cattle. Well, in my book he died a much richer man than you'll ever be!"

> *Takeaway:* Emotionally impactful scenes are about a clash of worldviews. Each character makes their moral argument about what is right and what is wrong. They make an argument about how the world works, how it should work, and how life should be lived.

The Turning Point

Remember that every scene culminates in a turning point where a story value changes. This turning point typically occurs the moment that new, significant information is conveyed. It's the reason the scene exists—to deliver new information. It might be the success or failure of a character in attaining their scene goal. It might have nothing to do with a scene goal and instead be a disruption that turns the story in a new direction and gives rise to a new desire. It might be an unexpected revelation or discovery. The turning point can often be thought of as a disruption where new information is revealed or unexpected action takes place.

33

PRINCIPLES OF DRAMATIZATION

Dramatization is about expressing story information through action. Instead of saying that a character desires a suitcase, we simply show a character who can't take their eyes off of it. Instead of saying that a character has died, we show a black curtain being lowered over their portrait. Instead of saying that a potential choice is fraught with danger, we show another character making that incorrect choice and being killed for it. Instead of saying that a character is angry with someone, we show them forcefully discarding an object belonging to the other character. These are all examples where we're expressing a piece of story information through action in the story world, but we're never explicitly stating it. This is the goal of dramatization.

As we discussed earlier, dramatization is at the heart of Andrew Stanton's rule of 2+2. We want to give the audience the puzzle pieces and let them put together the ultimate meaning. This forces the audience to remain mentally engaged at the same time as it provides a natural dopamine reward for figuring out story information. Let's explore a few principles of dramatization to help us more organically express story information.

Reactions

Reactions are a way of quickly expressing a character's emotions and internal state. We can use reactions to show how a character feels about a person, an object, a situation, etc. If a character says they're indifferent to a vase, but they cringe as it loses its balance, we now know that the character actually *does* care about the vase. If a man stands stone-faced in an elevator but then flashes a slight smile as a woman enters, we know how he feels about her. If a character begins to fidget as soon as a police officer walks in the room, we've created a mystery and the fidgeting character is immediately suspect.

Reactions can also be used to show the audience how they should feel about something. This technique is used in the beginning of *Arrival* when we see the classroom's stunned reaction to the news reports, but we don't know exactly what's at the heart of the reporting. The looks tell us that whatever's happening is worthy of a stunned response—even if we don't yet know what it is. We can use this principle to show that a character is dangerous, for example. We see this technique in *Harry Potter* where even the mention of Lord Voldemort's name incites fear.

Objects

We can use objects to physically represent information, characters, relationships, events, trauma, and even ideas. In this way, physical objects can function as symbols.

For instance, let's consider how we might use an object as a symbol of a relationship. Let's say we have two characters meet for the first time at a deli when one accidentally spills ketchup on the other's white shirt. By tying a stain to an emotional moment in their relationship—the first time the two met—we've made it significant. Now anytime the character looks contemplatively at their stained shirt (or any stain for that matter), we know they're thinking about the other character. The stained shirt is now symbolic of the relationship and provides subtext to any scene in which it may appear.

In *The Umbrella Academy,* one of the male antagonists requests a jelly donut from a woman at a donut shop. The two of them have a long conversation about the donut and how she's fluffy like the donuts. In a later scene, he's seen eating a jelly donut, which instantly brings to mind the woman from the donut shop.

Objects can be used to connect any two story elements. In the opening of Hitchcock's *Sabotage,* we see a group of men inspecting a broken machine and pulling sand from its insides. They confirm that the machine was deliberately sabotaged and wonder who could have done this. We then see a character, Verloc (giving us a tentative answer via the Kuleshov Effect). Verloc arrives back at home and we see him washing his hands. The sink fills with sand. We've got our saboteur. By having an unusual (i.e. "out of place") or noteworthy object appear both at the sabotaged machine and on Verloc's hands, we connect Verloc to the scene of the crime.

We can put a unique object (or an action, behavior, gesture, quirk, line of dialogue, etc.) in a situation so that when we see another situation with the same unique object, we can quickly draw a connection between the situations or events. This is done in the show *Das Boot* when a man is having bad dreams. After he wakes up, he takes a particular pill from a container. When we see that the man has a bad dream again in the future, he takes the pill from his container again. We connect the two and remember the previous recurrence.

We can even use objects as measurement devices to let us know how close we are to a deadline. In *Beauty and the Beast,* the decaying rose and its petals tell us how much time before the curse is permanent. To stress the time remaining, the storytellers need only show a single rose petal fall. In *E.T.,* the flowerpot is a symbolic representation of the health of both E.T. and Elliot. When the flower is dying, E.T. is dying. When E.T. comes back to life, the flower comes back to life as well. By tying health and time to these symbolic objects, we can use visual metrics to countdown the time remaining in the dramatic situation.

We can use objects to highlight how someone (or something) is different to those around them. We do this through contrast. In *Office*

Space, Joanna is a server at Chotchkie's where the employees are required to wear pins ("flair") on their outfit. In contrast to the rest of the employees, Joanna actively chooses not to add more flair than is necessary. Her boss approaches her and says, "What do you think of a person who only does the bare minimum?" She responds, "You know what, Stan, if you want me to wear 37 pieces of flair like your pretty boy over there, Brian, why don't you just make the minimum 37 pieces of flair?" From the way her outfit contrasts with the outfits of her co-workers, we can tell she doesn't belong at Chotchkie's.

Objects can also be used to symbolize achievements. In these instances, the object acts as a sort of trophy. In the show *Dexter*, Dexter keeps blood slides of his victims, which act as trophies. Each slide symbolizes a different kill. An astronaut might have a moon rock that symbolizes her accomplishments. A clock repairman might have trophies of particularly difficult cases throughout the years. These trophy objects also tend to act as memory triggers (which can be particularly helpful when the story uses a narrator).

Richard Price said, "The bigger the issue, the smaller you write. Remember that. You don't write about the horrors of war. No. You write about a kid's burnt socks lying on the road. You pick the smallest manageable part of the big thing, and you work off the resonance." This is a key principle for dramatization. We want to prefer and focus on those concrete objects that are involved in a substantial, impactful, important, and/or traumatic experience.

When we include a unique or noteworthy object in a significant or emotion-filled moment, the object becomes intrinsically tied to the elements of that moment. If the object isn't inherently unusual or noteworthy in its environment, we must draw special attention to it via narrative weight (i.e. focus).

Takeaway: Objects can be used as symbols of relationships, events, accomplishments, people, and even time. Objects can also be used to highlight connections between people, places, situations, crimes, etc.

Relativity and Comparison

Comparing story elements is a particularly effective way of high-lighting their differences and similarities. For instance, we might show how a character reacts to a situation and then show how a different character reacts to the same situation entirely differently. This draws attention to the differences between the characters doing the reacting. We might show a woman who smiles at one man and glares at another man. This draws attention to the differences between the men and how the woman feels about them.

We can draw a comparison between a character's choice at one point in time and the same character's choice in the same situation but at a different point in time. This draws attention to the character's change over time.

Comparison can be used, for example, to show how an element *should* be versus how it actually *is*. This is used in *Ocean's Eleven* where we preview the way that the heist should go down before we see it in action. When we see it in action, the difference between the expectation and reality is highlighted. We wouldn't get this effect if we hadn't first dramatized the plan for the heist. This allows a direct comparison.

Comparison can be used to establish the stakes of a dramatic situation by showing what happens if a character fails. This is what happens in the climax of *Indiana Jones and the Last Crusade* where Indie must correctly choose the Holy Grail. We first see a Nazi choose the wrong Grail and die horribly. When it's Indie's turn to choose, we understand the consequences of an incorrect choice and the suspense is heightened.

We can also compare two elements through the use of parallelism. We can show the two elements acting in a similar way simultaneously. We might have one character start a line of dialogue and then cross-cut to another character finishing that same line of dialogue, for instance. Less directly, we might show one character discussing a particular topic and then cross-cut to another character discussing that same topic (even if their lines of dialogue aren't identical). We can also show two settings that have strikingly similar occupants or characteristics such as Kansas and the Land of Oz in *The Wizard of Oz*.

We can compare characters, reactions, situations, decisions, emotions, etc. in space, time, or medium in order to highlight differences, similarities, and change. We previously discussed additional techniques to draw comparisons via the Kuleshov Effect as part of our dramatic tools.

Takeaway: Comparing two people, events, plans, or reactions allows us to quickly highlight differences in a dramatically interesting way.

Measure Change

We've discussed how we can explore a theme by showing how characters, settings, and situations change for good and bad. For this to be an effective technique, however, we've got to be able to dramatize that change has occurred. So how do we do that?

Change is dramatized by measuring a value at one point in time and then measuring it again at another point in time. To highlight that a man's demeanor has changed from calm to angry, we have to have first seen his calm demeanor in order for his new angry demeanor to mean anything. We must understand what something was *before* the change in order to appreciate what it is *after* the change. Change is inherently relative. This point is sometimes so obvious that it can be missed. We might mistakenly assume that the audience understands or simply infers the "before" state. It's not a mistake we can afford when dramatizing change.

A key to dramatizing change is to pick the correct (or most interesting) measurement device to show the changed value. If we want to highlight that a man's demeanor has changed from calm to angry, then we must figure out how we're going to dramatize demeanor. One way is to show how the man reacts to a stressful situation. By first showing his calm reaction and then later showing his angry reaction to a similar or identical situation, we highlight the change in his demeanor.

Some measurement devices require more mental engagement from the audience than others (and are potentially more interesting). If we want to dramatize that someone has gained weight, the most obvious measurement device is a scale. We can show the character's weight via the scale and then later show an increased number. We might, however, consider other measurement devices to signify a change in weight. Perhaps the character's pants no longer fit. Perhaps the character's wedding band no longer slides past their knuckle. Perhaps the character is no longer comfortable with their space on a bus or plane. These are all different measurement devices we can use to dramatize a value.

In certain circumstances, we may be able to get away with dramatizing change without showing a "before" state. We might be able to do this by dramatizing a strong character reaction to the value's measurement. If a character reacts in disbelief or joy to a value, for instance, it's implied that the value has changed. If a character struggles to button their pants and that's immediately followed by disbelief or noticeable concern (by either themselves or by someone else), the change is implied. This technique would probably not work if our measurement device were the character's comfort on a plane or bus, for instance. This technique can be subtle depending on the measurement device and if we really want to highlight a change, then we should be sure to first dramatize the "before" value.

> *Takeaway:* Change is dramatized by comparing the measurement of a value at two points in time. In order to show change, we must usually highlight the "before" value in order to give the "after" value meaning.

Imply and Suggest

Dramatizing something's value is about suggestion and implication. There are many cases where we want to make something known without showing it explicitly.

For instance, if we want to show that a character has stumbled into a spider's lair, our first thought might be to show a spider. But what if we instead focused on evidence that *implies* a spider's lair? We see the webs before we see the spider. We see the wrapped bodies before we see the spider. We see the *effects* of the thing before we see the thing itself.

To imply or suggest a war, we show the bodies being taken away on stretchers. We show walls riddled with bullets. We show tattered and burnt clothes in the street. We show discarded dolls and bloody footprints. We show the *consequences* of the thing before the thing itself.

A few questions we might ask of a thing we want to dramatize: What would be the effects of [x]? What would the reactions to [x] look like? In what kind of environment would [x] live or exist? What would it look like to prepare for [x]? What would the aftermath or consequence of [x] look like?

Show its tracks, its echoes, its influence, its wake, its destruction, its creations, its ripples, its reflection. But don't show it—yet.

> *Takeaway:* Implying or suggesting something before showing it allows the audience to use their imagination. We should prefer showing the effects and consequences of something before we show the thing itself.

Direct Audience Emotion via Character Emotion

It's often the case that if we want the audience to feel something, we can first make a character feel it. This works best when the audience is already emotionally bonded to the character experiencing the emotion. To create anticipation, we can give a character a fear or desire for a particular outcome. To create a sense of joy, show a character sharing their success with loved ones. To create a feeling of sadness, show a character experience a loss and sulk in hopelessness. To make the audience feel a sense of wonder, we can show a character who feels a sense of wonder and awe (such as Wall-E looking at the flame in Eve's hand). This technique derives its effectiveness from a principle called social proof. The premise is that we look to others to help understand how we should feel. In the words of the band *Local Natives*, "If I didn't know to be afraid, the faces made me sure that I know now."

Dramatizing With Thematic Tools

Any opportunity to further explore or argue our story's thematic question should be pursued. With this in mind, we want to consider whether we can use any of our thematic tools to dramatize information.

Recall that a clone character (or situation) is a way for us to show what could, should, or might happen to a character if they take a particular path. Can we use a clone character to convey information about where the character is headed or might be headed either philosophically, emotionally, or physically? We might show a clone character suffering due to their inability to make the correct choice in a thematic dilemma, for instance. How can we dramatize through clones the thing that the character fears most or hopes for most?

Another thematic tool is that of the worldview. Can we convey information about how the world works by showing a character with a strong worldview and belief system? This character is usually a thematic mentor or thematic opponent. Perhaps the character expresses their worldview and belief system through actions and deeds. We want to see how their approach to life dictates and guides the decisions they make under pressure and the actions they choose to take. We might also have this type of character deliver a philosophical aria where they either champion their worldview in general or argue it specifically to another character.

And finally, we can use the thematic tool of choice. Can information in the scene be conveyed through a difficult character choice? Can we learn something about a character, not only from a decision they make under pressure but also from *how* they make that decision? Can we learn something about the world based on what kind of difficult decisions are thrust upon the character?

Takeaway: We can use clone characters, worldviews, philosophical arias, and moral dilemmas to dramatize information in a way that enforces our story's theme.

34

OTHER SCENE TOOLS

Directionality and Urgency

Just as we want our overall story to have a clear direction and end point, we also want this for our scene. The easiest and perhaps most natural way of doing this is to give the scene some sense of urgency in the form of a ticking clock or deadline.

This urgency doesn't necessarily need to be an explicit count-down, but there should ideally be something that's pushing the scene's protagonist to accomplish their goal sooner rather than later. It might be as simple as one character being late for a meeting. It might consist of one character saying, "You shouldn't be here." This creates urgency and the implicit threat that the two could be caught talking to each other.

To heighten the urgency, we might tie an explicit deadline to the character's goal. There might be an approaching threat, for example. Or perhaps one character literally says, "You have thirty seconds before I walk away."

We might also simply place in the audience's mind an implicit end point for the scene. It might come from a microwave timer that's counting down. It might come from a child that's on their way home from school. We know that when the microwave starts beeping or when the child arrives, the scene's over. It's a subconscious end point, not necessarily a concretely logical one.

Whether urgency is logically tied to the character's goal or whether it merely serves to implicitly mark an end point to the scene, this urgency can be used to generate narrative drive and keep the audience engaged.

Setting

The right setting can take a scene from interesting to captivating. Let's explore a few principles when crafting the right setting for our scene.

First of all, the scene's setting should support the purpose of the scene. What feeling are we trying to convey in the scene? Is it a suspenseful scene where we may want to prefer a closed-in, claustro-phobic space? Or is it a pensive, introspective scene where we may want to prefer a more open landscape? Would the purpose of the scene be heightened by making the setting bustling or empty? Would it be better at day or night? Dusk or dawn? Raining or as dry as parched lips?

What feeling are we trying to evoke in the characters? Do we want a character to be tense or afraid? What physical environment would cause the most fear or discomfort consciously or subconsciously? What would remind the character of what they fear most? Do we want a character to be hopeful? What setting would cause them to consider change and opportunity? Crafting a setting to evoke a particular character emotion can help convey that same feeling in the audience.

Setting isn't merely a place where action happens to take place. Setting itself can enable action that might not otherwise be taken. We can consider how a character might use the setting itself to carry out their objective or strategy. If two characters are in an elevator and one is angry at the other, the angry character may light up all the buttons on the elevator or they may sound the emergency alarm.

A setting should be a unique expression of the story world. If a story takes place on a planet with an advanced alien civilization, but the scene occurs in a common human cafeteria, we may not be making the best use of the story world. We should consider which locations and aspects of the story world are unique and could be incorporated into the scene's setting. We want settings that are unique to our story world.

How does the setting affect the character's strategy for good or bad? How can the setting be incorporated into the character's plan? If we were to switch out the setting, would it have a noticeable effect on how the scene unfurls? These questions can serve as a litmus test for whether a setting is personalized to a character. If our setting doesn't pass this litmus test, we should ask how the setting might be changed so that a character can either make use of it in their strategy or be punished by it.

We may want to consider how we can incorporate movement into a setting. An argument that takes place on a roller coaster will generally be more interesting than one that takes place in a living room, for example. Might the characters be having a conversation while jumping hurdles during track practice? Is there any type of natural movement that occurs in the setting? How can character action take place in or around this movement? Introducing movement tends to create opportunities for mistakes, distractions, and agitation.

We previously discussed a dramatic tool called "agitation" where we introduce a distracting element that makes it more difficult for a character to accomplish their goal or to simply have a conversation. With this in mind, we want to consider whether our setting has any natural agitators. Are there any loud noises? Any inclement weather? Anyone or anything physically getting in the path of a character? Any approaching danger?

> *Takeaway*: A setting should support the specific feeling we want to
> convey in a scene. Setting should be incorporated into a character's
> plan or strategy. Setting should contain the unique elements of the

story world. Movement and agitation can heighten the drama of a setting.

Objects

After we've chosen a setting that best supports the purpose of the scene, we'll want to consider what kind of objects are naturally found there. We might also consider the objects that each character could have brought with them to the setting from elsewhere. Recall that objects can be a powerful way to symbolize characters, relationships, situations, and ideas.

Objects in the setting can be used by characters as part of their strategy. For instance, in *The Office* S6E20, Michael and Dwight are having an argument at a landfill. As the disagreement escalates, they start to throw pieces of trash at each other in anger. In *The Office* S4E13, Michael and Jan are hosting a dinner party for a few people from the office. During the climax of a disagreement between Jan and Michael, Jan throws Michael's Dundie at his cherished plasma screen TV. The Dundie becomes a part of Jan's strategy to inflict pain on Michael.

Objects can also act as scene agitators. Maybe one character finds an organ in a church and decides they need to learn to play while the other character is trying to carry on a conversation. Could one character be using a duster in a library and discover that they can send the other character into a sneezing fit as the argument escalates?

There's value in giving a character a background task that they're working on while talking. They might be making toast, lifting weights, or tinkering with a broken radio. We want to prefer an active task so that the objects involved in the task can become part of the conversation. A character may be in the middle of their task when another character interrupts them. We see this in *Toy Story* when Buzz is in the middle of trying to repair his spaceship and Woody interrupts him.

We may want to take the opportunity to have a character subtly show off or foreshadow a skill that they'll later use. A character might be throwing darts, for instance, at a bar. That skill might later payoff in the climax against an antagonist.

> *Takeaway:* An object can be used by a character as part of their scene strategy. Characters should have background tasks they're performing during a scene so that the objects from the task can be used in their conversation. These objects can function as agitators.

Blocking

Blocking is the movement and placement of characters within the scene. The physical relationship between characters can tell us a lot about their feelings and their personal relationship. Two characters who don't like each other might keep their distance. As a disagreement begins to escalate, they might get closer and closer as they begin to get in each other's face. A change in each character's physical location can help provide a feeling of escalating tension.

Blocking can be used to dictate a change in character strategy. If a character is trying "to attack," they might continually inch closer and closer to the other character as the confrontation escalates. Once they learn some information that causes them to switch to "stonewall," they might fold their arms and take a step back. The physical movement and relationship between characters conveys their internal state as well as the strategy that they're trying to enact. In this way, physical change can visually denote strategy change.

We can also play with the grouping of characters within a scene. If we have a scene with three or more characters, then perhaps two of the three excuse themselves for a sidebar. Perhaps a few of the characters talk over the heads of another group of characters at a board meeting. There can be small group dynamics within a larger group.

We want to consider which characters are physically *doing* something. We may want to give each character a physical goal (or destination) apart from their scene goal and consider how new information can cause that physical goal to change.

Takeaway: Blocking is the movement and placement of characters within a scene. Blocking can be used to convey how characters feel about each other or about a situation.

Character Tests

There are endless debates about the best way to craft a character. Is a character a collection of traits that we can pick from a list? Or is a character something that can only be discovered through the process of writing a story? There's a technique that can allow us to flesh out a character before they make their grand appearance in the story and that can also give us the benefit of organic character discovery.

This character development technique is to write a scene where we administer the character a test. This test is designed to help us discover what the character would do in a difficult situation. There are three distinct tests and each measures a different aspect of the character. Each of these tests relies on measuring character action. After all, character is defined first and foremost by action. Let's explore each character definition test individually.

The Elevator Test

Pixar has crafted an important test for defining a character called "the elevator test." The idea is that we want to put our character in an elevator, cause the elevator to break down, and then watch how the character responds. The goal here is to measure how a character responds to disruptions and particularly to stress. The journey of a character through a story is going to be filled with endless disruptions and stress so we need to find out how the character is going to react to their inevitable problems. This tells us about the character's "reaction cycle."

We can take this test a step further by amplifying the disruptions and problems. We now know how the character would react to a broken down elevator, but how does their reaction change if they believe that no one will be able to get there for eighteen hours? How does their response change when they find out that the SWAT team has been called in because there's a bomb wired to the elevator? How does their response change when they find out that someone lied to them about the SWAT team? How does their response change when they find out that the elevator is actually a staged set built to take the character to a different location?

We can further escalate the problems as we attempt to push the character to their breaking point and watch how they respond. We can use this test to write a scene and discover how a character would respond to a stressful situation.

The test, of course, doesn't require the use of an elevator. We can use any stressful situation that's likely to spur the character to respond. The more personal we can make the stress test, the better for defining the character. This can also allow us to discover what specifically triggers stress in a character.

> *Takeaway:* The elevator test allows us to use a disruption to put a character through a stressful situation. We then watch their reaction cycle and coping mechanisms.

The Velociraptor Test

Another helpful test for defining a character is something we can call "the velociraptor test." The idea with the velociraptor test is to put a character in a situation where they must make a seemingly impossible choice. It's a dilemma meant to measure what the character values most, their ability to make a decision, and their ability to be creative and clever in the face of seemingly limited options.

In this dilemma, a character and their best friend are desperately trying to escape a velociraptor. They're both scrambling to reach a blast door that's quickly closing. The raptor's barreling toward them and closing the distance. The character's best friend trips and gets their leg caught in a piece of debris. The character must decide if they will continue toward the blast door and leave their friend to die or if they will stay back and risk their own life to attempt to fight the raptor. A character's values are those things they're willing to defend or champion in the face of danger, loss, and consequences (i.e. that for which they're willing to risk and sacrifice).

From this test, we'll determine how quickly the character can make a decision (since the raptor is fast approaching), what they value most (their friend, their life, etc.), and whether they're able to come up with any creative solutions that aren't presented on the surface (such as constructing some sort of bait or distraction from the gear they have).

This core concept can be expanded, of course. We can put a character in a series of different moral dilemmas that all test what a character is willing to do in a tough spot.

Takeaway: The velociraptor test allows us to put a character in the middle of a moral dilemma to determine what they value most and how creative they are in a tight spot.

The Mission Test

One defining aspect of a character is what they're willing to do to get what they want. What do they believe is acceptable in the pursuit of their goal? To measure this aspect of character, we can put a character through a "mission test." The idea here is to assign a character a mission—a clear, objective goal—to get something from someone. We give the character no constraints on how they can complete this goal.

The character must then concoct a plan and enact a strategy to complete the mission. How do they do it? Do they use persuasion, manipulation, deception, or coercion? Do they use physical action or dialogue? Do they lie about their true goal and offer a pretext for their actions? How morally flexible is the character? Let's consider one of Rick's goals in *Casablanca*. He wants to convince Ilsa to leave her husband. How might our character convince someone to do that? Would they try persuasion? Would they stoop to manipulation and lies?

Consider the tactics that Darth Vader would use to accomplish this mission versus the tactics Luke Skywalker would use. Would our character reject the mission itself?

How a character takes action reveals their true nature. The methods they use, the risks they're willing to take, and the sacrifices (of either themselves, of others, or of values) they're willing to make all tell us exactly who they are.

Takeaway: The mission test allows us to discover the tactics and strategies a character may use to accomplish a goal. It also allows us to test their morality based on which tactics they deem permissible.

35

ENDING A SCENE (OR NARRATIVE UNIT)

The end of a scene offers the audience a clear, logical point at which they can walk away from the story. That's not good. For this reason, we need to ensure that the end of a scene uses a dramatic tool to make the audience want to know what will happen next. In essence, we want some form of a cliffhanger, even if it's subtle.

Recall from our dramatic toolbox that traditional cliffhangers tend to make use of either suspense or the introduction of a disruption (i.e. a problem or an opportunity). In other words, we can leave the audience wondering whether the protagonist will get what they want or we can upend the situation with a disruption (often the turning point of the scene) and make the audience wonder what the protagonist will do now. Recall also that a disruption is typically either an unexpected event or a surprising discovery. This may also include a character taking a surprise action or having a revelation or a self-revelation.

We can end a scene by raising a question or explicitly introducing a mystery. Cutting away from a scene early without showing an impending revelation or discovery is one way of raising a question and implicitly promising that the answer will come later. We can use the Kuleshov Effect as implicit commentary and irony. A character might say, for instance, "There's no way that they'd do that" and then the next scene opens with them doing that.

We can also use promises that project into the future or introduce a deadline or future event of some kind. We can telegraph the next event through a promise of a meeting or event, for instance. We can create a dangling cause by showing an action or event that implies a response (such as a marriage proposal), but then cut away before the response occurs. And finally, we might imagine the introduction of a dramatic irony where the audience is made aware of an important piece of information that a character doesn't know. The audience will tend to want to stick around to see the knowledge gap resolved.

> *Takeaway*: At the end of a scene, we may want to use some form of a cliffhanger to entice the audience to stick with us while we set up the drama and essential context of the next scene. This principle applies more broadly to the end of any narrative unit including a sequence and an act.

Scene as Story (The Dramatic Structure)

Many scenes follow a particular structure that we might view as the general structure of any narrative unit (i.e. a scene, a sequence, an act, and even the global story). Let's review this common dramatic structure.

First we set up any information that the audience may need to know in order to understand or emotionally appreciate the events of the scene. This is the scene's essential context. We want to use this time to subtly set up anything that will be part of a payoff.

We might ask the following questions:

- Are there any character desires that need to be established?
- Are there any plans or strategies that need to be previewed?
- Are there any "rules" that must be followed within this

scene? If artificial gravity has been disabled on the space
station for the duration of this scene, we need to know
that.

- Are there any character skills or physical tells that we need
  to know about?
- Are there any aspects of the setting that may become
  important?
- Is there any technology or magic that we need to
  foreshadow or explain? Are there any limitations or costs
  to this technology or magic?
- Are there any fears, vulnerabilities, insecurities, secrets,
  relationships, regrets, or weaknesses that will play a role in
  a character's actions or decisions?
- Are there any objects that will become important in the
  scene?
- Are there any promises we need to make in the form of
  warnings, threats, suggestions, predictions, requests,
  demands, assurances, etc.?
- Is any character weighing a decision that will become
  important?
- Are there any stakes that need to be established in the
  form of things of value?

We previously explored the value of a "sequel" scene. A sequel
follows a scene and explores the aftermath and emotional fallout of
the scene's disruption. In the same way, we might also consider a
"prequel" scene. Like a sequel, a prequel isn't a "proper" scene because
it doesn't have a disruption (i.e. a turning point). Its purpose is to
provide the essential context that will be necessary to understand or
appreciate an upcoming scene. The downside of a prequel scene is
that, like a sequel, it may slow the pace of a story.

In *Outbreak*, a team of virologists is about to land in a "hot zone"
full of infected patients. Dustin Hoffman's character warns Cuba
Gooding Jr.'s character not to be afraid of what he's going to see. If
anyone panics, it'll put the whole team in danger. Gooding's character

is book-smart but has never seen a nasty disease in the flesh. He acknowledges the warning and promises that he's ready. This is a "prequel" scene where we're foreshadowing and making promises about what's to come (via a warning). When the scene does play out, Cuba Gooding Jr.'s character *does* panic.

In our scene setup, we must also consider what dramatic tool will drive the scene forward. If the scene will be driven by a dramatic question, we need to define the protagonist's desire, their plan, what's at stake if they fail, the opposition, and any urgency in the form of a deadline or ticking clock. If the character's desire will be created within the scene via a disruption (i.e. an inciting incident), we need to first see the value of the thing threatened, removed, or offered by the disruption.

Once the desire has been defined, we may want to set an expectation about how the protagonist's plan *should* go by either having the protagonist lay out the details (as in *Ocean's Eleven*) or by having one or more clone characters enact the plan successfully or unsuccessfully. We can also use this time to define or emphasize the chances of success or failure. This technique of previewing the details of a character's plan should typically only be used if the plan will *not* be successful. If it *will* be successful, we can use the technique of unstated desire to show the enactment of the plan without explaining what the character is seeking.

If the scene will be driven by a dramatic irony, we must reveal to the audience the piece of information that one or more other characters won't initially know. This might be a secret, a fear, the plan of an opponent, the identity of an opponent, an approaching danger or opportunity, etc. If the scene will be driven by convergence or a promise, we need to start the scene with a promise of what's to come by the end. If the scene will be driven by mystery, we've got to show the audience that information is missing. We might also drive a scene forward with mystery via the dramatization of a character's plan without a stated desire (i.e. the tool of "unstated desire").

Much or all of the essential context of the scene may have been defined in a previous scene. In these cases, we can jump right into the action. This is the optimal situation if we're trying to maintain a quick pace, particularly toward the end of the story. While taking the time to convey context is essential to understand and appreciate the decisions and actions within a scene, we must be aware that if setup isn't done efficiently, it can slow the pace of the story.

Once we've defined the essential context, we can dive into the core of the scene. This is where the protagonist and antagonist of the scene enact their respective plans. Each character tries to sabotage the other's plan as they both work toward their desires. We see a chain of escalating disruptions. Each character must improvise as their plan is foiled or diverted. They make use of the resources and tools in their immediate environment. We may see a moral decay as the protagonist becomes more and more desperate in the face of failure. Their tactics and strategies may take on more risk and have increasingly lower odds of success. We may see the stakes rise as the action or dialogue moves from a place of relative safety to a place where mistakes aren't tolerated.

In this middle section of the scene, we tend to see a general escalation of action and emotions. A chase becomes a confrontation. Ranged combat becomes close-quarters combat. Veiled agendas are uncovered. The scope and depth of problems are discovered. The easy solution is replaced by the difficult solution. Emotions move from below the surface to out in the open. Indirect dialogue is replaced by direct dialogue. Safe plans are replaced by reckless plans. Façades are torn down. That which was hidden is revealed. The truth comes out.

This gradual transition from hope to desperation and from the unknown to the known tends to crescendo with an ultimate disruption—the scene's turning point. This is an unexpected action, event, revelation, or discovery that often results in the apparent defeat or false victory of the scene's protagonist. The protagonist is either backed into a corner or an opportunity arises that puts victory just within their grasp. It may result directly from the antagonist's words or actions or it may result from some outside force that intervenes in the confrontation, turning the story in a new direction. This turning point typically raises a new desire in the protagonist to address the problem or opportunity raised by the disruption. When this moment results in a dilemma for the protagonist about what to do next, it's sometimes known as the "crisis point."

At this point, we've entered the disruption cycle. Some scenes will end at the moment that this disruption occurs, effectively creating a cliffhanger. They'll leave the character's response to the disruption to a future scene. In this way, they effectively make use of the technique of a dangling cause by making an implicit promise that the disruption will be resolved later. Other scenes, however, will continue to the reaction cycle within the same scene. We'll see the character's emotional and analytical reaction to the disruption (even if it occurs quickly) as they deliberate their next action. We'll see them weigh their options and consider whether they can still pursue their desire given the information of the new disruption.

The character will then make a decision and take action to address the scene's central disruption (i.e. the turning point). This is the scene's climax. It's the moment when final action is taken to determine whether the scene desire will be attained or lost. After the protagonist's decisive final action, we enter the scene's resolution. It's here that we see the fallout and consequences of the protagonist's final scene decision.

> *Takeaway*: Every narrative unit (i.e. scene, sequence, act, and global story) tends to follow a common structure. We might call this the dramatic structure. This structure consists of the unit's essential context (which may include an inciting incident), escalation, turning point, reaction, climax, and resolution. Some scenes end at the turning point, effectively creating a cliffhanger.

36

FINAL THOUGHTS

Is the Story Actually on the Page?

We've spent a considerable amount of time crafting the elements of our story. We've discussed theme, character, plot, structure, and how to explore each of these elements. But when all is said and done, crafting these elements is meaningless unless they actually make it to the page. The audience won't be reading our story outline. We've got to ensure that we're actually *dramatizing* these elements through action.

Even though we know our characters and theme inside and out, the reader doesn't know them unless they're on the page. If the character's backstory is never explained or their motivation is never made clear, we may certainly understand what's going on as the writer, but the reader will likely be left confused and frustrated.

We need to allow other people to read and experience the story exactly the way that we did while writing it. We have an implicit assumption that the story playing in our head is the same story playing in the reader's head. But that's not necessarily the case. It's our job to ensure that we're communicating the context of our story clearly.

If a reader thinks our story is boring or confusing, it may not be because we've crafted a boring or confusing story in our head—it may be because we simply haven't communicated our story properly. Is the character's motivation actually on the page? Are the stakes actually there? Has the character's flaw and how it negatively affects others been clearly dramatized? Is the urgency explicit or is it merely implied? It's especially important to ask these questions during and after the revision process because some of these elements that were originally on the page may come out or be reduced to mere implication during the revision process. Is the story in the reader's head the same one we had in our head while writing it?

To help ensure that the story in our head does actually make it to the page, we can and should take time to list the story elements that each scene is responsible for dramatizing. Is a scene responsible for showing the character's flaw? Is it responsible for setting the urgency or deadline in the story? Is it responsible for defining the stakes? Is it responsible for foreshadowing the use of some piece of technology? Does it actually accomplish its task in conveying this information? After we've got a list of the story elements that each scene conveys, we must ensure that each critical story element is contained somewhere in the list.

> *Takeaway*: After we've written our story, we need to verify that what we intended to convey actually made it to the page. Have we successfully dramatized all of the critical story elements that were in our outline? Is the story in our head the same one that actually made it on to paper?

Quantity over Quality

"Make a list of alternative choices a character could make—
especially if you've fallen in love with the ones you've already
chosen. You might be surprised where it'll take you."

— ADAM SKELTER

We often hear about aiming for quality over quantity. In the
realm of creativity, it's inverted. We want to aim for quantity above all
else (while maintaining quality when we can achieve it). Nowhere is
this a more helpful mindset than in the realm of scene work.

Our first scene idea doesn't need to be our last. In fact, it shouldn't
be. We shouldn't expect ourselves to come up with the right imple-
mentation of a scene on our first go. Once we've determined the
purpose that the scene will need to fulfill, we should brainstorm
multiple scenes that might all fulfill that purpose.

When it comes to brainstorming, the more answers we expect of
ourselves, the more creative our answers will *need* to be in order to
keep coming. We might consider creating a numbered list and
forcing ourselves to fill it with up to fifty scene ideas. The key here is
not to judge the value of any one idea. We're not looking for the
"right" idea or the "correct" solution. Instead we're looking for the
largest *number* of ideas. That's our only metric. By doing this, we tap
into those ideas that are hidden behind all of the traditional clichés
that first come to mind. Of course, as we continue it'll become harder
and harder to come up with another idea. But we must keep going—
that's where the creative gold is.

Takeaway: Creative problems tend not to have only one right answer.
They have multiple right answers. We must remember to prioritize
quantity over quality in all elements of our writing. Quantity will
lead to quality.

Story Engines

In the context of story, an engine is anything that continually generates story energy. A story engine generates interesting situations and dilemmas. It's a source of continued drama and theme. Wherever possible, we want to pack our story with engines.

Perhaps the most fruitful story engine is one that has at its heart a structural conflict. In other words, the engine consists of two forces that are diametrically opposed.

An important aspect of a story engine is that it's something that exists throughout the story, not just at one point in time. A character engine, for example, consists of a character who has at their core an internal conflict. This internal conflict isn't one that exists at one particular moment in the story but rather it spans throughout the character's existence. We place an internal dilemma at the center of the character's nature. What's the central dilemma that pulls this character between two ways of living?

In *The Office*, Michael Scott epitomizes a character engine. He has at his core a conflict between wanting to be a good boss and wanting to be loved by others. This is a conflict between duty and love. In almost every episode, Michael is pulled between these two forces. He knows he must keep the branch productive, but he wants nothing more than to be liked by his officemates.

We might imagine a character who lives in a world of faith. This character wants to fulfill their role as one who believes and trusts and at the same time they have a natural personality tendency to question and search for evidence. This pull between faith and reason might cause persistent dilemmas and problems for this character within their community. A character's Great Decision Moment may be where they need to make a final choice in their persistent inner dilemma.

To create an engine for our story world, we can create multiple communities that are all thematically opposed. They all have different worldviews and approaches to life. This will ensure that when those communities meet, sparks will fly.

We can also imagine a story engine sitting at the heart of a relationship between two characters. If the two characters are fundamentally opposed in their worldviews, beliefs, and value systems, all interactions will create story energy.

Story engines are perhaps our most powerful tool when writing. When we create something that keeps on producing story energy, the engine does much of the story's heavy lifting for us. In fact, this book has been filled with story engines.

A character void (including a worldview, lie, ghost, or obsession) consistently produces character action and energy. It's driven by a pull between what the character wants (to fill, conceal, or validate their void) and what they need (to become individuated). Desire and dramatic opposition produce plans that must be continually reshaped and reworked. Thematic opposition generates fierce battles over ways of life. Relationships between characters of different worldviews produce endless conflict.

When we identify the models, patterns, and tools that produce story energy, we let the tools do the work. As storytellers, our job is to pick the *right* tool to make the story work *for* us, rather than against us.

> *Takeaway*: A story engine consists of two forces that are diametrically opposed. This oppositional structure produces an endless supply of story energy.

Our Power and Responsibility as Storytellers

We as storytellers have more influence than we may recognize.

The themes at the heart of our stories can affect beliefs and behavior. People internalize the choices their favorite characters are willing to make. They see the actions they're willing to take. They see the value systems that they embrace. They learn what's possible. They learn what's rewarded, what's punished, and what's overlooked.

Stories aren't just told through cinema. They're not just told on a page. They're told all around us, all day.

With our ability to shape beliefs through story, we as storytellers are perhaps the most influential members of society. We have the power to influence and change minds.

There's truth to the idea that those who tell the stories rule society. Let's remember this as we set off to write our stories and change the world.

Join Us

Join us at Kiingo to help bring imaginary worlds to life through story. Find us at https://kiingo.com

NOTES

17. The Disruption Chain

1. http://penultimateword.com/editing-blogs/characterization-in-fiction-writing-realistic-character-reactions/

29. Irony

1. https://www.vocabulary.com/dictionary/irony

ACKNOWLEDGMENTS

This book was as enjoyable to write as it was challenging. I couldn't have written it without the rock-solid support of my loved ones. Thank you.

As with almost every journey of discovery, "if I have seen further it is by standing on the shoulders of Giants." Thank you to John Truby, Paul Gulino, Brian McDonald, John Yorke, Matt Bird, Steven James, Karl Iglesias, Andrew Stanton, Michael Arndt, K.M. Weiland, Shawn Coyne, Pamela Jaye Smith, Chuck Wendig, Peter Russell, Sacha Black, Pilar Alessandra, Adam Skelter, Michael Hauge, Amnon Buchbinder, Jim Mercurio, and Alan Watt. The storytelling content of this book would not have been possible without the groundwork you all have laid for future generations of storytellers.

Thank you to all the creators who have been generous in sharing their knowledge and resources. I'd particularly like to thank Karen Worden and David Branin of FilmCourage for the immense value they provide to the storytelling community through their interviews. It's a veritable treasure trove of story information. Thank you to all the bloggers and podcasters out there who share their knowledge with the world.

Thank you to the beta readers who helped make this book what it is. A special thank you to Louise Skeats for your immensely valuable time, feedback, and advice.

Thank you to Esther Chilton for the excellent editing.

Thank you Sacha Black, Meg LaTorre, Lauren Eckhardt, and Danielle Harrington for helping me navigate the publishing process.

Thank you to everyone who supported and encouraged me during the long process of writing this book. Thank you Riley Hagan, Star Jeries, Bijou Schmidt, Orlando Viera, Courtney Borkowski, Heather McLaughlin, and Meghan Neilsen. Thank you Courtney and Riley for the long talks on irony. Thank you to the virtual family I've collected in the writing community. Thank you Brenda Wilson, Lauren Eckhardt, Danielle Harrington, Charlotte Taylor, Taylor Ferguson, Kalie Cassidy, Jayde Rossi, Jessica Scurlock, Kate Akhtar-Khavari, Gabrielle Villalba, Shannan Johnson, Joshua Townshend-Zellner, Natalie Banks, Paul Gilbert, and the Writing Champions Project team. You all have made this a great journey.

And most of all, thank you to my family. Thank you to my parents and sisters. You always support me no matter what crazy direction I decide to pursue. I love you all very much. Thank you.

ABOUT THE AUTHOR

Ross Hartmann is the Creative Director at Kiingo. Kiingo is dedicated to bringing imaginary worlds to life through storytelling. Join us. https://kiingo.com

 facebook.com/kiingocreative
twitter.com/kiingocreative
instagram.com/kiingocreative
patreon.com/kiingo